A Vision of Service

Celebrating the Federation of Sisters and Daughters of Charity

A Vision of Service

Celebrating the Federation of Sisters and Daughters of Charity

Geraldine Anthony, SC, Ph.D.

Sheed & Ward
Kansas City

Sheed & Ward™ is a service of The National Catholic Reporter Publishing Company.

Library of Congress Cataloguing-in-Publication Data
Anthony, Geraldine, 1919-
A vision of service : celebrating the Sisters of Charity / Geraldine Anthony.
p. cm.
Includes bibliographical references and index.
ISBN 1-55612-972-6 (alk. paper)
1. Sisters of Charity Federation in the Vincentian-Setonian Tradition—History. I. Title.
BX4452.A58 1997
271'.91073—dc21 97-20334
CIP

Published by: Sheed & Ward
115 E. Armour Blvd.
P.O. Box 419492
Kansas City, MO 64141-6492

To order, call: (800) 333-7373

www.natcath.com/sheedward

For my grandniece, Alison Leigh Anthony,
And her generation
Who will arrive at maturity in the twenty-first century,
That they may keep the spark of charity alive
And kindle it into a fire –
This history of women is dedicated.

Also by
Geraldine Anthony

This is Barbara's Life
Halifax: Sisters of Charity, 1956.

John Coulter
Boston: G.K. Hall & Co., 1976.

Gwen Pharis Ringwood
Boston: G.K. Hall & Co., 1981.

Stage Voices
New York & Toronto: Doubleday & Co., 1978.

Profiles in Canadian Drama
Toronto: Gage Educational Publishers, 1977.

Rebel, Reformer, Religious Extraordinaire: The Life of Sister Irene Farmer
Calgary, Alberta: University of Calgary Press, 1997.

The Congregation of the Sisters of Charity of Halifax
(Filmstrip and record)
New York: Sisters of Charity, 1958.

Nunc et Semper: A Call to Radical Sisterhood (Play)
Halifax: Sisters of Charity, 1988.

Contents

We must pass, my sisters, from affective love to effective love, and that is a love which takes flesh in works of Charity, service of the poor which is undertaken with joy, constancy and tender love.

– St. Vincent de Paul (*Documents,* vol. 11, p. 593)

Take great care to serve the poor; above all live together in great union and cordiality; loving one another in imitation of the union and life of our Lord.

– St. Louise de Marillac (Last words, Sr. Vincent Regnault, D.C., *Saint Louise de Marillac* [Rockford, IL: Tan Books, 1983], p. 121)

It is expected I shall be the Mother of many daughters.

– St. Elizabeth Ann Seton (letter to Cecilia Seton, October 6, 1808)

I see your holy order diffusing itself in the different parts of the United States, spreading everywhere . . . teaching by . . . angelical lives . . . how to serve God in purity and holiness.

– Bishop John Cheverus (letter to Mother Seton, Boston, April 13, 1809)

Acknowledgments

This popular history of the Sisters of Charity Federation in the Vincentian-Setonian Tradition could not have been written without the generous support of more than 400 Sisters and Daughters of Charity in the thirteen congregations, who graciously consented to be interviewed on their current individual ministries and their vision of the future. Although space did not permit the inclusion of more than a representative number, I thank all those who contributed. The descriptions of their ministries will be preserved in the archives.

I also am grateful to those sisters who contributed articles on their congregations' histories, their work in the fields of health care, social services, education, and their current Associate programs. Their names appear in the notes following each chapter.

My gratitude extends especially to the General Superiors and Provincials who welcomed me so wholeheartedly to their Motherhouses and Provincial Houses. The results of their sharing with me their visions of the future of religious life and the Federation, has enriched the concluding chapter of this book.

Finally and most particularly I wish to name the dedicated, hardworking archivists and two General Secretaries who became my mentors. Without them I would have been lost indeed. Their organization of my visits and interviews, their generosity in allowing me access to the material in their archives, is deeply appreciated. I thank the following Daughters and Sisters of Charity, with whom I spent many fruitful hours: Sisters Aloysia Dugan, DC, Emmitsburg, MD; Elaine Wheeler, DC, Albany, NY; Genevieve Keusenkothen, DC, St. Louis, MO; Margaret Flynn, DC, Evansville, IN; Margaret Rodericks, SCN, Mary Collette Crone, SCN, Nazareth, Kentucky; Anita Marie Howe, SC, Cincinnati, Ohio; M. Anne Francis Campbell, OLM, Charleston, S.C.; Rita King, SC, Riverdale, NY; Francis Teresa Martin, SC, Halifax, N.S.; Marion Murray, SCIC, Saint John, NB; Imelda Guignard, NDSC, Moncton, NB; Helen Forge, SCL, Leavenworth, Kansas; Elizabeth McLoughlin, SC, Convent Station, NJ; Sara Louise Reilly, SC, Mary Catherine Seli, SC, Greensburg, PA; Anne Kremenik, VSC, Pittsburgh, PA; Margaret Mach, VSC, Bedford, Ohio.

For those readers unacquainted with Catholic Sisters' congregations in North America, mention should be made of the work of other Orders, such as the Sisters of Mercy, the Sisters of St. Joseph, the Sisters of Notre Dame, the Sisters of the Immaculate Heart of Mary, the Franciscans, Dominicans, Benedictines, Ursulines, and countless other congregations who, like the Sisters of Charity, also pioneered free health care, education, and social services before government agencies ever were established to provide for these needs. Inspired by gospel values, thousands of religious women dedicated their lives to the poor, regardless of race, color, age, culture, or religious and political affiliations. The works of the Sisters of Charity can be multiplied innumerable times by the efforts of all those congregations. Today, though smaller in number and older than average in age, the sisters continue to contribute their services. Where there is a need, the sisters try to respond despite all odds. Their common goal is to create a world where children are given a loving start and adults are helped to conquer obstacles in their lives.

S.G.A.

Introduction

If you are planning a Federation or Union of your communities with common founder and charism, you may profit by this story of the Sisters and Daughters of Charity – their birth, growth, present achievements, and future hopes. Born in 1947 and originally given the title of "The Conference of Mother Seton's Daughters," it was formed for the express purpose of lending corporate support to bring about the canonization of Elizabeth Ann Seton, foundress of the Sisters of Charity and of the parochial school system in America. "Conference" was used at the time to indicate meetings of major superiors of those congregations claiming Elizabeth Seton as their foundress, whereas "Federation" is the term first used in this context in 1965 in response to Pope Paul VI's recommendation in *Perfectae Caritatis* that institutes of common origin and charism should unite or federate. The Sisters and Daughters of Charity use the term loosely to mean a sharing of spirit or charism while still remaining autonomous.

When congregations of like spirit and history decide to join together in a Federation, the very first step is to examine and deal with the reasons that have initially separated them. These may have been geographical, social, developmental, diocesan or hierarchical, national, international, sociological. All or several of these may have contributed to the early isolation and independence of communities who owe their spirit and origin to the same founder. The history of the Daughters of Charity and the several congregations of Sisters of Charity in North America offer an apt example of this phenomenon. This is the story of a developing organism that has not yet reached full maturity as a Federation. Celebrating its Fiftieth Anniversary in 1997, the Federation's leaders decided it was time to trace its history of development since 1947.

The Sisters of Charity Federation in the Vincentian-Setonian Tradition has expanded from its original number of six congregations in 1947 to thirteen in 1997, with 7000 members. A brief look at the foundations of those first six communities will cast light on a family that had an almost insurmountable problem when the member communities were very young. The mother, Elizabeth Ann Seton, had, unknowingly in a sense, begot from her original foundation six separate congregations. Her founding group was born in Emmitsburg on July 31, 1809 and named the Sisters of Charity of St. Joseph. Its purpose was the education, health care, and social ministry of the poor, especially the enormous number of immigrants coming in from European countries in the 19th century. So many young women joined her little community that she was able to send some of the earliest members to New York in 1817 to help the poor and destitute children and mothers. After her death in 1821 Sisters of Charity continued to be missioned: to Cincinnati in 1829, to Pittsburgh in 1835, from New York to Halifax, Nova Scotia, in 1849, to New Jersey in 1859, from Cincinnati, Ohio, to Greensburg, Pennsylvania, in 1870.

Meantime in 1847 Mother Seton's original congregation of Sisters of Charity in Emmitsburg was being encouraged by the French Sulpician Bishop and priests in Maryland to join the international congregation of

Daughters of Charity founded in France in 1633 by Vincent de Paul and Louise de Marillac, with its Motherhouse in Paris. When Elizabeth Ann Seton founded the first truly American religious order, which did not owe its origin to any European foundation, she had, at the suggestion of the hierarchy in Maryland, adopted the Constitutions of St. Vincent de Paul's Daughters of Charity in France, with appropriate modifications for an American order. When, in 1847, the Sisters of Charity in Emmitsburg decided to join the Daughters of Charity in France, they recalled their sisters from New York and Cincinnati, as both groups were caring for orphan boys, forbidden by the Daughters of Charity rule. Thirty-three of the sisters in New York decided to retain their American roots and become, at the suggestion of Bishop Hughes, a New York diocesan congregation. The sisters in Cincinnati did likewise, becoming the Sisters of Charity of the Cincinnati diocese. Communities eventually branching from those also became diocesan congregations: Halifax, Nova Scotia; Convent Station, New Jersey; Greensburg, Pennsylvania. Over the years most of these congregations became Pontifical Institutes under the patronage of the Pope.

As a result of this break between the congregations of Sisters of Charity and the Daughters of Charity of St. Vincent de Paul in Emmitsburg, a deep division developed that lasted well into the next century. By 1947, some 100 years later, the rift had not healed as the story of the division was handed down from one generation of sisters to the next. This was the dilemma in 1947 faced by Sister Isabel Toohey, Visitatrix of the Daughters of Charity in the United States. The five diocesan congregations of Sisters of Charity considered themselves true children of Mother Seton, loyal to her original intention of being an American congregation, while the Daughters of Charity now were the daughters of Vincent de Paul and Louise de Marillac with an historical allegiance to their original foundress, Mother Seton. Their Provincial House was situated on the very spot where Mother Seton founded her first community; her precious body buried in the graveyard there. Did not all six congregations owe their foundation directly or indirectly to Mother Seton, while at the same time accepting the Constitutions of St. Vincent de Paul, with modifications to suit the Sisters of Charity?

This was the situation that Sister Isabel faced. Without the cooperation of all six congregations working together for the canonization, their goal might never be realized. Single-handedly she worked the miracle of reconciliation, but it took many decades to achieve it fully. What she did accomplish through visits and letters to the five Mothers General was to bring them together in Emmitsburg on October 27, 1947 to found "The Conference of Mother Seton's Daughters." They would continue to meet twice a year at various Motherhouses over the next twenty-eight years until their goal was reached: the Beatification of Mother Seton in 1963 and her Canonization in 1975 – the first American-born saint canonized by the Roman Catholic Church. As a thoughtful gesture to those five congregations whose loving relationship to Mother Seton had persisted through more than one hundred years, Sister Isabel had the White House restored, the home of Mother Seton and her first small band of Sisters of Charity. Sister Isabel graciously offered it as a retreat house to any Sister of Charity who might wish to visit Emmitsburg.

What to do next? By now the General Superiors of the six congregations had formed deep and lasting ties. Why end the Federation? But what to do with it? The first meeting after the Canonization occurred the following year in Halifax in 1976. The Halifax News Release on May 4, 1976, summed up the meeting and stated the Federation's future goals:

> The twenty-one members present affirmed the value of uniting when possible wherever the strength of their corporate response might alleviate any injustice; of raising the status of women and not only in North America but in all countries of the world; of utilizing the creative talents of women in the service of the Church, and of working with other women for an understanding of our responsibility to society.[1]

It is interesting to note that their corporate response is to women's problems. Obviously the Feminist Movement had a strong impact on the Daughters and Sisters of Charity. Gradually the Federation began to gain momentum, slowly at first when the annual meetings revolved around academic papers, educating the sisters to their congregations' past history and great leaders. Papers too were given on common problems faced by all religious congregations in the wake of Vatican II: revisions of the Constitutions, local community lifestyles, individual ministries, the charism of charity that united them. Papers and discussions also examined the spirituality of Elizabeth Ann Seton, Vincent de Paul, and Louise de Marillac. As early as 1977 Federation members were beginning to suggest some corporate action in advertising job offerings to all six congregations, in offering to share central services, and to explore joint projects, but not much action resulted from these initial tentative offerings.

The first actual stirrings of change came in 1979 when the Canadian Sisters of Charity of the Immaculate Conception in Saint John, New Brunswick, applied for admission to the Federation. They had indirect links to Mother Seton. What to do? The six founding congregations had not established any criteria in the by-laws for admitting other congregations. They solved the problem temporarily by admitting this congregation as an Associate member of the Federation.

As the annual meetings continued, so did new ideas benefit the members. The necessity for professional archives for each congregation resulted in a special meeting at the Archives of the Sisters of Charity of Seton Hill, Greensburg, to which all the archivists were invited. Other needs suggested a central file for the Federation, a constant update of the by-laws, a Policy Handbook. In 1982 the Sisters of Charity of the Immaculate Conception were finally and warmly received as full members into the Federation, and a turning point had been reached. Eventually any congregation owing its spirit to either Elizabeth Seton or Vincent de Paul would be admitted, after due course, into the Federation. The 1982 Annual Meeting Evaluation stated: ". . . there seems to be a new spirit in the Federation, a greater sense of what binds us together."[2]

Thus the Federation had taken hold of itself, at least theoretically, as a single body. Two years later, in 1984, it discovered its dynamism when the major superiors gave their solid support to a group of their young, highly-motivated Formation Directors. The proposal presented was that:

> The sisters in initial formation from all the congregations of the Federation, . . . come together, possibly for a four to six week period in the summer, to share an experience and to exchange ideas that would . . . deepen and broaden their understanding of religious life and of the charism of Elizabeth Seton and Vincent de Paul. Formation Directors would be directly involved in the study and planning for such a program.[3]

Perhaps no one realized how creative and dynamic those young Formation Directors were. Together they formed the *CCFP – Company of Charity Formation Personnel*. From this think tank emerged two major programs that would involve not only sisters in formation but also the grass-roots sisters, those out in the field of a variety of ministries. Thus far only the leadership members of the congregations were involved in the Federation. The Formation Directors, therefore, offered the following two programs:

Roots

In 1985 a program was developed called From These Roots inviting Formation Directors, their novices and the Daughters' seminary sisters to Convent Station, New Jersey, June 21 to July 5, to become acquainted, discuss formation programs, and make plans for future collaboration. Twenty-five sisters from six congregations participated in what proved to be, for the novices and seminarians, a wonderful experience. This continues, usually every two years at various Motherhouses.

Roots-on-the-Road

In 1987, from May 24 to June 12, nineteen novices and eleven directors from nine communities participated in a summer bus tour to all the historic sites of Mother Seton's life, and to many of the Motherhouses of the Sisters of Charity.

Roots Revisited

Programs held regularly for those who participated in the Roots program to help them keep up the contacts they made in the Roots program and to look at Mission and Charism.

A Final Vow Retreat

This took place in June 1994 at the summer homes of the New York Community at Ventnor, and the New Jersey Community at Harvey Cedars. It consisted of two weeks devoted to Vincentian spirituality in a feminine mode, with emphasis on ministry to the poor, community, feminism, the vows, vision, prayer.

The next project that these Formation Directors presented was the idea of a collaborative novitiate house where the novices of all the Federation congregations might be trained. Established in Fort Lee, New Jersey, in January 1989, it has very successfully carried out its program for those congregations interested. Although all the congregations opted for the Roots programs, not all participated in a central Novitiate due to the international ties of the Daughters of Charity, and the cultural as well as the language differences of some Canadian congregations.

A very successful venture of the Federation was the result of a resolution taken at the 1986 Formation Planning Conference. "Resolved: That common renewal and revitalization programs . . . be developed and extended to the larger body of sisters in our communities as part of a collaboration and on-going formation effort in the Charity Family of Communities."[4] The Federation, therefore, in the person of Sister Judy Metz and her colleagues created a one-week annual summer program called *Charity – A Shared Vision* for the so-called grass-roots sisters. It consists of conferences, papers, discussions, liturgies, and social events designed to acquaint the sisters with each other and with the charism they all share. Some sixty or seventy sisters representing all the congregations would gather at the designated Motherhouse in July for what proved to be a very inspiring and entertaining week in which the seeds of friendships were sown among sisters of different Charity congregations. Between 1988 and 1995 over 500 sisters have shared in this program.

Another project created by the Federation is the Seton Legacy program. Those who organized *Charity – A Shared Vision* saw the possibilities of an academic conference taking place once every three or four years in which scholarly papers are presented for discussion on the history and spirituality of the Sisters and Daughters of Charity. First held in 1992 in Dayton, Ohio, and Convent Station, New Jersey, it will be held again in 1996-97 in Nazareth, Kentucky; Albuquerque, New Mexico; Convent Station, New Jersey, and Halifax, Nova Scotia.

As the years passed, six more congregations of Sisters of Charity joined the Federation: in 1986 Les Religeuses de Notre-Dame-du-Sacré-Coeur of Moncton, New Brunswick; in 1989 the Vincentian Sisters of Charity of Pittsburgh, Pennsylvania; in 1990 the Vincentian Sisters of Charity of Bedford, Ohio; in 1991 the Sisters of Charity of Nazareth, Kentucky; in 1994 the Sisters of Charity of Our Lady of Mercy in Charleston, South Carolina; in 1995 the Sisters of Charity of Leavenworth, Kansas. This brings the total to thirteen congregations comprising in 1996 some 7,000 sisters – a tribute to a Federation that is fast proving itself a dynamic and challenging force for the future. In order to acquaint many of these sisters with the other congregations in the Federation some communities have arranged bus tours to Emmitsburg and other Motherhouses. The Cincinnati sisters call it a Heritage Tour, and about fifty of their sisters periodically take advantage of this.

At the 1989 meeting the need for an Executive Committee to handle the rapidly accumulating business of this growing Federation was discussed and initiated in 1990, becoming a working reality in 1991. Amended by-laws in 1991 defined the wider latitude of Federation admissions.

The following is a record of revisions and editing that were accepted by the Federation membership as the by-laws document was studied.

> Preamble
> *Phase III revision:* At the annual Federation meeting in 1989 a revision of the By-Laws was proposed providing for the admission of congregations that have no direct historical connection to Elizabeth Seton, but which share in the charism of charity through some adaptation of the Rule of Saint Vincent de Paul. In 1990, as a result of preliminary meetings which examined the basic purpose and structure in the light of present and future collaboration, this concept was approved. In addition, the name was changed to *The Elizabeth Seton Federation.*[5]

What direction is the Federation taking? In 1992 it was suggested that there should be a greater involvement of the general membership in projects and activities, as well as a greater involvement of the leadership sisters in putting Federation issues on their Council agendas. Many delegates felt that unification is inevitable, but fear was expressed at moving too fast. In 1993 a Federation Vision Statement was created as follows: "Claiming our future as women of faith, we are bonded by the charism of charity; impelled to respond to the needs of our day especially among the poor; committed to collaboration."[6] In 1996 the name of the Federation was again changed to accommodate all. It is now the Sisters of Charity Federation in the Vincentian-Setonian Tradition.

The latest project is Regional Meetings for the grassroots sisters planned geographically to bring as many sisters as possible together from different congregations of Charities. A Federation Newsletter was established; a Federation History commissioned, and the collection and publishing of the writings of Saint Elizabeth Ann Seton planned. Several sisters with creative ideas envision a future for religious sisters that may be surprising but also inspiring.

The idea of unification was positively discussed by many sisters, even by a few Daughters of Charity despite their international ties, which would make such a union difficult if not impossible. One Sister of Charity said wryly: "Together we have power, mutual support, diversity, increased enthusiasm, optimism for the future, holiness and financial resources."

However, in lieu of unification, there were many significant ideas expressed both by major superiors and grassroots sisters: sharing ministries, facilities, resources, within the present structure of autonomous congregations.

In future it is possible that the sisters of differing age-groups may come together occasionally for mutual support: the novices (with the exception of the Daughters of Charity) being trained together at the same Formation House; younger professed sisters who find themselves isolated by age, spending time together annually; middle-aged sisters in similar ministries meeting together on a consistent basis; retired sisters in close geographic areas sharing the same retirement houses; elderly sisters in need of health care sharing facilities in the same regions.

Observe the gradual growth of relationships among these communities of Charity sisters, slowly at first from 1947 to 1975; then gaining momentum as new ideas proliferated, new programs created for sharing, new congregations joining the Federation and adding their numbers and enthusiasms to nontraditional ministries. By and large the sisters are looking for unification of some kind; possibly in the distant future when numbers are considerably smaller, the creation of an entirely new kind of congregation to which all may belong.

One Daughter of Charity quoted an old saying: "Remember, pilgrim, there are no roads. Roads are made by walking." We Sisters and Daughters of Charity are making our own road and progressing along it.

Notes

1. Federation of the Daughters of Saint Elizabeth Ann Seton, 29th Annual Federation Conference Meeting, Mount Saint Vincent Motherhouse, Halifax, Nova Scotia, April 26-29, 1976, as appearing in *The Halifax News Release*, May 4, 1976.
2. Federation of the Daughters of Saint Elizabeth Ann Seton, 35th Annual Federation Conference Meeting, Mount Saint Vincent Motherhouse, Halifax, Nova Scotia, June 7-10, 1982, minutes, Annual Meeting Evaluation.
3. Federation of the Daughters of Saint Elizabeth Ann Seton, 37th Annual Federation Conference Meeting, Seton Hill, Greensburg, Pennsylvania, May 22-25, 1984, Report on the 1984 Federation Meeting.
4. Report on the Federation Initial Formation Planning Conference, Convent Station, New Jersey, April 15-19, 1986.
5. The Elizabeth Seton Federation, De Paul Center, Greensburg, Pennsylvania, 44th Annual Meeting, June 17-20, 1991, Federation minutes, p. 4.
6. The Elizabeth Seton Federation, Mount Saint Vincent Motherhouse, Halifax, Nova Scotia, 46th Annual Meeting, June 11-14, 1993, Federation minutes, "Vision Statement," p. 2.

Chapter One

Historical Background: Thirteen Congregations

Roman Catholic religious congregations of women in European countries had, as far back as the 17th century, sent small groups of their sisters to minister to the immigrant population in the new world and to establish American and Canadian branches of their own European communities. Sisters of European origin ministered to poor immigrant families in the fields of health care, social service, and education. But it was not until 1809 that an American-born woman founded a genuinely American religious congregation without any ties to European communities.

The woman was Elizabeth Ann Seton, member of a prominent New York family, a widow and mother of five small children, an Episcopalian convert to Catholicism. A well-educated young woman, she had moved to Baltimore in 1808 at the invitation of Archbishop John Carroll and Father Louis DuBourg, a Sulpician priest, founder and President of St. Mary's College in Baltimore. There she opened a Catholic school for day students and boarders. Her three daughters would be taught there; her two sons would be educated at St. Mary's College. Other young Catholic women joined her in her endeavors. Inspired by her leadership, they also followed her to Emmitsburg the following year where, through the instrumentality of a seminarian, Samuel Cooper, a permanent establishment was provided. There she founded the Sisters of Charity of St. Joseph. Fr. John Dubois, a French émigré, acquainted with the Daughters of Charity in France, was named Superior General. In June 1809 the sisters appeared in religious habit, the simple dress, cape, and black bonnet that became the hallmark of Mother Seton's Sisters of Charity.

New facilities had to be constructed to accommodate the burgeoning community as Mother Seton became the inspiration for many young women eager to give their lives to God in the service of the poor. The first building was completed in 1810 and a free day school for children was begun, which became the prototype of the free parochial school system in America. Until 1814 teaching at St. Joseph's School in Emmitsburg was the principal work, although the sisters nursed the sick in the neighborhood and performed other works of charity. In 1814 the sisters were asked to staff an orphanage in Philadelphia, which continued in existence for 175 years, and in 1817 an orphanage in New York for boys and girls.

The Sisters of Charity of St. Joseph were incorporated in 1817 for "works of piety, charity and usefulness, and especially for the care of the sick, the succor of aged, infirm and necessitous persons, and the education of young females."[1] Only four years later in 1821 at age forty-seven, Elizabeth Ann Seton, beloved by the sisters, clergy, and all those whom she had helped, died of tuberculosis in Emmitsburg at the "White House," the motherhouse she had founded. There were, at that time, fifty sisters working in five missions. They continued to increase rapidly in numbers and in the ministries of education, health care and social services, spreading out in a wide arc of charity to neighboring states: Maryland, Virginia, Washington, D.C., Delaware, New Jersey, New York, Massachusetts, Pennsylvania, Ohio, Missouri, Louisiana, Indiana, and California. For the next twenty-five years they remained a united community. Then in the mid-1840s the Sulpicians in the United States received a mandate from their Superior General in Paris requiring them to relinquish all works except the primary objective of conducting seminaries. This precipitated events leading to the union of the Emmitsburg Sisters of Charity with the Daughters of Charity in France.

THE DAUGHTERS OF CHARITY OF ST. VINCENT DE PAUL – UNITED STATES[2]

In 1846 the Sisters of Charity in Emmitsburg were urged by the French Sulpician clergy and Bishops to join the international Company of Daughters of Charity with Motherhouse in France. The sisters in New York were requested to give up teaching boys in their orphanage in accordance with the Daughter's rule. Thirty-three of them preferred to continue this work and remain an American-based community, becoming a diocesan community under Archbishop Hughes. The sisters in Cincinnati did likewise, both instrumental in founding other communities in Halifax, Nova Scotia; Convent Station, New Jersey, and Greensburg, Pennsylvania. The break was very painful for all concerned.

The union of the two communities – the Sisters of Charity in Emmitsburg and the Daughters of Charity in France – became effective on March 25, 1850, when the Sisters of Charity made the Vow of Obedience to the Venerable Superior General of the Congregation of the Mission in France, thus consummating the union and becoming Daughters of Charity of St. Vincent de Paul. Ties with the other five communities dedicated to the leadership of Mother Seton were thus effectively broken; the wound was deep and it would take another one hundred years, in 1947, for them to join with the Daughters of Charity in a Federation that has, over the next fifty years, united all the Sisters of Charity, and, in the United States the Daughters of Charity, in a common bond of friendship and dedicated service.

The Daughters of Charity in Emmitsburg grew in numbers and works, especially health care, throughout the states. One noticeable change after the union with France was in the sisters' attire. The black dress and bonnet, the habit adopted by Mother Seton for her community, was exchanged for the blue/gray garb and white-winged cornette of the Daughters of Charity in France and throughout the world, a picturesque habit made familiar by artists who depicted them on the battlefields in Europe and elsewhere nursing the wounded.

Throughout the 19th and 20th centuries the works of the Daughters of Charity of Emmitsburg spread across the nation, and the numbers of Daughters had, at their peak period in the 1960s reached over 2,500 sisters working in health-care, social services and education. Eventually they volunteered for missions in China until they were expelled by the Communist government. They served in Bolivia and Japan, and formed autonomous provinces of the Daughters of Charity there. Through their international headquarters in Paris individual American Daughters served with Daughters from other countries in several impoverished areas throughout the world. So numerous became the Daughters of Charity, their need for more direct communication with decision-makers so great, that in 1969 they divided into five provinces in the United States with headquarters in Emmitsburg, Maryland; Albany, New York; Evansville, Indiana; St. Louis, Missouri; and Los Altos Hills, California. Review and revision of works is an ongoing process reflecting their commitment to the poor and to health care. In 1986 they incorporated the Daughters of Charity

National Health Care System ensuring a greater percentage of finances available to be used for the poor.

The Daughters ministered to the sick on the battlefields during the Civil War and the Spanish-American War, in U.S. refugee camps, in epidemics. The Associate Program is not new to them. Lay women and men had been their associates in ministry since the time of Vincent de Paul and Louise de Marillac. This led the sisters to relinquish administrative positions to qualified lay colleagues. Changes today reflect a deep commitment to the poor and a thrust toward service in areas where the Catholic presence is minimal. The Daughters are working in Covenant House, thrift shops, soup kitchens, literacy programs, homeless shelters, family health centers, high-rise apartments for the elderly, work with the disabled, campus ministry, GED programs, chemical dependency programs, English and Spanish as second languages, services to HIV/AIDS mothers and babies, advocacy for refugees and migrants, catalysts in neighborhood development while maintaining traditional school and health-care programs.

In 1993 they numbered 1,280 sisters and eight Postulants. They continue today to be a vital force for good in the lives of hundreds of thousands of people in the United States and abroad. Their Provincial House in Emmitsburg houses the National Shrine of St. Elizabeth Ann Seton, proclaimed a Basilica in 1991, where Mother Seton's remains are interred.

THE SISTERS OF CHARITY OF NAZARETH, KENTUCKY[3]

The Congregation of Sisters of Charity of Nazareth, Kentucky, had its beginnings in 1812 at Bardstown under the direction of Father John Baptist David, a Sulpician priest and former Superior and Spiritual Director of Mother

Seton and her community in Emmitsburg. Because of the overwhelming number of Catholic families that flocked to Kentucky from Maryland in those days, Father David enlisted the help of Catherine Spalding and five other young women who wanted to dedicate their lives to the Church. On Easter Sunday 1813 they elected Catherine Spalding their first Mother Superior. Father David directed the Kentucky foundation after Mother Seton's model in Emmitsburg, adopting, as she had done, a modified rule based on the Constitutions of St. Vincent de Paul.

Father David, future Coadjutor to Bishop Benedict Flaget, carefully guided the religious formation of his sisters. An experienced educator, he also trained the first sisters as teachers. In 1814 Eleanor O'Connell, a well-educated teacher from Baltimore, entered the community and assisted Father David with that training. Nazareth Academy was opened at St. Thomas and later moved closer to Bardstown.

When the Emmitsburg community considered affiliation with the Daughters in France, Bishop Flaget advised the Kentucky Sisters to do likewise, but the sisters were unanimous in their desire to remain a distinct American institution. Mother Catherine Spalding pleaded their cause so effectively that Bishop Flaget yielded to her. As far back as 1829, its fiscal and legal status was secured when it became incorporated by the General Assembly of Kentucky. For nearly one hundred years the Sisters of Charity were a diocesan community, renewing their vows annually, but in 1910 they received Papal approval and with it the privilege of making perpetual vows.

In 1831 Mother Catherine opened Presentation Academy, the first Catholic school in Louisville still in operation more than a century and a half later. During the cholera epidemic in 1832 the teachers nursed the victims and cared for its orphaned survivors, later founding St. Vincent Orphanage and St. Joseph Infirmary, the first of their many future institutions of social service and health care. Eventually they taught at two colleges, more than thirty high schools, one hundred elementary schools, six orphanages, ten hospitals, and six nurses' training schools, working in Massachusetts, Kentucky, Washington, D.C., Virginia, Ohio, Arkansas, Alabama, Tennessee, and other areas. At their peak in the 1960s they numbered about 1,600 sisters.

A group of Sisters of Charity of Nazareth in 1842 established an academy and hospital in Nashville, Tennessee, at the invitation of the Bishop. In 1851 they separated from the Kentucky community and in 1858 they founded the Sisters of Charity of Leavenworth, Kansas, now a large and flourishing congregation.

In 1947 the Sisters of Charity of Nazareth provided health care and education to the poor in Mokameh, India, at the invitation of the Bishop of Patna Diocese in Bihar. In the following years they taught in schools and adult education centers, and worked in community development projects, a hospital, a school of nursing, outpatient clinics. They established a novitiate for native women to carry on their work in India. In 1975 they went to Belize, Central America, and in 1979 to Nepal.

As it nears the end of its second century of work, the Nazareth congregation continues to maintain its Motherhouse and central offices on the property that Mother Catherine Spalding purchased in 1822. The former college dormitories are now low-income apartments for the elderly and disabled. Other buildings on this extensive property house a Montessori school and a home health agency that meets the health-care needs of the people in eight nearby counties. Catherine Spalding Center in

Russell Hall, once the Novitiate building, is now a flourishing retreat center for lay people and religious.

In 1996 the congregation numbered 829 members and 240 Associate members. The sisters are engaged in education, health care, pastoral ministry, and social service. Today the priorities of the Sisters of Charity of Nazareth are: humanizing values, alleviating poverty, working against racism, effecting peace, public corporate stances, support of sanctuary for Central American political refugees, opposition to the nuclear arms race, opposition to the U.S. military involvement in Central America, the dignity and value of women worldwide, the abuse of natural resources. For the past ten years the congregation's nursing home in Louisville, Kentucky, has offered long-term care for persons with AIDS and support for their families. In June 1995 the Sisters of Charity of Nazareth and their Associates adopted a Mission Statement in which they committed themselves to work for justice in solidarity with oppressed people, especially the economically poor and women, and to care for the earth.

THE SISTERS OF CHARITY OF CINCINNATI[4]

High on a hill overlooking the Ohio River just west of Cincinnati stands an impressive red brick structure known as Mount Saint Joseph. Over one hundred years old, it presents an imposing face to the river and to the sisters' Kentucky neighbors. Few would suspect that the roots of the Mount can be traced to four women who arrived in 1829, answering the call of Bishop Edward Fenwick to serve the needs of poor Catholics.

Those four women, Sisters Fanny Jordan, Victoria Fitzgerald, Beatrice Tyler and Albina Levy, traveled a long and tiresome journey from Mother Seton's community in Emmitsburg by stage and riverboat to Cincinnati.

Undaunted by their fatigue, they immediately set to work taking care of five orphans and six other children, opening St. Peter's Orphan Asylum and Free School. During the dreaded cholera epidemic in 1832 the sisters cared for the sick and orphaned, whom they brought into their orphan asylum. Bishop Fenwick himself died of cholera. By the late 1840s the number of sisters increased to eleven, and the school and orphanage to several hundred children. At this time the sisters in Cincinnati learned that their superiors in Emmitsburg had made arrangements to join their congregation with the Company of Daughters of Charity based in France. The Emmitsburg superiors recalled three of the sisters from Cincinnati who had begun to staff a new orphanage for boys in 1845, as the rule of the Daughters of Charity forbade caring for orphan boys. Seven sisters under the leadership of their Superior, Sister Margaret George, refused to participate in this change and formed the diocesan community of the Sisters of Charity of Cincinnati on March 25, 1852, with Archbishop Purcell's permission and under the leadership of Sister Margaret George as first Mother Superior. Within a few months their work had expanded to include a boys' orphanage and the first Catholic hospital in Cincinnati. They opened a novitiate and, as their numbers grew, expanded geographically. By 1859 they numbered seventy-five Sisters of Charity of Cincinnati. When the Civil War broke out, one-third of the now one hundred sisters saw active service on the eastern front in Ohio, Maryland, and Virginia; and on the western front in Mississippi, Kentucky, and Tennessee. Sister Anthony O'Connell became widely known as the "Angel of the Battlefield" due to her outstanding medical work as well as her dynamic personality. The sisters moved with the army, serving at Camp Dennison where 12,000 men were camped, nursing the wounded at Cumberland, Shiloh,

Corinth, New Creek, Culpepper Court House, Gallipolis, Nashville, and Richmond.

Immediately after the war four Sisters of Charity were sent to Santa Fe to open St. Vincent's, the first hospital in the New Mexico territory. The sisters in the West supported their social service works by begging at the railroad and mining camps. By the 1880s the community had sisters in cities and towns along the front range of the Rocky Mountains in Colorado and New Mexico. Perhaps the most colorful of these sisters was Sister Blandina Segale whose book, *At the End of the Sante Fe Trail,* became the basis for articles, plays, and movies. Of particular interest were her contacts with Billy the Kid.

In 1866 two wealthy gentlemen acquainted with Sister Anthony's work for the sick poor purchased the U.S. Marine Hospital in Cincinnati and presented the deed to her on her birthday, naming it the Good Samaritan Hospital because of Sister Anthony's work for the sick poor. It has become a leading institution in the medical field – a teaching hospital with its own school of nursing.

As the community continued to grow, it was able to offer assistance in the establishment of two additional branches of Mother Seton's sisters, the Sisters of Charity of Convent Station, New Jersey (1859), and the Sisters of Charity of Seton Hill, Greensburg, Pennsylvania (1870).

Meanwhile the Sisters of Charity of Cincinnati widened the expanse of their work in the Midwest. Many new parish schools were accepted in the Cincinnati area and throughout Ohio and Michigan. In 1886 Mount Saint Joseph Motherhouse became a reality outside the city in Delhi. By the end of the 19th century the community became involved in work with Italian immigrants. The Santa Maria Italian Educational and Institutional Home was incorporated as the first Catholic Settlement House in the United States and became the foundation for an

Archdiocesan social service program. In 1920 the College of Mount St. Joseph was founded to respond to the increasing demand for higher education for women. In 1962 a new seventy-five-acre, eleven-building campus was constructed. In the 1920s the Sisters of Charity of Cincinnati also became a Pontifical Institute.

China became the first foreign mission field for the Sisters of Charity of Cincinnati. In 1928 six sisters arrived in Wuchang, a city about 750 miles up the Yangtze River from Shanghai. They opened a hospital and dispensary, cared for the aged and orphans, ran a school for young children and a training program for nurses. By the early 1930s Chinese women began to join the community. A novitiate was therefore opened in 1934. The sisters continued to work in China during the Japanese invasion and occupation in World War II and the Chinese Civil War but left in 1949 in the wake of the Communist takeover. Other foreign involvements included running an orphanage in Rome in the 1950s and 1960s, missions initiated in Peru in the 1960s, and a brief sojourn in Africa in the 1970s.

With the passing decades the community experienced continued growth, reaching its highest peak of over 1,500 sisters in the 1960s. The impact of the Second Vatican Council caused reassessment of ministry, lifestyle, sponsorship of institutions, and internal governance. An Associate Program initiated in 1975 invites friends and coworkers to share in the mission of the community. In 1979 all the Sisters of Charity of Cincinnati's Health Care Institutions were brought together in the Sisters of Charity Health Care Systems under the leadership of Sister Grace Marie Hiltz, becoming one of the largest Catholic health care systems in the United States. In 1996 it became part of Catholic Health Initiatives. In the 1990s the Sisters of Charity of Cincinnati number 700 sisters engaged in parish ministry, administrative positions, hospital chaplaincies, work with senior citizens and the poor. They sponsor grant and low-interest loan programs to assist community development and social justice organizations and projects.

THE SISTERS OF CHARITY OF OUR LADY OF MERCY[5]

The Sisters of Charity of Our Lady of Mercy is an American diocesan congregation founded by Bishop England in Charleston, S.C., in 1829. While in Baltimore attending the first Provincial Council of Catholic Bishops, England met four young women eager to enter a religious order to give their lives to God in the service of the poor. They were the American-born Mary Elizabeth Burke and three natives of Ireland – Mary and Honora O'Gorman and their fifteen-year-old niece, Teresa Barry. Bishop England invited them to form with him a new religious community in the diocese of Charleston, South Carolina. Using Mother Seton's Sisters of Charity in Emmitsburg as his model, the Bishop wrote a rule based on that of St. Vincent de Paul. Oral tradition testifies that their original religious habit came from Emmitsburg and was worn for over one hundred years, from 1830 to 1932.

At the time of Bishop England's death in 1842, the community numbered nineteen members who conducted an orphanage, a girls' academy, a free school for poor white girls and one for free black children. During the yellow fever and cholera epidemics the sister teachers became nurses, tending the sick in their homes and in temporary relief hospitals.

Bishop Ignatius Reynolds, a native of Kentucky, second Bishop of Charleston, wrote the Constitutions, basing them on Bishop England's rules and the Constitutions of the Sisters of Charity in Emmitsburg and those of the

Sisters of Charity of Nazareth, Kentucky, all of which were modified versions of those of St. Vincent de Paul. The original name of the Order was Sisters of Our Lady of Mercy, but in 1949, one hundred years later, they adopted a new Constitution and name – the Sisters of Charity of Our Lady of Mercy. The insertion of the word *charity* was intended to identify the congregation with those congregations based on the rule of St.Vincent de Paul and its American adaptations.

In 1844 young Sister Teresa Barry at age thrity was elected Mother Superior, a position she held for thirty-nine years. She is looked on today as the foundress of the Sisters of Charity of Our Lady of Mercy. Under her leadership during the Civil War the sisters staffed a Confederate Hospital in Montgomery White Sulphur Springs, Virginia. While Charleston was being bombarded, the sisters moved their academy boarders and their orphans to Sumter, S.C. There they founded St. Joseph's Academy, a day and boarding school which continued in operation until 1929. The remainder of the community stayed in Charleston, visiting Union soldiers in prisons and hospitals. After the Civil War, the United States Congress granted an appropriation of $12,000 to the sisters to help rebuild the Motherhouse/orphanage in Charleston. During the Reconstruction era they also received financial assistance from the "carpetbag" governments. The sisters established convents in Georgia and in North Carolina that eventually amalgamated with Mother McAuley's Sisters of Mercy.

From 1880 to 1929 the congregation of Sisters of Charity of Our Lady of Mercy doubled its membership and broadened the scope of its ministries, establishing St. Francis Xavier Hospital and School of Nursing in Charleston, and Divine Savior Hospital in York, South Carolina, which later included a nursing home. The sisters also taught in parochial schools throughout South Carolina. In the 1940s and 1950s they opened schools in New Jersey in the Trenton and Camden dioceses. At their peak they numbered about one hundred sisters. The sisters succeeded in breaking down prejudices against Roman Catholics in the South by their work for people of all denominations in their Catholic hospitals. St. Francis Xavier Hospital in Charleston expanded its services to include the Neighborhood House, a social services agency, providing home nursing care for the sick and poor. In the 1960s Catholic Charities took it over, assuming responsibility for orphans and children of broken homes while the sisters continued to work in the Diocesan Home for Children until it was closed in 1991.

At present the congregation numbers thirty-three sisters living and working in the Diocese of Charleston. The Motherhouse on James Island overlooking Charleston Harbor, offers facilities for laity, both Catholics and non-Catholics, interested in retreats or professional programs. In 1989 the sisters transferred ownership of St. Francis Xavier Hospital and Divine Savior Hospital and Nursing Home to the Bon Secours Sisters. However the Sisters of Charity of Our Lady of Mercy continue their hospital work with their visits to the sick and elderly. They have, for some time, been running a highly successful Outreach Facility and program providing direct service to the poor and elderly of every denomination and color on John's Island, James Island, and Wadmalaw Island. Some sisters continue to teach and serve as Principals of parochial schools, parish ministers, on church councils and in choirs. They also provide education programs.

Their former General Superior, Sister Bridget Sullivan, was Assistant Vicar General of the Diocese of Charleston and Executive Secretary of the Diocesan Synod (1990-1995). She gave an overview of what a small community of sisters is able to accomplish. Although never numbering more than one hundred sisters at any given time, they have a reputation for answering the call to a new work, getting it started, and then leaving it to capable people to carry on. These sisters lay the groundwork, do the hard spade work, then pass it along to others and hold no grudges. They are rugged individualists who had to struggle in the deep South, where Catholics are a minority group. In 1994 they celebrated their 165th anniversary – a testimony to almost two centuries of ministry to the African-American and the white people of South Carolina. In 1996 Sister M. Anne Francis Campbell was elected General Superior. Though a small community these sisters are big in energy, creativity, and hard work, totally dedicated to the needs of God's people.

THE SISTERS OF CHARITY OF NEW YORK[6]

In 1817, only nine years after Elizabeth Seton's departure for Baltimore and Emmitsburg, her Sisters of Charity returned to New York to begin their long and fruitful work there in hospitals, orphanages, infants' homes, schools, and colleges. In 1850 when the Sisters of Charity of Emmitsburg decided to join the Company of Daughters of Charity in France, thirty-three of the Sisters of Charity in New York preferred to remain there and become a New York diocesan community. They continued with great success the work of charity so dear to Mother Seton throughout the five boroughs of New York, on Long Island, and in upstate New York. Manhattan and the Bronx have been the center of their work. Sister Elizabeth Boyle was elected first Mother of this new community of Mother Seton's sisters. With the approval of Bishop Hughes the Cathedral trustees lent Mother Elizabeth $10,000 to purchase for the Motherhouse the property at McGown's Pass near Fifth Avenue at East 107th Street, now part of Central Park.

On January 23, 1849, the Community was incorporated under the legal title of Sisters of Charity of St. Vincent de Paul of New York, with five sisters appointed legal trustees for the first year. That same year marked the founding of what would become one of the major establishments of the Sisters of Charity of New York – the opening of St. Vincent's Hospital in a rented house on East 13th Street. That year also marked the beginning of the congregation of Sisters of Charity of Halifax. Bishop Hughes agreed to the request from Bishop Walsh of Halifax for sisters. He sent four Sisters of Charity to Canada to serve in education, health care, and social service.

Other establishments were founded: St. Joseph's School on Oliver Street, St. Patrick's Academy on Mulberry Street, the New York Catholic Protectory, and the Roman Catholic Orphan Asylum. The Motherhouse of the Sisters of Charity was, in 1859, transferred to an estate of fifty-five acres along the Hudson River, south of the village of Yonkers, owned by Edwin Forrest, the distinguished actor, who had built on the property a Norman Gothic Castle called Font Hill. It was providentially purchased and on this beautiful site rose the many fine buildings of Mount Saint Vincent-on-the-Hudson. Established at the Motherhouse were the Postulate, Novitiate, and Juniorate of the congregation which at its peak period in the 1960s numbered over 1,200 Sisters of Charity. By 1855 there were almost 200 students in the Academy of Mount Saint Vincent, which eventually became the highly esteemed College of Mount Saint Vincent.

In 1853 four sisters were sent to open a mission in Jersey City at St. Peter's Parish. There they conducted a free school for the poor and a select school for tuition-paying students. The money thus derived helped the sisters to continue the work for the poor. Bishop James Roosevelt Bayley, a nephew of Mother Seton, was the first Bishop of Newark and later Archbishop of Baltimore. Father Bernard McQuaid, who said he owed his vocation to the Sisters of Charity, asked for New York Sisters of Charity to staff St. Patrick's Orphan Asylum for boys in Newark, October 1853, some months after a group of Sisters of Charity had arrived in Jersey City. Three sisters were sent, followed later on by three more.

Mother Jerome Ely was now Mother General of the New York community, having been elected in 1849. By 1858 Bishop Bayley and Father McQuaid were convinced that a new diocesan community of Sisters of Charity of New Jersey should be founded. Accordingly Sister Mary Xavier Mehegan and Sister Mary Catherine Nevins were sent to take charge of the new Motherhouse in Newark. Sister Xavier was appointed the first General Superior of the New Jersey Sisters of Charity. The Motherhouse was moved to property near Madison and given the name of St. Elizabeth after Mother Seton. The first novices were trained by the Sisters of Charity of Cincinnati under Sister Margaret George, friend of Mother Seton. The New Jersey Sisters of Charity were an offshoot of the Cincinnati congregation.

Another new community established in Canada in 1854 was also linked to the New York Sisters of Charity. Mother Mary Vincent Conway, foundress of the Saint John, New Brunswick, Sisters of Charity, later called the Sisters of Charity of the Immaculate Conception, received her religious training at Mount Saint Vincent Novitiate in New York. The concluding paragraph of a folder published by the Saint John Sisters of Charity in 1947 stresses the spiritual relationship of this community with Mother Seton and the New York community: "She [Mother Mary Vincent Conway] left to her own community the spirit of

Mother Seton's Sisters of Charity communicated to her by Mother Mary Jerome Ely during that period of intense religious training prior to her departure from New York in September 1854."[7]

An industrial school for young people was taken over by the Sisters of Charity on West 42nd Street. Here during the Civil War in 1861 the students made the red and blue uniforms for the Fire Zouaves, a regiment of picked troops. The sisters contributed three years of military service at home by opening the old Mount Saint Vincent Motherhouse in Central Park as a military hospital, accommodating 250 patients, where they nursed the wounded soldiers. In 1866 the sisters nursed the victims of cholera on Wards Island. One of the most outstanding works of the New York Sisters of Charity was the foundation in 1869 of the New York Foundling Hospital for abandoned infants. This was greatly needed in the many desperately poor areas of the metropolis of New York where so many young, unmarried mothers abandoned their infants. Almost a century later a ten million dollar building project for the Sisters of Charity was initiated by Cardinal Spellman in 1954 with the purchase of a new site for the ten-story New York Foundling Hospital at Third Avenue between East 68th and 69th Streets, accommodating more than 300 infants and small children, a nurses' training school and residence, a shelter for unmarried mothers, and a residence for the sisters.

The community multiplied in numbers as did the schools in which the sisters taught and the health care centers where they worked. In 1936 they were asked to found a native community of sisters at Nassau in the Bahamas where the New York Sisters of Charity had taught in many schools since 1889. At home in New York the large influx of Puerto Rican families into the city required sisters to learn Spanish and become involved in teaching and social work for these impoverished families.

In 1984 the Sisters of Charity Health Care System Corporation was inaugurated; in 1989 they celebrated their hundredth anniversary working for the poor in the Bahamas; in 1992-93 the 175th anniversary of their presence in New York; in 1994 the 125th anniversary of the New York Foundling Hospital. At their peak period the Sisters of Charity of New York numbered almost 1400 sisters. Today there are about 650 sisters in this New York community still engaged in social work, health care, and education besides several nontraditional ministries.

THE SISTERS OF CHARITY OF HALIFAX[8]

On May 11, 1849, four Sisters of Charity of New York arrived at Market Wharf, Halifax Harbor, via the ship Cambria, which carried 110 passengers and 300 tons of cargo from Boston. It was a two-day journey. The sisters had set out at the behest of Bishop William Walsh of Halifax through the permission of his good friend, Bishop Hughes of New York. Led by Sister Basilia McCann, a former pupil of Mother Seton in Emmitsburg, the sisters brought with them the spirit and inspiration of Mother Seton to this new foundation, of which Sister Basilia would be the first Mother. A young Haligonian, Catherine McNeil, was there on the wharf to see the new arrivals. She was to become their fourth Postulant and eventually Mother General of the congregation.

By November the sisters, with the help of lay people, were teaching 400 students, caring for orphans, directing Sodalities and Sunday School classes. By 1855 six Halifax girls had gone to New York to make their novitiate and return to Halifax as professed Sisters of Charity. In the same year Bishop Walsh arranged with the New York

Sisters to make the Halifax community a separate diocesan congregation. It was formerly approved by Pope Pius IX in 1856. After Mother Basilia's term of office expired in 1858, she chose to return to her own New York Congregation to the genuine regret of the little Halifax community who revered her as their foundress. The Sisters of Charity were incorporated by statute of provincial legislature. Sister Mary Rose McAleer, one of the original group of New York sisters, became the second Mother (1858-1864). In the years that followed new schools and convents were opened in Nova Scotia and New Brunswick by the Sisters of Charity of Halifax. In 1864 Sister Mary Josephine Carroll took office as the first Canadian Mother General. Two years later the passenger ship *England* arrived in Halifax Harbor carrying 1,300 Irish immigrants, many of whom were stricken with the dread Asiatic cholera. They were quarantined on McNabb's Island. Although all the sisters volunteered to nurse them, only three were allowed to do so with the doctor and a priest. After it was over, the sisters were able to bring back many orphaned children. The sisters opened St. Joseph's Orphanage in Halifax in 1868.

In 1872 Mother Catherine O'Neill purchased twenty-five acres of woodland in Rockingham, a suburb of Halifax, on the shores of Bedford Basin. It was a beautiful site. On it was constructed the first Motherhouse, similar to Mount Saint Vincent Motherhouse on the Hudson River in New York. The sisters gave this new Motherhouse the same name. Over the years one wing after another was added. A huge and gracious building resulted, including a Postulate, Novitiate, Academy and College. Completely destroyed by fire in 1951, it remains a precious part of the history of the Sisters of Charity of Halifax, some 1,500 or more of whom had been trained and educated there. A new and even larger Motherhouse replaced it, as did separate buildings for Mount Saint Vincent University.

During the 1870s the very existence of the congregation was threatened by the opposition of Archbishop Michael Hannan of the Archdiocese of Halifax, to the Sisters of Charity and their ministries. Many outstanding Canadians including Bishop John Cameron of Arichat, Nova Scotia, and Sir John D. Thomson, Attorney General of Nova Scotia, later to become Prime Minister of Canada, appealed to Rome. Two Sisters of Charity, Sister Mary de Sales Dwyer and Mary Aloysia Holden, traveled to Rome and were given an audience by Pope Leo XIII to explain their just grievances. The Pope placed the community under the direct protection of Rome, and in 1913 it became a Pontifical Institute, thus giving the congregation new stability and status.

The Sisters of Charity of Halifax included health care in their ministries, opening the Halifax Infirmary which became a large, highly successful hospital and school of nursing. Other hospitals included St. Elizabeth in Cape Breton and four hospitals in Alberta and British Columbia. In 1917 during World War I the collision of two ships in Halifax Harbor, one of which was loaded with dynamite, caused a deadly explosion that leveled the north end of Halifax seriously injuring and killing some thousand people and children. The sisters nursed the sick, brought orphaned children into their orphanage, and continued to teach their pupils, although many of the schools were demolished.

The main ministry of the Sisters of Charity of Halifax was education, and they developed a reputation for excellence. They built and staffed Mount Saint Vincent Academy, later Mount Saint Vincent University, and taught in the public schools in Nova Scotia, the separate and parochial school system in New Brunswick, Quebec,

Ontario, Alberta and British Columbia. They also staffed large numbers of elementary and secondary parochial schools in Massachusetts and New York, and a few schools in New Jersey and New Hampshire. In 1890 they were asked to staff an academy and school in Bermuda, where they still teach. The sisters were sent on for doctorates at Catholic University, Washington, D.C.; Fordham University, New York; Notre Dame University, Indiana, and many other higher institutions of learning. The first Ph.D.'s were earned: in 1916 Sister Evaristus Moran, in 1917 Sisters Maria Rosaria Gorman and Mary Gervase Kelley, in 1924 Sister Maura Power, and some fifty more in subsequent years.

The sisters also engaged in social work, taking care of unwed mothers and their infants at the Home of the Guardian Angel; orphans at St. Joseph's; the elderly at St. Theresa's Retreat and St. Vincent Guest House – all in Halifax – and at St. Bridget's Home in Quebec. They taught in two residential schools for native children. In the 1960s they opened missions in Peru, the Dominican Republic, and the Northwest Territories. By the 1960s the total number of Sisters of Charity reached a peak of over 1,600.

In the 1970s the congregation divested itself of the ownership of most of its institutions but retained ownership of the Motherhouse in Halifax and Mount Saint Vincent of Wellesley Hills, Massachusetts, for their health-care facilities and living quarters for retired sisters.

A wide variety of individual ministries have been initiated since the 1960s for battered women, single parents, the victims of AIDS, abused children, mentally handicapped young people, victims of alcohol and drug abuse, prisoners and immigrants. Literacy programs for illiterate adults and minority groups, programs for the unemployed, the lonely, the aged have also been maintained. Despite reduced numbers (860 sisters in 1996), half of these sisters are still employed either full- or part-time. Many retired sisters in their 70s and 80s are actively employed as volunteers in part-time ministries. The spirit of charity is life-giving.

THE SISTERS OF CHARITY OF THE IMMACULATE CONCEPTION[9]

In 1852 Honoria Conway, a young educated woman from County Galway, Ireland, volunteered to help her friend, Bishop Thomas Connolly, in Saint John, New Brunswick, Canada, with the care of the orphaned children of Irish immigrants whose parents had died in the cholera epidemic. Shortly after, perhaps on Bishop Connolly's advice and her own interest in religious life, she entered the Congregation of Sisters of Charity of New York. After completing the Postulate and Novitiate training in 1854, Honoria was present with other novices when Bishop Connolly, with Mother Jerome Ely's permission, told them about a new diocesan community he was founding in Saint John, N.B., and asked for volunteers. Honoria and three others offered to go. One was Mary Routanne, a former member of the Emmitsburg community (1842-1847). They left for Canada and took their vows in Saint John in October 1854 as professed Sisters of Charity dedicated to "the care of orphans, the instruction of the poor, and the attendance of the sick" (Original Rule). The name of the community was lengthened in 1918 to the Sisters of Charity of the Immaculate Conception. Through Mary Routanne's association with the Emmitsburg and New York Sisters of Charity, and Honoria's novitiate in New York, the spirit of Mother Seton became their inspiration.

Bishop Connolly appointed Honoria Conway, now Sister Mary Vincent, the first Mother General. He held her in high esteem. In the fall of 1854 two more young women joined them – Mary and Bridget O'Toole from New York. Mary had been with Honoria in the New York Postulate. St. Vincent Convent and Orphanage for girls on Cliff Street became their base. In 1892 a wing was added as a select school for girls, thus providing the sisters with an income to spend in their work for the poor. In 1880 St. Patrick's Industrial School, an orphanage for boys, was opened by the sisters. They continued to teach there for seventy years. In 1949 the two orphanages merged with accommodations for all at St. Patrick's just outside the city. Classes were provided for the orphans only. In 1888 Bishop Sweeney collaborated with the sisters in building Mater Misericordia Home for the Elderly which was the forerunner of the present fine building, Rocmaura Nursing Home on Parks Street.

Besides education and social work, the sisters also became involved in health care, establishing the first Catholic Hospital in the diocese, the Saint John Infirmary, which opened in 1914, the foundation for their excellent St. Joseph's Hospital today. Throughout New Brunswick and in various cities across Canada the Sisters of Charity of the Immaculate Conception ministered in hospitals, orphanages, social agencies, and schools in western Canada in the provinces of Saskatchewan, Alberta, and British Columbia. At Prince Albert, Saskatchewan, their dedicated service to the needy was notable. There they ministered to orphan children and opened the congregation's first hospital in the West.

Although dedicated to the care and education of the children of Irish immigrants, the sisters' pioneering spirit inspired them to open a school for the large population of French children at Madawaska on the northwestern corner of New Brunswick. Its most thriving center was Saint Basile, where the first Catholic parish was established. In December 1857 three Sisters of Charity established a school there in the wilderness among the Acadian people whose language and culture was so radically different from the Irish. Nevertheless the Acadians gave them a warm welcome, accepting English as the language of the school since this would facilitate their social and economic future. The sisters also prepared young Acadians for teaching. *The Carlton Sentinel* as quoted in *The Morning Freeman* July 11, 1863, noted that seventeen of the sisters' students had left to take teaching positions in Maine, with forty-seven remaining scholars with the sisters at Madawaska. The paper noted "Up till the middle of the 19th century, education for the Acadians was practically non-existent."[10]

It was with considerable regret in 1924 that the Irish Sisters of Charity of the Immaculate Conception were faced with a division. The Acadian sisters, with the approval of the Bishop, decided to found a new French community, Les Religieuses de-Notre-Dame-du-Sacré-Coeur. Fifty-three Acadian sisters would minister to the French Acadian families of New Brunswick. It caused a deep break between the two groups, difficult to heal. But time is a great healer and today, some seventy years later, they are closely united in spirit.

The Irish Sisters of Charity of the Immaculate Conception continued in their excellent work for the English-speaking people of eastern and western Canada. They also opened, in the 1960s, a mission in Peru for the Latin American people in impoverished areas. At their peak period in the 1960s they numbered 400 sisters. At the present time, with the readiness of the lay population to assume leadership in ministry, and with the decrease in the number of religious, the Sisters of Charity of Saint John have gradually withdrawn in part from many of their former areas of service. As individuals they have become more involved in ministries of greater advocacy and solidarity with the poor and the marginalized, with the formation of lay leadership and ongoing formation within the wider Church, with groups and organizations fostering the dignity and worth of all persons, with the ministry in rural areas especially among native peoples, and with housing for the underprivileged. In 1994 they numbered 214 sisters. Most of the sisters, even the retired members, are still working in full- or part-time ministries.

LES RELIGIEUSES DE NOTRE-DAME-DU-SACRÉ-COEUR[11]

This new congregation, founded in 1924 with fifty-three French Acadian Sisters of Charity of the Immaculate Conception from Saint John, New Bruswick, had freely chosen to leave their community of English-speaking sisters in order to minister to the French Acadians in their own language and culture.

The history of this break began as far back as 1871 when Suzanne Cyr (Sister Marie-Anne), a resident of Saint Basile, New Brunswick, entered the Congregation of the Irish Sisters of Charity of the Immaculate Conception at Saint John. As a young professed Sister of Charity, her first mission was to an almost entirely French Acadian parish, Saint Joseph at Memramcook. There she organized French classes for the boarders and day students in the convent school, where formerly they had been taught exclusively in English. An intelligent woman and a capable administrator, she realized the ethnic problems of an Irish Order of sisters, not bilingual, ministering to French Acadian people and children. She could at least partially solve the problem. She worked and taught there for thirty-five years with great success. But in 1908 she was unexpectedly transferred to Bouctouche, New Brunswick, where she faced the same problems. It was then that she came to the realization that only a French Novitiate for the Acadian girls entering the Sisters of Charity would solve the problems, guaranteeing adequate formation for the sisters who would be working in French-speaking areas.

In 1914, when the congregation numbered less than 200 members, Sister Marie-Anne with a group of Acadian sisters, and the consent of Bishop Edouard LeBlanc, made an official request for a separate French Novitiate to the Superior General of the Sisters of Charity in Saint John, and to the Sacred Congregation of Religious in Rome. Her request was refused by both, no doubt because a separate novitiate would require a separate province and the small number in the congregation did not permit two provinces. Eight years later, in 1922-23, Sister Marie-Anne repeated the request and this time Mother Alphonse suggested a complete separation, that is, the founding of a French Acadian Order for the fifty-three Acadian Sisters of Charity willing to join it. On February 8, 1924, permission was granted and on February 17 the foundation was made, the first General Council formed, and Sister Marie-Anne at age 74 was elected General Superior (1924-1936) of Les Religieuses de Notre-Dame-du-Sacré-Coeur. She had spent a lifetime as a Sister of Charity of the Immaculate Conception; she loved that community and was a close friend of their General Superior. Only circumstances and her own good judgment forced her to do what her own heart would forbid. She did it for the good of the Acadian people, for the preservation of their language and culture. The new community grew rapidly in numbers and works of education, health care, and other services to the poor, the needy, the downtrodden and outcast. On February 23, 1924, only six days after the foundation, seven young women entered the new community and at the end of the year there were twenty-nine Postulants of whom twenty-three persevered. At its peak in the 1960s it numbered over 500 members. They were noted especially for their work as educators and for the numbers of sisters whom they sent on for higher degrees beyond the Bachelor's degree which most of their sisters achieved. Interestingly they continued to promote the spirituality and the ideals of Mother Seton that they had inculcated as members of Honoria Conway's community. Over the seventy-three years of its existence (1924-1997) this small community engaged in a surprising number of good works. Boarding schools were established at Grand-Sault, Saint-Joseph, Bouctouche, and Saint-Anselme. The sisters opened schools in Moncton, Sackville, Petit-Rocher, Ville-Platte in Louisiana (1931-1939). Between 1937 and 1941 five missions were opened at Drummond, Lewisville, Cap-Pelé, Dieppe, and Pointe-Sapin – all still open today except for Drummond and Cap-Pelé. By 1941 there were over 200 sisters in the community.

In 1943 the sisters opened a college at Saint-Joseph. It soon became obvious that better and larger facilities were needed and Notre Dame d'Acadie College (1949-1982) was built at Moncton, New Brunswick. It prospered for thirty-three years developing programs in the arts and enriching the students with a knowledge of their own history, culture, literature, and language. Two new houses were opened in Minto and Port Elgin in 1949. By 1950 four more houses were opened in New Brunswick. Their first establishment in Nova Scotia was made in 1951 at Weymouth. That same year four more houses were opened in New Brunswick, two in Prince Edward Island, and in 1955 the community assumed the direction of a small hospital in Bouctouche. In 1969 four sisters left for Peru. In the 1960s eight more houses were opened in Nova Scotia – at Berwick, Annapolis, Digby, Plympton, Quinan, West Pubnico, Kentville, and Buttes-Amirault.

Of these, three are still open to this day. The works of education in the congregation flourished.

The members of Les Religieuses de Notre-Dame-du-Sacré-Coeur are confident of the work of the sisters in the future. They ask with faith: "Why would we not grow? Have we not arisen from the Sisters of Charity of the Immaculate Conception, who were an offspring of Mother Elizabeth Seton . . .?"[12]

The sisters believe that tomorrow will be different from today; yet it will be the same as far as their profound commitment to the service of the Lord and His Church is concerned. They note that it was the same during Elizabeth Seton's time at the dawn of a new century; the same in Bishop Thomas Louis Connolly's and Mother Honoria Conway's time during the epidemic; the same in Mother Marie-Anne (Suzanne Cyr's) time. Each time there was a challenge to be faced, a people to help, and a God Who guides.

THE SISTERS OF CHARITY OF LEAVENWORTH[13]

The Sisters of Charity of Leavenworth, founded by the Sisters of Charity, Nashville, Tennessee, identify in themselves the spirit of the pioneer and immigrant, a lively American spirit imbued with deep faith; a spirit that marks collectively and individually the sisters themselves as they meet the needs of the times with trust in God. Their heritage through their founders, formation, and their background is both Vincentian and Setonian.

In 1851 five Sisters of Charity of Nazareth serving in Nashville, Tennessee, agreed to respond to a plea from Bishop Richard P. Miles to form a diocesan community. This was done with the reluctant approval of Mother Catherine Spalding. The small group continued to follow the rule of St. Vincent. Their rapid growth in Nashville necessitated more space, which Father Ivo Schacht, their ecclesiastical superior, appointed by the Bishop, moved to provide. He bought land and built a Motherhouse, an Orphanage, and an Academy, using monies deposited by parishioners. The sisters occupied these in 1856, unaware of the deepening trouble between Bishop Miles and Father Schacht, which resulted in Father Schacht's leaving the diocese. Upon learning of his departure, the parishioners began demanding their money, but there was none to give them. The now ailing Bishop refused to honor the debt. The sisters then were faced with debts not of their own making. They decided they would meet these and did so by selling land, furniture, and some supplies.

Now homeless and almost penniless, the sisters' problems were solved by prayer and by their Mother Superior, Mother Xavier Ross, who met with the well-known Father de Smet, Jesuit missionary to the Indians. He arranged a meeting for her with Bishop John B. Miege of Kansas Indian Territory. That good Bishop urged Mother to send her sisters to Leavenworth, Kansas, in these words: "Come North as soon as possible." Thus it was that the new Congregation of Sisters of Charity of Leavenworth was born.

In 1858 Leavenworth, "Where the West begins," was filled with a conglomeration of trappers, hunters, Indians, settlers heading West, frontier merchants, scouts, gamblers, and soldiers stationed at Fort Leavenworth. Those were years of terror and violence in the Kansas Territory as pro-slavery and anti-slavery factions contended for supremacy. Such a milieu seemed out of place for religious women to begin a new congregation, but the stark contrast fertilized new growth. On November 11, 1858, three years before Kansas became a state, five sisters, two postulants, one novice, and an orphan girl arrived at the wharf in Leavenworth, having traveled by train and riverboat from Louisville, Kentucky. The other sisters soon followed – sixteen in all. Immediately the sisters began teaching in the boys' school, which had been under the direction of a Jesuit Brother. They rented another cottage and opened an Academy for girls. They taught Black children, took in orphans, cared for the sick in their homes and wagon trains. The very presence of the sisters was reassuring in that turbulent era.

By February 1859 they had settled in their new home. Bishop Miege opened a canonical novitiate in which Mother Xavier would give instruction and the Bishop weekly conferences. A Motherhouse was built on Kickapoo Street in 1860, which would also serve as an Academy. The cottage, St. Vincent's, would house the growing orphanage.

In 1864 the sisters opened the first private hospital in Kansas with Sister Joanna Bruner, the first trained nurse and first woman in the Western Territory to run a hospital. It was she who trained the other sisters in nursing skills. Their patients arrived before the doors were opened – a poor family of refugees from Alabama fleeing Sherman's army. Bathed, fed, treated for sores and bruises, clothed in fresh garments, the family rapidly improved.

In 1868 the community received its state charter incorporated under the laws of Kansas as St. Mary's Female Academy. The following year five of the sisters and a music teacher, Rosa Kelley, traveled eleven days by rail line and stagecoach to Montana Territory, at Father de Smet's request, to open a hospital, orphanage, and school in Helena. Three families gave the sisters lodging until the Jesuits moved out of the newspaper office and the sisters moved into the "Gazette Shanty." During the summer and fall two sisters traveled to mining camps and frontier towns by coach, horseback, and on foot to solicit money for the new school and to build a hospital. In 1870 the first school for white girls in the territory was opened, and in October St. John the Baptist Hospital was ready to receive patients. The Academy and Hospital caught fire several times, but the sisters hauled water from the wells to quench the flames. In the first half of the twentieth century earthquakes totally destroyed their missions in Helena but the sisters regrouped and rebuilt. They opened a hospital in Deer Lodge, one in Butte, the largest mining camp in the world, and then St. Ann's in Anaconda and St. Vincent's in Billings, as well as elementary and secondary schools. The sisters developed a spirit and an energy unique to Montana as large numbers of Montana's young women entered the community.

The turn of the century brought the establishment of schools of nursing. In 1873 they opened St. Joseph Hospital in Denver, today a leader in the health field; another hospital in Laramie, Wyoming, St. Vincent's Hospital in the silver camp of Leadville, Colorado; St. Mary's Hospital in Grand Junction, Colorado; St. Anthony's Sanatorium, later a Hospital in Las Vegas, New Mexico. Today they operate a system of clinics for the sick-poor in Leavenworth, Kansas City, Topeka, Billings, Grand Junction, and Santa Monica – all under the Sisters of Charity Community's Health Service Corporation. They also draw on the generosity of medical personnel. Expenses are defrayed by gifts, contributions from charitable groups, and small payments made by some patients. Three sisters are qualified Physician Assistants. Hospitals continue to be part of their service.

Education was not neglected as the sisters opened many schools in Kansas and Nebraska as well as children's homes. Denver's Mount St. Vincent (1883) is today a viable and caring home for emotionally scarred children. The sisters knew starvation and extreme poverty;

they suffered through cyclone, drought, flood, earthquake, and grasshopper plague, but the community continued to grow, becoming in 1915 a Pontifical Institute. In 1923 they opened St. Mary Junior College, which later became a senior college for women educating the sisters and thousands of young women from across the country. In 1988 young men were also accepted as students. In the 1930s the sisters became part of the National Religious Instruction Vacation School Movement. They responded in rural areas during weeks of their summer vacation. The number of prisons in the Leavenworth area drew the sisters' interest in education as well as in prison ministry – an outreach program from St. Mary's College. Since the 1970s faculty give courses for inmates at federal and state prisons. In 1963 the sisters opened a school and clinic in Peru, where many Peruvian women have become Sisters of Charity in a canonically approved Formation Program. Today 400 Sisters of Charity of Leavenworth meet the needs of the times, still resourceful, willing to endure hardships, nurtured by prayer, trust in God, and mutual support, and looking forward to new challenges in the twenty-first century.

THE SISTERS OF CHARITY OF SAINT ELIZABETH, CONVENT STATION, N.J.[14]

The Sisters of Charity of Saint Elizabeth, a branch of Mother Seton's Emmitsburg foundation, was founded in 1859 in Newark. Mother Seton's nephew, Bishop James Roosevelt Bayley of the Diocese of Newark, New Jersey, appealed to the New York Sisters of Charity to help him form a new diocesan community. Sister Mary Xavier Mehegan, who had already worked in Newark, was loaned to him. He had recruited five young women whom he had sent to the Sisters of Charity of Cincinnati to be trained in their novitiate. These were to be the nucleus of the new community.

Assisted by Sister Mary Catharine Nevin of the New York congregation, Sister Mary Xavier opened the first Motherhouse in Newark, and they were joined by the five novices from Cincinnati. After three years the two New York sisters were free to remain or to return to New York. They chose to stay. In 1860 ten sisters, including Sister Xavier, moved to Convent Station, then Madison where a permanent Motherhouse including an Academy was established. Sister Mary Xavier was, in 1873, appointed by Bishop Michael Corrigan, successor to Bishop Bayley, to the office of Mother for life.

During Mother Xavier's tenure of fifty-six years, the congregation experienced a remarkable growth in membership and missions: schools, hospitals, day-nurseries, orphanages, a home for the incurable ill, and a residence for working women were established. The sisters' ministries had extended to New York, Connecticut, and Massachusetts. Between 1923 and 1963 the Sisters of Charity of Saint Elizabeth undertook missionary foundations in China, Puerto Rico, the Virgin Islands, and Bolivia. Within the United States the congregation opened the first Catholic parochial school for African-American children in the state of Florida.

The painful struggle to discern their charism and ministries often tested their sense of identity and purpose in those early days, even as it does now. The questioning of whether the higher education of women could be included in the purpose for which they were founded resulted in the opening in 1899 of the College of Saint Elizabeth, one of the first Roman Catholic colleges for women in the United States, and the first college in New Jersey to grant degrees to women.

In 1957 the status of the congregation was changed from a diocesan community to that of a Pontifical Institute. Shortly thereafter the Second Vatican Council and its aftermath became a watershed in its history. The directives to make the following of Christ in the Gospels the norm of religious life, to return to the spirit of its founders, and to adjust themselves to the changed conditions of the times presented undreamed-of challenges. There was a proliferation of new ministries, a revitalization of traditional ones, and an increase in small community living. There were shifts from a juridically-based approach to religious life to a more Biblically and theologically-oriented approach; from separation from the world to an involvement in the world as the locus of God's action in history.

The congregation in 1967, at its peak period numbering over 1,700 sisters, submitted to a directive from the Vatican, dividing the congregation into three provinces, all of which have provincial houses in New Jersey. Hitherto they had had one central government. The three provinces are still functioning; all of the institutions belong to one province or another, as do all the sisters in the congregation. The governing body of the congregation consists of the General Superior and the General Council that is composed of the Assistant General Superior, the General Secretary, the General Treasurer, and the three Provincial Superiors.

Since Vatican II the sisters' ministries have multiplied and diversified to a great extent. Approximately nineteen sisters work individually in social services, in addition to those who work in their sponsored institutions. Their responsibilities include administration of agencies and departments, alcohol rehabilitation, ministry to the elderly, parish social services. Elizabeth Seton House for single mothers provides a haven for troubled young women and their children. In the past few years the sisters have expanded the scope of their work in diocesan offices as Chancellors, Vicars for Religious, members of retreat and mission teams, leadership in contemporary parish life. At present approximately sixty-seven sisters serve in health care institutions sponsored by the congregation in positions of administration, pastoral care, mission effectiveness, therapy, nursing, social service, dietetics, and technology. Three sisters are physicians, one of whom is devoted exclusively to the care of AIDS patients.

The long-standing educational ministry is both complex and diverse in its efforts and accomplishments. The Sisters of Charity of Saint Elizabeth, numbering 792 sisters in 1994, serve in sixteen states, thirty dioceses, but predominantly in New Jersey, Connecticut, Massachusetts, and Florida. The sisters are also in El Salvador, Mexico, and the Virgin Islands. As of 1992 some two hundred sisters, assisted by twenty-five volunteer sisters, minister full-time as administrators, teachers, and staff in one private school, fifty-five parish elementary schools, eight parish high schools, three regional high schools, five of the Sisters of Charity academies, and their College of Saint Elizabeth.

THE SISTERS OF CHARITY OF SETON HILL[15]

The Sisters of Charity of Seton Hill, Greensburg, Pennsylvania, is the youngest of the communities that branched off from Mother Seton's original group in Emmitsburg. In 1869 Bishop Michael Domenec of Pittsburgh appealed to the Cincinnati community for sisters to found a house in his diocese, and, on August 20, 1870, Sister Aloysia Lowe and three other sisters arrived in Altoona, Pennsylvania, and began their work teaching in St. John's School.

The Sisters of Charity were legally incorporated in Blair County, 1874, and Westmoreland County, 1885.

Sister Aloysia Lowe was appointed the first Mother Superior. She had made her novitiate under Mother Margaret George, who was a close friend of Mother Seton and a member of the Emmitsburg community, before going to Cincinnati. Hence the new community of Sisters of Charity of Seton Hill had strong ties to Mother Seton. Mother Aloysia sent her sisters to establish schools in Blairsville, Johnstown, and Pittsburgh. It was expected that the Sisters from Cincinnati would remain only long enough to establish a school and assist in the formation of a new community. By 1882 all of them had been recalled except Mother Aloysia and her assistant, Sister Anne Regina Ennis. In 1888 they formally petitioned their Superiors to remain permanently with the new congregation. On Christmas Day they renewed their vows, this time as Sisters of Charity of Seton Hill.

The Sisters were at the service of people in times of emergencies, such as the Johnstown Flood, the small pox and flu epidemics, and the 1936 flood, caring for patients during periods of strike at Westmoreland Manor, Kane Hospital, Torrance State Hospital. In the 1918 epidemic of influenza the sisters served at temporary hospitals set up at Youngwood Town Hall, the Greensburg Armory, the clubhouse of the Greensburg Country Club, as well as at many locations in Pittsburgh.

In the field of education the Seton Hill sisters made an impact early on in their history, staffing more than ninety elementary and secondary schools. In 1882 Mother Aloysia purchased the 200-acre Jennings farm in Greensburg and named it Seton Hill. There she founded St. Joseph Academy and St. Mary's School for Boys. Seton Hill College was built in 1918. It has a present enrollment of 700 students. Besides granting degrees in the humanities, in arts and music, in science, home economics, and pre-medical technology, they today have a very strong Continuing Education Program. It offers thirteen scholarships besides supported scholarships. They conducted an Undergraduate Teaching Program during the 1950s and 1960s, giving scholarships to young women in exchange for their teaching service in parochial schools. "Project Forward" since the 1960s has been searching out talented youth and opening up educational opportunities for them. Sisters and students have given and continue to give volunteer service to Westmoreland Correctional Facility and other institutions. As Professors and Administrators they also served at Catholic University of America, Washington, D.C.; Duquesne University, Pittsburgh; Fordham University, New York, and other institutions of higher learning. A notable service of the Seton Hill Sisters was the instruction of the Holy Family Sisters, an African-American community in New Orleans, victims of segregation laws, barred from attendance at southern colleges. From 1921 to 1957 Sisters of Charity conducted a summer normal school for these sisters. From 1942 to the early 1970s Seton Hill College established a scholarship program for them, nineteen of whom earned college degrees there. From 1967 to 1979 they had a teacher exchange program designed to bring about racial integration at the religious faculty level in the Catholic elementary schools.

The late nineteenth and early twentieth centuries witnessed the extension of ministries into health care and social services. The sisters opened Roselia Foundling and Maternity Hospital (1891-1971), Pittsburgh Hospital and School of Nursing (1897), Providence Hospital and School of Nursing (1909) in Beaver Falls, Pennsylvania, Jeannette District Memorial Hospital and School of Nursing, and McGuire Memorial Convalescent Home (1950s).

The sisters have administered DePaul Institute for hearing-impaired children.

The Sisters have expanded their work into numerous dioceses in the United States. In 1960 a mission was established in South Korea, where in the Seton tradition the sisters named their first school Saint Joseph's. In 1972 a Korean Novitiate was canonically erected and in 1976 the Korean Region was formally established in accordance with Article 138 of the *Constitutions*. For the good of the life of the Congregation in Korea and the Church there, the need to have its own authority over personnel and finances led the Region to propose at the General Chapter of 1993 its establishment as a Province. Today the Province numbers over 150 Korean sisters, novices, and postulants. Originally a diocesan congregation, the Sisters of Charity of Seton Hill were granted pontifical status on May 3, 1957.

The Sisters of Charity of Seton Hill in 1996 number over 550 sisters. They devote themselves to education, to apostolates of evangelization and religious education, and to a variety of services in health care and works of charity and mercy. By 1995, the 125th anniversary of their foundation, the Sisters of Seton Hill have been serving in the dioceses of Greensburg, Pittsburgh, Altoona-Johnstown, Washington, Baltimore, Tucson, Phoenix, Los Angeles, and New Orleans. They serve also in the cities of Chicago, Cincinnati, Columbus, Erie, Nashville, New York, Orlando, Paterson, Raleigh, St. Petersburg, Santa Fe, Stuebenville, and Wheeling-Charleston. The history of the Congregation reflects a spirit of courage founded upon a strong faith and trust. Impelled by that spirit, the Congregation looks to the future with hope and with renewed dedication to the mission of Christ and His Church.

THE VINCENTIAN SISTERS OF CHARITY OF PITTSBURGH, PENNSYLVANIA[16]

In 1902 five Slovak Sisters of Charity of St. Vincent de Paul from Szatmar, Rumania, arrived in Braddock, Pennsylvania, to serve the large Slovak population there at the request of Rev. Adalbert Kazincy. Four more Slovak sisters joined them in 1907. To distinguish them from the Sisters of Charity of Seton Hill in Greensburg, Pennsylvania, Bishop Canevin named them the Vincentian Sisters of Charity. Their roots were entirely Vincentian, descending from the Daughters of Charity in France founded by St. Vincent de Paul. In 1938 they established their independence from the Szatmar community in Rumania in an amicable separation, with the St. Vincent's charism continuing to unite them spiritually. This congregation and its future branch, the Vincentian Sisters of Charity of Bedford, Ohio, are the only congregations in the Federation without ties, either direct or remote, to St. Elizabeth Ann Seton.

Their first duty was to learn the English language, although their native Slovak was happily acceptable to the Slovak people whom they served. The sisters immediately began their ministry doing church work by caring for the sanctuary, linens, vestments, and decorations. Their skill in art needlework and embroidery resulted in beautiful new vestments, tabernacle veils, and altar linens to enhance the House of God. They trained altar boys, enrolled girls in Sodalities, gave religious instruction, visited the sick in their homes, and helped young mothers in the care of their children. After twenty-five years they had established schools in twenty-seven Slovak parishes and three schools for the children of Irish, Italian and Croatian descent. They acquired normal school teachers certificates. Some of the sisters became nurses, caring for the sick. During the flu epidemic the sisters took care of orphaned children whose parents had died. In 1910 the sisters purchased nine acres of land in Perrysville to build a Motherhouse. The first General Superior was Mother Emerentiana Handlovits.

The sisters established a Novitiate for the many young women of Slovak descent who desired to enter the congregation. The novices engaged in work unlike that of many of their American colleagues in American-founded novitiates. These young Slovak novices were taught to milk cows, make apple butter, plant, cultivate, and harvest crops. They merited a prize-winning photo in *The New York Mirror* when a news photographer caught a scene of the novices making hay. The novices also raised chickens, entertaining them with phonograph music to encourage egg-laying, and feeding them with cod liver oil to insure good health. They were taught cooking and baking, caring for the plants in the greenhouse, and open gardens. Other skills taught them were carpet-weaving, embroidery, and fine lace-making. They also learned the heavy work of construction, laying cement for walls and paths.

One of the major works of the Vincentians of Pittsburgh was health care. In 1924 the Vincentian Home for Invalids was built by volunteers from East Pittsburgh. The sisters, without any outside help or remuneration, took care of their patients at the home for the next forty-three years. A program was begun to prepare many sisters for the R.N. degree and the Bachelor of Science in Nursing. They purchased an estate in Pittsburgh and converted the building there into a nursing and convalescent home, Villa de Marillac. In 1939 they traveled west to Illinois and Missouri, teaching and nursing, and south to Montgomery, Alabama, to minister to African-Americans. Their ministry there continues to the present day, and also in Phenix City, Alabama. In Montgomery the Vincentian sisters helped during the polio epidemic, extending hospitality to the Selma marchers on their Civil Rights March to Montgomery. Offered a gift of a small hospital in Monett, Missouri, they renamed it St. Vincent Hospital. In 1928 the Vincentian Sisters of Charity of Pittsburgh were asked to establish a separate congregation in Bedford, Ohio, to minister to the Slovak people there. This was in the Cleveland Diocese where, in Bedford, they were offered a beautiful estate on which to establish their new community Motherhouse. Five sisters from Pittsburgh began the new community, which became totally independent of the Pittsburgh Vincentians. This congregation grew and flourished over the next seventy years.

Sister Eulalia of the Pittsburgh community started a printing shop at the Motherhouse in 1928 for the printing of hymnbooks in English, Latin, and Slovak, of stationery, envelopes, and greeting cards. This work continues to the present, through the dedicated work of Sister Maurice and her volunteers. During the depression they also continued their services to the poor, although the sisters themselves were on the brink of poverty. They used all their Slovak ingenuity in encouraging the boys in their schools, for example, to collect lumps of coal along the railroad tracks to keep the classroom stoves heating the schoolrooms. In 1932 their boarding school, Vincentian Academy, met the approval of the State Department of Instruction. Later known as Vincentian High School, it has continued to flourish. In the 1990s, in conjunction with Duquesne University, it is launching an international baccalaureate program. The official title is Vincentian Academy/Duquesne University.

Their missionary work included three years in Puerto Rico, working on the missions with the Capuchin Fathers from 1930 to 1933. In 1983, they established a mission in Peru. The sisters also taught in the Canadian Separate

School System in Ontario. At home at the Motherhouse they conduct retreats for laypeople as well as sisters. One of the famous émigrés who courageously stood up to the communists in Slovakia, Sister Cecilia Barath, visited the Motherhouse in Pittsburgh in 1955, to the delight of the Slovak people in the area. Sister Cecilia was the writer and heroine of the best-selling *The Deliverance of Sister Cecilia,* in which she describes her experiences at the hands of the communists in Czechoslovakia.

The Vincentian Sisters of Charity of Pittsburgh continue to work in their nursing homes, social service centers, and in education, as well as in individual nontraditional ministries, answering the needs of children and adults today. The realities of their problems as the sisters approach the twenty-first century require new and creative ministries which the descendants of the Slovak people, as Sisters of Charity are eminently capable of doing. At the peak of their ministry in the 1960s they numbered 410 sisters. Today they number about 200, almost all of whom are actively engaged in either full or part-time ministry regardless of their age. They are a hardy lot who cannot be discouraged by decreasing numbers and increasing needs. The spirit of their Solvak foundress in America in 1902, Mother Emerentiana Handlovits, continues to inspire her daughters today.

THE VINCENTIAN SISTERS OF CHARITY OF BEDFORD, OHIO[17]

The Congregation of Vincentian Sisters of Charity of Bedford, Ohio, was established in September 1928 by Bishop Joseph Schrembs of the Diocese of Cleveland for the needs of a large Slovak population in the area. He applied to the Vincentian Sisters of Charity in Pittsburgh, but permission had to be granted from the Congregation in Szatmar, Rumania, to which the Pittsburgh community was still attached. Permission was granted, and five sisters left Pittsburgh for Bedford, Ohio. Like the Pittsburgh Vincentians, the Vincentian Sisters of Charity in Bedford trace their origins to Empress Caroline of Austria, who adapted the original rule of St. Vincent de Paul, inviting the Sisters of Charity of St. Vincent de Paul to Austria on September 15, 1835. It was this foundation in Austria from which the sisters in Szatmar, Rumania, came and eventually, in 1902, established the Vincentian Sisters of Charity in Pittsburgh and, twenty-six years later, the Bedford, Ohio, community.

The Bishop offered the sisters an estate on the outskirts of Cleveland with the provision that they establish a novitiate there. The first two women to enter the community as Postulants came on September 15, 1928, and were joined by another Postulant in October. From 1929 to 1939 the Pittsburgh community supported and nurtured its Bedford extension until it became an autonomous community in 1939. The membership had grown to forty-four sisters in ten years. Mother Mary John Berchmans Fialko was appointed the first General Superior in 1939, a position that she held until her death in 1959.

In the beginning years the sisters responded to Bishop Schrembs' purpose to minister to Slovak immigrants, teaching in elementary schools in Slovak parishes. By the 1950s the commitment to elementary education extended to non-Slovak parishes in the suburbs as the Diocese expanded. In 1963 they opened their first high school class in a temporary building until Lumen Cordium High School for girls was finished in 1965. The sisters owned and operated this school until 1987, when it was closed and the building was retrofitted for a senior citizen complex that the sisters own and operate. The sisters were also engaged in nursing at various hospitals and domestic services, especially for priests. As new needs arose, the Vincentian Sisters of Bedford responded in the spirit of St. Vincent who had urged his Daughters ". . . to be open to the needs that God lets us see." The first major renewal took place in 1969 with an interim Constitution, modification in dress, approval of personal stipends, openness to new ministries, and, in 1974, a Community Self-Study Project that resulted in further changes and renewal, including plans for the completion of a Motherhouse of which one wing was completed in 1981. Construction began in 1974 with the demolition of the original house given to the sisters in 1928. Following the construction of the Motherhouse, the sisters began to evaluate their ministries. As a result of this self-probing the sisters began to terminate all domestic services. They took a distinct turn to mission work in California with Cesar Chavez in the summers; with immigrants in Indiana and Michigan in the summers; in census-taking in the parishes; in inner-city Bible Schools. In 1975 a sister established a local community of L'Arche for Handicapped Adults in the inner city of Cleveland. In January 1980 they opened staffing of Villa Sancta Anna Home for the Aged in Beachwood, Ohio. They also began St. Joseph Ministry to the Terminally Ill, a traveling hospice. The sisters intensified their commitment to social justice through workshops calling them to be sensitive to women, race, the aged, minority groups, and in general, respect for all life.

Additional involvements include the missionary work in the Cleveland Diocesan mission in El Salvador; ministry to the illiterate in Pineville, Kentucky; visiting as members of the Marymount Health Care Group, the homes of elderly former patients who need assistance; counseling and bereavement programs to help those in need of compassionate understanding; cooking for the mentally handicapped residents of Bradley House; working at Fr. Berard Godspeed Center on the east side of Cleveland, where the poor are fed and clothed; organizing a hospice home, Isaiah House in Rochester, New York; sponsoring a Vietnamese family; working with Catholic Social Services in Cuyahoga County assisting immigrants through migration and refugee services. The Bedford Vincentans continue to expand their ministries in their care of the elderly, mentally-handicapped adults, and the terminally ill. The congregation owns and operates a ninety-two unit senior adult facility for independent and assisted living in a beautiful building named "Light of Heart Villa." This is the building that was formerly their high school.

Having remained faithful to the call to renewal since Vatican II, the community embarked on a month-long Chapter in 1980 to create a new Constitution and an articulation of the congregation's servant theology. In 1991 the Chapter mandated the community to engage in strategic planning to address issues of future viability. As a result of this initiative, and after four years of study, discussion, and hard work, the community made a week-long discernment retreat in July 1996. The Community reached a unanimous decision to pursue merging with another community. They now embark upon a risk-taking journey, knowing that the providence of God is leading them.

Thus the Vincentian Sisters of Charity of Bedford, Ohio, continue the charism of St. Vincent de Paul and St. Louise de Marillac to make God's love visible as servants of the Word of God, of the poor, and of charity. At their peak period in the 1960s they numbered over 150 sisters. Today they number just seventy-six sisters, all of whom continue their lives of work and prayer in the spirit of their foundress. "Relying on the Providence of St. Vincent dearly loved, we give our lives simply to those needs which God lets us see."

The history of the Daughters and Sisters of Charity with its roots in Vincentian and Setonian Spirituality and traditions reached its peak with the Beatification and Canonization of Mother Seton. It was perfectly expressed in the words of Sister Hildegarde Marie Mahoney, SC, former General Superior of the New Jersey Sisters of Charity of Saint Elizabeth, and former President of their College of Saint Elizabeth, who in an article for *The Beacon* referred both to the Beatification and Canonization of Elizabeth Ann Seton and the pontificate of Pope John XXIII, pointing out the sisters' ". . . faith-filled dynamic heritage" that "prepared them to respond to the special call of the Church":

> At Mother Seton's beatification in 1963 Pope John XXIII spoke of her in relation to the establishment of the Catholic hierarchy of America and the laying of a sound foundation for a "marvelous growth of Catholic works such as can be seen today in full maturity." He declared that Elizabeth Seton "gave a new impetus to the practice of charity" and that in her spiritual daughters she "bends down . . . to countless persons in spiritual and temporal need."
>
> The pontificate of Pope John XXIII will be recalled in history especially for his convocation of the Second Vatican Council. The faith-filled, dynamic heritage of the Sisters of Charity prepared them to respond to the special call of the Church to religious communities to assemble their highest governing body to examine their way of life and ministries in the light of the Gospels, their founding spirit, and the needs of the times. This representative governing body was given extraordinary powers by the Church to initiate experimentation to bring about desirable changes and renewal.

The canonization of Mother Seton in 1975, confirming once more the charism of the American Sisters of Charity, gave great joy to the Church in the United States, as its first native citizen was honored as a saint in the universal Church. Her canonization gave special joy to all the communities who trace their origin to the community founded in America by Mother Seton.

Sisters of Charity are called to make visible the love of Christ for every human being and, animated by that love, to reach out by every means in their power to alleviate spiritual and material need. They are to have complete trust in Divine Providence even when they seem to be deprived of every resource. They are not to be afraid to use means and procedures and structures different from those commonly used by religious when such are required to carry out their ecclesial mission.[18]

Notes

1. Sisters of Charity of Saint Joseph, incorporated 1817, p. 2.
2. From Sister Daniel Hannefin, DC, *Daughters of the Church* (Brooklyn: New City Press, 1989), and the writings of Sisters Aloysia Dugan, DC, and Elaine Wheeler, DC.
3. Sister Mary Collette Crone, SCN, archivist, Nazareth, Kentucky.
4. Sister Judith Metz, SC, Cincinnati, Ohio.
5. Sister M. Anne Francis Campbell, OLM, archivist, Charleston, South Carolina.
6. From the history by Sister Marie de Lourdes Walsh, SC, *The Sisters of Charity of New York*, and other articles on this congregation.
7. Sister Marie de Lourdes Walsh, SC, *The Sisters of Charity of New York* (New York: Fordham University Press, 1960), vol. 1, p. 177.
8. Sister Geraldine Anthony, SC, Halifax, Nova Scotia.
9. Sister Marion Murray, SCIC, archivist, Saint John, New Brunswick.

10. *The Morning Freeman,* July 11, 1863, p. 2.
11. Sister Imelda Guignard, NDSC, Moncton, New Brunswick.
12. Soeur Marie-Dorothee Maillet, NDSC, *Une Pierre de la Mosaique Acadienne* (Ottawa: Les Editions Lemeac, 1984), p. 158.
13. Sister Mary Seraphine Sheehan, SCL, Leavenworth, Kansas.
14. Sister Anne Gertrude Coleman, SC, Convent Station, New Jersey.
15. Sister Sara Louise Reilly, SC, archivist, Greensburg, Pennsylvania.
16. Sister Anne Kremenik, VSC, archivist, Pittsburgh, Pennsylvania.
17. Sister Margaret Mach, VSC, General Superior, Bedford, Ohio.
18. Sister Hildegard Marie Mahoney, SC, *The Beacon* (Convent Station, NJ: Sisters of Charity of St. Elizabeth, 1984).

Chapter Two

Health Care

THE DAUGHTERS OF CHARITY IN THE UNITED STATES[1]

In 1850 at the time of the union with France and the establishment of the first diocesan communities of Sisters of Charity, Emmitsburg became the headquarters of the Daughters of Charity in the United States. During the period before their division into two provinces in 1910, there was a good deal of expansion. Daughters of Charity were sent as far as California and Virginia City, Nevada, where they established orphanages, schools, and hospitals. As works in the West grew and the Civil War began in the East, combatants on both sides were nursed by both Daughters and Sisters of Charity. Many sisters who had been engaged in teaching and other works were recruited for battlefield nursing or for service in the military hospitals.

During the war, Providence Hospital in Washington, D.C., and St. Agnes Hospital in Baltimore were established. There the Daughters of Charity provided care primarily to civilians, although military casualties were also admitted. Today they continue to provide quality health care. The changing times have seen expansion of services, including home health and hospice care, subacute units, in/out surgery, and care of AIDS patients. Following the Civil War, hospitals were established in a number of the cities where the Daughters had nursed the wounded. In spite of the threat of the Know-Nothings, their work prospered.

In 1910 the number of Daughters and works, combined with the enormous distances, led to the creation of a second United States province of Daughters of Charity with its provincial house in St. Louis, Missouri. The dividing line for the two provinces of the East and the West was the Mississippi River. This left the province in the East with 1,000 sisters. Its health-care facilities alone included sixty-nine missions, fifteen hospitals, and three psychiatric institutions. In the Eastern province several hospitals were accepted, among them Allegheny, now Sacred Heart, in Cumberland, Maryland, and hospitals in Pensacola and Jacksonville, Florida. As standards were established for hospitals the Daughters began formal studies for degrees, principally during summer programs at St. Joseph's College in Emmitsburg, enabling them to combine necessary education and ministry without detriment to either.

When the influenza epidemic struck in 1917, schools were closed and the school sisters, as well as those in hospitals, cared for the sick. Seventeen Daughters of Charity in the Eastern province were among the people who died of influenza in the United States. Combining these with the other province and with the many Sisters of Charity who nursed the influenza victims, the number was much higher.

In 1922 Father Francis Verdier, Superior General, invited the Daughters to open a mission in Kiangsi, China. St. Margaret's Hospital as well as an orphanage and lace workshop were opened. The sisters were forced to flee several times during the Chinese Civil War, but continued to return until they were expelled by the Communists in 1952. However Daughters from several provinces now serve in Taiwan.

In the post-World War II period, hospitals throughout the Eastern province rebuilt and expanded with the help of the Hill-Burton Act. Nursing schools were gradually phased out as more and more colleges offered degree programs to nurses.

The two provinces were split up into five in 1969. At this period the Daughters of Charity numbered more than 2,500 sisters. The advantages were obvious: smaller territories and fewer sisters would enable the visitatrix and her council to serve better the poor and sick in their territory. The Southeast Province now covers the area from Maryland south to Florida. It was also responsible for missions in Bolivia, but this is now a province. Recent developments in health-care delivery have caused vast changes over the last ten years. In 1986 the Daughters of Charity of the five provinces formed the Daughters of Charity National Health System with headquarters in St. Louis and a regional office in Baltimore. The System provides professional and financial support for all the members. In addition to membership in DCNHS, most hospitals are also part of a local network aimed at providing more complete health care for all patients. The declining number of sister nurses led to the formation of sisters in pastoral care and the creation of vice president for mission services. Advisory Boards with a Daughter of Charity always serving as Chairperson help maintain quality health care and service to the poor.

St. Agnes Hospital in Baltimore has been a leader in establishing a program known as Villa Louise to provide care and education for pregnant adolescents, currently operating in conjunction with Bon Secours Hospital. St. Agnes Hospital is also a leader in cardiac care, establishing the first cardiac emergency room in the United States. In Washington, Providence Hospital, which had a unit for the care of alcoholics almost since its inception in 1861, developed a rehab program for substance abuse in a freestanding building on its campus. It also has a group of outreach clinics in the inner city that provide immediate access to health care for the poor. Several hospitals including St. Vincent's in Jacksonville, Sacred Heart in Pensacola, Sacred Heart in Cumberland, and most recently Providence in Washington, D.C., have acquired or have built freestanding nursing homes as an adjunct to the acute care they provide. In all of these facilities the sisters help to provide pastoral care for the patients. A unique development was the opening of the Care Clinic in Fayetteville, North Carolina, made possible through the donations of local health-care professionals and grants. For those without health insurance, free medical and dental care is provided.

After the division into two provinces in 1910, the province of the West with center in St. Louis, Missouri included 700 sisters. Its health-care facilities included fifty missions, twenty-two hospitals, two psychiatric facilities, and six infants' homes, including maternity hospitals. The sisters took on only two new hospitals; one begun and destroyed by the earthquake in San Francisco before the division, and the other, the supervision of nursing service of a state charity hospital. Existing health-care institutions were standardized and improved by joint meetings and training sessions for sisters in administration, bookkeeping, pharmacy, nursing supervision, nursing education, and other hospital duties. Degrees were sought from universities with special training programs.

During World War I ten sisters served in Italy with a nursing staff recruited from hospitals served by Daughters who were an international congregation. Hospital sisters and school sisters back home nursed soldiers and civilians suffering from smallpox and the Spanish influenza in overcrowded hospitals, in the tents surrounding them, and in homes.

In 1921 the state leprosarium in Louisana, staffed by the Daughters of Charity in the Western Province, was transferred to federal ownership, but the sisters were retained in charge of nursing services. Natural disasters were met by first-aid and relief stations set up by the sisters as they occurred. During the Depression, hospitals managed to continue to care for the poor, stretching resources to the maximum, doubling occupancy sometimes by the sharing of beds by two patients.

The Daughters of Charity from the Western Province went to Poyang, Kiangsi, China, in 1923, opening a dispensary and other services until they were expelled in 1929. They returned to train others to carry on the work until their final expulsion in 1948.

During World War II their hospitals intensified nursing education programs and built new schools of nursing to increase the number of nurses available for military and civilian service. After the war, government funding and Medicare brought new regulations. To accommodate the regulations affecting administration, nursing care, medical care, and every department in the hospital, expansion, renovation, and the building of new hospitals was necessitated. No new hospitals were accepted between 1940 and 1970.

Health care in Latin America was improved by accepting sisters from various countries to study nursing and hospital administration in the United States. Sisters were sent to help organize a nursing school in Nicaragua in 1945, and assist in a government hospital in Equador in 1953. Other sisters participated in consultative work in nursing education and in teaching in the nursing program in Quito for six years until Ecuadorians could be prepared to replace them in 1970. Similar consultations and cooperative efforts were done in other Latin American countries.

Missions were begun in Japan and Taiwan involving the sisters in care of the sick poor in their homes and in the local hospital, organizing clinics in outlying areas and building a hospital in Wakayama.

During the 1970s and 1980s lay collaborators were replacing sisters in many of their positions of leadership within the hospital. Sisters were expanding their efforts to new areas of health care, targeting medically underserved in the area. As of 1996 sisters serve in many capacities in Daughter-sponsored hospitals and clinics for the poor, as well as in the offices of the regional and national Daughters of Charity Health System. Others serve in state and federally sponsored health services.

In 1969, when the two provinces of the East and West were further divided into five provinces, the East Central Province with center in Evansville, Indiana, became a reality, composing nine states: Alabama, Mississippi, Tennessee, Kentucky, Illinois, Indiana, Wisconsin, Ohio, and Michigan where Daughters of Charity were already serving in those nine states. Seventy sisters from the Emmitsburg Province and 331 sisters from the St. Louis Province formed the new East Central Province. Although an inland province, it is actually almost surrounded by waterways: the Great Lakes, the Mississippi River, the Gulf of Mexico, and smaller rivers to the east. The cycle and depth of change marks this province. Changes in health-care environment, society, and the Daughters' community have demanded alterations in the health ministry. With the founding in 1986 of the Daughters of Charity National Health System, including all five provinces, they provided systemwide management leadership and shared service programs. Since then local health ministries have responded to market forces in order to serve better their communities. Current issues include formation of the laity, forging strong partnerships, and delivering holistic/spiritually-centered care to individuals and communities with the distinctive vision of seeing Christ in the service of the poor.

The 1980s and 1990s have dramatically affected health care with the rapid growth of managed care and for-profit health services. Computers and technology have revolutionized how and where care is delivered. The number of Daughters has continued to decrease while their average age has continued to rise. The Daughters therefore elected to pursue a strategy of placing greater reliance upon laity rather than reducing the size of their health ministry. Part of this strategy was the establishment of the Daughters of Charity National Health System. DCNHS, founded in 1986, as an integrated structure of local, regional, and national health-related organizations. Members may be sponsored or cosponsored by Daughters of Charity or affiliated with DCNHS. The mission of the system is to make a positive difference in the lives and health status of individuals and communities, especially the poor, by providing spiritually-centered, affordable health services. The core values of the system are respect, quality service, simplicity, advocacy for the poor, and inventiveness to infinity. The vision of the system is to be a values-driven health system that serves the health needs of the total individual – body, mind, and spirit, while promoting a healthy and just society through community-based networks and collaboration with those who share these values. Much more transformation in governance, service models, and thinking is expected to achieve this vision. The regional corporation board based in Evansville, acting on behalf of the canonical sponsor, evaluates the sponsorship and governs the health-care organizations and activities within the region. This responsibility includes carrying out certain reserve powers: approval of mission, philosophy, mergers/organization, strategic plans, and budgets. The Daughters of Charity Regional Information Center (DC-RIC) also based in Evansville, serves the information needs of the local health ministries.

The East Central Province sponsors over fifty-five health facilities in six states: Michigan, Wisconsin, Illinois, Indiana, Tennessee, and Alabama. In Michigan, Providence Hospital has added multiple satellite facilities, including outpatient surgical centers, family health centers, and medical office buildings. In 1995 Mission Health was formed through a joint operating agreement with the Mercy Health System. In Saginaw, St. Mary's Medical Center offers many highly specialized services, including neurosurgery, burn care, open-heart surgery, and oncology treatment. In Wisconsin St. Mary's Hospital in Milwaukee is part of Columbia-St. Mary's Inc., an operating corporation formed in 1995 that governs and operates both St. Mary's and Columbia Hospitals in Milwaukee. In Illinois St. Joseph Health Centers and Hospital merged with Columbus/Cabrini Health System in 1995 to form Catholic Health Partners sponsored by the Daughters and the Missionary Sisters of the Sacred Heart of Jesus. In Indiana St. Vincent Hospitals and Health Services opened St. Vincent-Carmel Hospital in 1986 and in the 1990s transitioned over 120 mentally-impaired residents to residential facilities with assisted-living services provided by New Hope. St. Mary's Medical Center in Evansville has been on the top 100 hospitals' list published by HCIA, Inc. for 1994 and 1995. The Daughters accepted sponsorship of Warrick, St. Joseph, and Mercy Hospitals in those two years.

In Tennessee St. Thomas Hospital focused on the development of primary and outpatient care during the 1990s. Middle Tennessee Medical Center is a jointly owned health ministry with Baptist Hospital in Nashville. In Alabama, St. Vincent Hospital, established longer than any other hospital in the Birmingham area, is noted for high-quality services. Seton Home Health Services serves the poor in over twenty-five counties. St. Margaret's Services provides for the frail elderly in Montgomery while Providence Hospital serves the community of West Mobile.

Progressive empowerment of the laity by the Daughters of Charity in governance and executive management from 1985 to 1995 has led to 90% lay CEOs and Board composition, which is strengthening the Daughters' values-based health ministry. Ownership and control are giving way to influence and partnership at many levels challenging the partners' ability to trust and respect each other. Their plan is to direct attention and resources to ministry formation of the laity, who will continue to carry even greater responsibility in future.

In 1969 the newly formed Province of the West embraced a vast geographical area of almost two million square miles in thirteen states including Alaska and Hawaii. The 243 Daughters of Charity for that province lived in six of those states: California, where the Provincial House is established in Los Altos Hills; in Washington, Nevada, Utah, Arizona, and Colorado. The rapid change in health care in California demanded a flexible and courageous response. The Daughters served in three long-standing hospitals and assumed sponsorship of health facilities in four new locations. In 1995 they merged their regional health-care system with that of the Sisters of Mercy of Auburn, Burlingham, and the Dominicans of Adrian, Michigan. In recent years they have developed many innovative programs for the poor: the largest Meals-on-Wheels program in Los Angeles County, clinics for the poor, both mobile and at various sites, e.g. the RotaCare Clinics in cooperation with the

Rotary Club; the founding of an on-site school for licensed vocational nurses; a more comprehensive organization of emergency referral services.

The Northeast Province, with its Provincial House in Albany, New York, is the smallest geographically but the most urbanized. Here Catholicism is the majority religion in many of the older urban centers, and there is much ethnic diversity. There are more Hispanics and blacks than in any other region except the South and Southwest. In New York State the Daughters served in hospitals in four areas. Originally asked by the Bishop of Buffalo, John Timon, CM, to staff a hospital there, the Daughters arrived from Maryland and in one year they had cared for the cholera victims and had served 1,513 patients, half of them charity cases. In 1832 they had worked in the Albany-Troy area caring for cholera victims in their homes and makeshift health centers until St. Mary's Hospital, Troy, opened in 1848. In 1996 it is still operating, developing new programs as part of the Seton Health System.

Under the supportive organization of the DCNHS the Daughters face challenges in seven cities of the Northeast: Buffalo, Troy, Rochester, Boston, Bridgeport, Binghamton, and Pottsville, Pennsylvania. They have, since 1969, created procedures to develop cost-effective health-care delivery models, to continue collaboration with physicians, to provide health-care education programs, and to extend all types of health-care service to the local community. These outreach programs include wellness promotion, health education, clinics, screenings for specific problems, and medical research. New focus has been given to Mission Services, the study of ethical issues, and pastoral care in multicultural environments. At Sisters' Hospital in Buffalo, Labouré College in Boston, and St. Vincent's Hospital in Bridgeport, Associate Degree Programs in Allied Health have replaced the former programs in nursing education.

The Northeast Province is composed of ten states: Maine, Massachusetts, Connecticut, Delaware, Pennsylvania, New York, New Hampshire, New Jersey, Rhode Island, and Vermont. At that time there were in the United States over 2,500 Daughters of Charity in the five new provinces. In the Northeast Province since 1969 many services for the aged and those with chronic health needs have been increased. St. Louise House, Albany, serves the aged and infirm Daughters of Charity. At St. John of God Hospital and St. Joseph's Nursing Home in Boston, and St. Mary's in Troy, residential care is provided. In 1996 the Daughters strengthened health services in Buffalo by establishing a network of providers in collaboration with the sponsors of seven hospitals. The Eastern Mercy Health System and the DCNHS – East region became cosponsors of several facilities. That same year another collaborative relationship was established in Connecticut with the St. Vincent's Health Services, Inc., St. Joseph's Medical Center in Stamford, and Stamford Health Systems, Inc. This collaboration seeks to address the major changes in the delivery of health care in this section of Connecticut. The goal of all these efforts is to provide new services, plan for future needs, and collaborate with others to renew the commitment of the Company of Charity to serving the poor, the sick, and the disenfranchised.

THE SISTERS OF CHARITY OF OUR LADY OF MERCY[2]

In Charleston, South Carolina, another community of Sisters of Charity had for their original purpose to "care for the sick and infirm." The Sisters of Charity of Our Lady of Mercy, founded by Bishop John England in Charleston, South Carolina, in 1829, had for the next twenty-five years, cared for the sick at a time when neither the modern hospital nor the nursing profession, as we know them, existed. The sisters cared for the sick in their homes and in temporary relief hospitals.

Yellow fever and cholera epidemics were frequent in the Carolinas during the nineteenth century. Schools closed; sister teachers became nurses. The people of South Carolina saw the sisters wading through muddy streets lugging baskets filled with food and medicine for the sick poor. Yellow fever was called "strangers' fever" because so many victims were recent immigrants, often Irish Catholic laborers living in overcrowded boarding houses. To help these working men and their families, Bishop England established a society called the Brotherhood of San Marino and rented a house as a temporary hospital for the members. For the duration of its existence (1838-1841) the sisters cared for fever victims there as well as in Augusta, Georgia, in 1839. They staffed a relief hospital on the second floor of the as yet unopened Roper Hospital in Charleston in 1852, and in Wilmington, North Carolina, in 1862.

The Civil War expanded the sisters' experiences in health care by providing an opportunity for caring for sick and wounded soldiers in Union and Confederate military hospitals and prisons. From December 1861 until the closing days of the Civil War, several Sisters of Charity of Our Lady of Mercy staffed a Confederate military hospital at Montgomery White Sulphur Springs, Virginia. The Charleston sisters brought food, clothing, and medicines to Union soldiers, addressed their spiritual and emotional needs by listening to them, writing letters to their families, and bringing them mail.

The following decade witnessed the birth of the modern hospital with skilled doctors, trained nurses, medical science, and advanced technology. In 1880 the Sisters of Charity of Our Lady of Mercy built St. Francis Xavier Hospital, two wood-framed two-story buildings on the corner of Calhoun and Ashley Avenues in Charleston. When it opened on October 1, 1882, it had five patients and five sisters in attendance. The ambulance was a horse-drawn covered wagon. There was no elevator nor any wheelchairs, and patients had to be carried upstairs on chairs. Financial records reveal that the sisters sold a cow and a calf at one point to meet expenses. Some sister nurses gave piano lessons and china-painting lessons to supplement the hospital income. In time, so successful had it become that the sisters added new wings, new buildings, new services. In 1900 they opened a training school for nurses. It continued with great success until 1966, when nursing education had become part of the general educational system. In 1968 the Nursing School graduated its last class.

Bishop Emmet M. Walsh saw the establishment of Catholic hospitals staffed by sisters as an opportunity to introduce the Church in sections of South Carolina where it was almost unknown and often the victim of prejudice. In 1938 the Carroll residence in York became part convent, part health-care clinic, and later a new hospital named Divine Saviour. In 1943 the sisters had to leave York due to the urgent need for them in Charleston at St. Francis Xavier Hospital during World War II, returning in 1947 when they purchased the hospital from the Diocese. They continued to operate their two hospitals until 1989, when the General Superior and her Council, due to the declining number of sisters and the increasing complexity of providing health-care in the U.S., transferred ownership to the Bon Secours Sisters.

The Congregation continues to be involved in health care through work in the Pastoral Care Department of St.

Francis Xavier Hospital and on its Board of Governors. The former General Superior, Sister Bridget Sullivan, is Diocesan liaison for health-care concerns. Sister Mary Joseph Ritter is Director of the sisters' Outreach Services on Johns Island, seeking with her staff better ways of providing health care for the poor, elderly, and migrant population on the sea islands off Charleston. Sisters in parishes visit the sick and elderly in their homes.

THE SISTERS OF CHARITY OF NEW YORK[3]

Just as the cholera epidemic in South Carolina was the incentive for the Sisters of Charity of Our Lady of Mercy to dedicate themselves to health care, so did a similar epidemic in New York in the 1840s incite the Sisters of Charity of New York to open a small house, rented for $900 per year on East 13th Street in lower Manhattan, to care for numerous immigrants arriving in New York afflicted with cholera. This small beginning of the first Catholic hospital in New York became in time the internationally respected St. Vincent's Hospital and Medical Center. Originally accommodating thirty patients, it had 813 beds and a staff of over 4,000 in 1996. The sisters learned to care for patients under the direction of outstanding New York physicians. Patients receive quality care regardless of race, color, creed, or ability to pay. Its School of Nursing opened in 1892 and became one of the best institutions of its kind.

In 1876 St. Vincent's Hospital in Harrison, N.Y., opened for the care of the mentally ill; in 1888 St. Joseph's Hospital in Yonkers was founded; in 1903 St. Vincent's Hospital in Staten Island. There were others too: St. Mary's and Holy Family Hospitals in Brooklyn; Seton Hospital in the Bronx to care for patients with tuberculosis, and St. Lawrence Hospital in Washington Heights.

But as needs changed and new religious orders came to New York, the sisters entrusted some of their works to these sisters; other works were discontinued.

Nearly every major work was initiated in response to an appeal for help during a critical period of national or civic history. When requesting sisters for a military hospital during the Civil War, a New York politician, Edward Pierpont, wrote to the Secretary of War, ". . . we want the nurses of this hospital to be the Sisters of Charity . . . Their tenderness, knowledge and religious convictions of duty render them by far the best nurses." The request was granted and twelve Sisters of Charity nursed the sick and wounded until the end of the war in St. Joseph's Military Hospital located in the vacated original Motherhouse of the Sisters of Charity in Central Park. The graves of the Sisters of Charity nurses of the Civil War are honored with government markers, and their names are inscribed on "The Nuns of the Battlefield" Memorial erected in Washington, D.C., in 1924.

The New York Sisters of Charity hospitals have continued to expand to meet the needs of the times offering a wide variety of inpatient and outpatient programs and services. St. Vincent's and Bayley Seton Hospitals of Staten Island form part of the large Sisters of Charity Health Care System, begun in 1984. The newest entity in this system is the St. Elizabeth Ann Nursing Home, dedicated January 4, 1994, and serving AIDS and ventilator-dependent patients as well as geriatric/chronic-care residents. The other hospitals are medical centers, and of these St. Joseph's Medical Center has a 200-bed nursing home.

A mission of mercy for which the New York Sisters of Charity were to become internationally known was the establishment in 1869 of the New York Foundling Hospital by Sister Mary Irene Fitzgibbon in an effort to reduce infanticide. Today it is a huge complex considered one of the best in its field.

The 1990s demonstrated the need for drastic changes in health-care ministry. Networking of services became necessary because it was obvious that no organization could stand alone and survive. In July 1994, the Archdiocese of New York and the Sisters of Charity of St. Vincent de Paul of New York announced their commitment to work together to form an integrated delivery network. Using recommendations of an advisory committee of representatives from area hospitals and nursing homes, archdiocesan officials and the past President of the Sisters of Charity, Sister Carol Barnes, with Sisters Regina Bechtle and Regina Murphy, worked on a plan to achieve this goal. They initiated the Catholic Health Care Network (CHCN) on January 1, 1995.

THE SISTERS OF CHARITY OF HALIFAX[4]

Four Sisters of Charity from New York came up to Halifax in 1849 to staff a school for Catholic girls. A few days after their arrival the sisters found they had some orphans to care for and so began their ministry with orphan children. Having come basically as educators, it was not until May 1866 that the sisters fell "accidentally" into emergency care of cholera victims quarantined on McNabb's Island at the mouth of Halifax Harbor.

In 1886 Mother M. Clephas Connors, Mother General, opened a home for Elderly Ladies. The following year a local surgeon did emergency surgery for one of these residents. He was so pleased with the help provided by the sisters that he and the other medical doctors asked the sisters to continue with hospital work. Thus was born the famous Halifax Infirmary (a name used in England and Scotland to denote hospital). Gradually new wings were added and in 1908 a School of Nursing. The first three nurses graduated in 1911. Also in 1908 a hilltop mansion in North Sydney, Cape Breton, Nova Scotia, was donated to become Hamilton Memorial Hospital with a Nurses Training School. These two hospitals on the Northeastern Atlantic coast grew, struggled, prospered, and did notable work for the people of area, including the sailors of the Merchant Marine in both World Wars. In December 1917, two ships, one of them loaded with dynamite, collided in the Halifax Harbor. The resulting explosion leveled the north end of the city. The Halifax Infirmary was headquarters for the Red Cross Emergency Team from Rhode Island. In 1922 the American College of Surgeons gave full accreditation to the Halifax Infirmary, the first of many, which in later years were given by the Canadian Council on Hospital Accreditation.

With the growth of Halifax, there was need for expanded facilities. Planning and fund-raising resulted in the Halifax Infirmary on Queen Street, which was opened in January 1933 with a capacity of 228 beds and 60 bassinets. It was noted for its School of Nursing and a number of schools in the Health Sciences: Medical Records, X-Ray, Medical Lab, and others. In 1961 the Halifax Infirmary became one of the teaching hospitals for Dalhousie University Medical School, resulting in further expansion. Over the years the Halifax Infirmary gained a reputation for excellence. The sister nurses were so highly appreciated that many mothers of different denomination wanted their infants to be born at the Halifax Infirmary. With the passing of years sister nurses and personnel gradually declined, and expenses became too high for the sisters to manage, even with government grants. In 1973 ownership of the Halifax Infirmary was transferred to the Government of Nova Scotia. Today it is part of the Queen Elizabeth II Health Sciences Centre, a complex embracing the amalgamation of six hospitals in the City of Halifax.

Meanwhile the Sisters of Charity's hospital in Cape Breton, Hamilton Memorial, had also expanded to such a degree that the large new Saint Elizabeth's Hospital was built in North Sydney. Many more of the highly qualified sister nurses were added to the staff there and for many years this hospital served well the people of Cape Breton. But like the Halifax Infirmary it too became a financial burden to the Congregation and in 1975 ownership was transferred to the Government of Nova Scotia. It is now known as the Northside General Hospital.

Several thousand miles west, in the Archdiocese of Edmonton, Alberta, a plan to establish a network of Catholic hospitals in the small towns of Alberta was inaugurated in the 1920s. Several religious congregations were approached. The Sisters of Charity were able to comply with some requests by sending qualified sister nurses and administrators from Nova Scotia. In Westlock, a small town north of Edmonton, a zealous young Pastor had acquired a small house for the care of sick and injured. Immaculata Hospital, a modern brick building for thirty patients, was formally opened on July 22, 1928, with all essential services. Administered and partly staffed by the Sisters of Charity of Halifax, it continued to grow and expand until, in 1995, a large new hospital was formally opened by the municipality. As the congregation was no longer able to supply staff, ownership was transferred to the Alberta government for a partial consideration of equity.

Meanwhile in a village twenty-seven miles west of Westlock a doctor had, in 1929, organized a primitive hospital with one nurse in charge, and rented it to the village of Barrhead. The people were trying to engage a community of sisters from eastern Canada to come and take charge. In the meantime the sisters at Immaculata Hospital were asked to assist in keeping the accounts. From 1929 to 1932 Sisters Elizabeth Seton Belwood and Mary Anacletus Power frequently traveled the twenty-seven miles to Barrhead in snow, mud, and dust. When the new hospital was built, it was called Elizabeth Seton Hospital and the Sisters of St. Joseph of Pembroke took over responsibility for it.

At approximately the same time in 1928, in another small Albertan town, Hardisty, on a branch railway for the wheat pool, a doctor was providing emergency service in a storefront. Seriously injured patients had to be kept overnight for transfer the next morning by train to Edmonton. Therefore the doctor appealed to the Archbishop of Edmonton for a community of sisters who would build and operate a hospital. The Sisters of Charity of Halifax responded and St. Anne's Hospital in Hardisty was born. With the discovery of oil in Alberta and the building of a pipeline near Hardisty, prosperity had arrived. The sisters operated the hospital for many successful years until, in 1972, ownership was transferred to the Alberta Provincial Government after which a District Board took over the direction of the hospital and appointed a new administrator.

In 1929 at the request of Archbishop Alfred A. Sinnott of Winnipeg, the Sisters of Charity took over the administration of a small hospital in the town of Swan River, Manitoba, where the population was mainly Protestant. Twenty years later when the municipality built a new hospital, they were forced to withdraw. The people who had originally resisted the arrival of the sisters where sad to see them leave.

The Sisters of Charity of Halifax were able to answer a request to staff a hospital in the town of Jasper in the heart of the Canadian Rockies, and four sisters went there in 1930. The request for women religious had come to Archbishop O'Leary from Sir Henry Thornton, President of the Canadian National Railway. The hospital was built and partly supported by the CNR to give priority treatment to railway emergency cases. It also served victims of skiing accidents and the occasional bear-mauling of unsuspecting tourists, as well as the people of Jasper and the surrounding area. Over the years the town of Jasper expanded and the hospital facilities were updated and enlarged. Eventually a new hospital was built in 1971. The ownership was transferred to the Alberta government but the name Seton Hospital was kept.

The Sisters of Charity of Halifax engage in many other fields of health care besides hospitals. They operate Health Care Facilities at their Motherhouse in Halifax, and for their elderly and sick American sisters at Mount Saint Vincent, Wellesley Hills, Massachusetts. Elizabeth Seton Residence was built there and licensed for the chronically ill and disabled. Both facilities accept the sisters' parents, and recently laypeople in need of health care.

In the sisters' foreign missions, especially in Bani, the Dominican Republic, the Sisters of Charity of Halifax work in a health-care center and have extensively treated mothers and their children. In Lima, Peru, they help staff an inner-city clinic. In the Northwest Territories one Sister of Charity worked assiduously as a Public Health nurse for many years. In this final decade of the twentieth century individual sisters are dedicated to health care. Dr. Nuala Kenny, a pediatric specialist and noted educator, has medical ethics as her present priority. For some years Dr. Kenny has been Chief of Pediatrics at the Izaak Walton Killam Hospital for children, Professor and Head of the Department of Pediatrics at Dalhousie University, and presently Chair of the Medical Department there.

Several sisters have taught in nursing schools and colleges and are chaplains in hospitals.

THE SISTERS OF CHARITY OF CINCINNATI[5]

In 1852, shortly after becoming a diocesan community, the Sisters of Charity of Cincinnati began their ministry in health care by opening the first Catholic and first private hospital in Cincinnati. Five sisters inaugurated the twenty-bed St. John's Hotel for Invalids on November 13. Doctors and sisters from St. John's rendered heroic service during the Civil War, both at the hospital and on the battlefields. The hospital, re-christened Good Samaritan after the War, built a new facility in the early twentieth century that eventually grew to a 639-bed capacity. A teaching hospital from its inception, many medical firsts occurred there. Good Samaritan continues to be one of the leading health-care facilities in the Cincinnati area.

In 1865 the Congregation opened its first hospital in the New Mexico Territory. Tales of courage and heroic response accompany the story of the early days of St. Vincent's in Sante Fe. Originally a one-story adobe structure, the hospital was supported by the sisters' begging trips to mining and railroad camps. One of the sisters at St. Vincent's became the first woman in the Territory awarded a medical license based on surgical and diagonostic skills she had developed over many years of service.

Between 1865 and 1902, the congregation took on four additional hospitals in Colorado and New Mexico. In 1882 St. Mary's was opened in Pueblo, and in 1889 Mount San Rafael in Trinidad. Glockner Sanitarium in Colorado Springs was donated to the Congregation in the early 1890s, and shortly after the turn of the century, St. Joseph's in Albuquerque. Besides being general hospitals, all of these western hospitals, with the exception of Trinidad, served as tuberculosis sanitariums.

By the turn of the century, the congregation opened additional hospitals: San Antonio in Kenton, Ohio; St. Joseph's in Mt. Clemens, Michigan; and Seton in Cincinnati. In the early decades of the twentieth century, facilities were also undertaken at St. Joseph's in Wuchang, China, and Good Samaritan in Dayton, Ohio. An increasing number of sisters became professionally prepared as nurses, dietitians, medical technologists, X-ray technicians, and in other health-related areas to meet the needs of the growing hospital ministry.

The majority of sponsored hospitals conducted schools of nursing as well as other health-related educational programs. Sister of Charity nurses, administrators, and other professionals have consistently been active and have often served in leadership positions in local, state, and national professional organizations.

As health-care delivery in the United States expanded after World War II, Sister of Charity-sponsored hospitals were involved in extensive facility expansion and replacement programs. These involved three new buildings in the West, two new wings in the East, and remodeling and updating in all community hospitals. The financial picture became more complex as construction costs rose and federal aid and foundation grants became available. At the same time, sisters working in health care continued to advance their professional skills and credentials.

By the middle of the twentieth century local advisory boards were organized to participate in governance of the hospitals. Eventually this led to separate incorporation with local boards of trustees that included both sisters and laypeople. Simultaneously, a centralized approach to operating the hospitals was introduced, including programs in shared services, capital construction financing, insurance, employee benefits, and purchasing. This approach makes these institutions more efficient and financially viable. Ongoing evaluation of the health-care ministry led to Sister of Charity facilities in Kenton, Ohio; Trinadad, Colorado; and Santa Fe, New Mexico, being turned over to the local communities.

In 1979, as economic and societal factors continued to influence health care in the U.S., the Sisters of Charity anticipated the need for more comprehensive, integrated health-care services by forming the Sisters of Charity Health Care Systems (SCHCS). During the next decade SCHCS expanded its membership to include health and elder-care facilities operated by the Sisters of St. Francis of Colorado Springs and by Sunny Acres Villa of Denver.

After several years of planning, SCHCS consolidated with two other Catholic health-care systems to form Catholic Health Initiatives (CHI) in 1996. This new entity represents nine religious congregations and has a presence in seventy-two urban and rural communities in twenty states. It is one of the largest Catholic, not-for-profit health organizations in the United States.

Through the nearly 150 years of involvement in health care, the sisters and the institutions they served reached out to meet the needs of the communities in which they are located. They continue to do this through the hospitals and their many outreach programs. In addition, in recent years, sisters are rendering health services in rural, inner-city, and parish settings as well as in a few third-world areas. Several Sister of Charity physicians have expanded the scope of the sisters' involvement as well. Although health care continues to change dramatically, the Sisters of Charity are poised to continue their long tradition of service in this ministry.

THE SISTERS OF CHARITY OF THE IMMACULATE CONCEPTION[6]

A Canadian congregation, the Sisters of Charity of the Immaculate Conception, in Saint John, New Brunswick, has been involved in the healing ministry since its founding in 1854. Initially they visited the sick and took care of the elderly in their homes. Elderly ladies were cared for in the Motherhouse. Mater Misericordia Home was the first institution established by the Bishop of the Saint John Diocese in 1888 and operated by the sisters.

The SCIC's first venture into hospital ministry was in 1910 in Prince Albert, Saskatchewan. Holy Family Hospital was built on land provided by Bishop Pascal but the building costs were provided by the sisters with assistance from local lumber camps whose employees along with the native people were the first patients. The hospital grew from its initial twenty-five beds to 150 beds in 1963, when a completely new hospital was built. A Nursing School was opened in 1914 and continued until 1971, when all nursing schools were centralized. Currently Holy Family Hospital is being used for long-term care with some outpatient clinics.

St. Joseph's Hospital was opened in 1914 in a private residence, expanding through the years to a 125-bed hospital with a School of Nursing (1915-1971). A new hospital was built in 1958. Eventually it became part of the Saint John Regional Hospital District. It continues to operate day-care surgery, a smaller emergency department. Inpatients are limited to geriatric assessment and rehabilitation units. There are several special units, one of which is eye surgery.

In Vancouver, B.C., in 1939 the Sisters of Charity of the Immaculate Conception opened St. Vincent's Hospital at the request of Archbishop Duke, who felt the need for another Catholic Hospital for this rapidly growing city on the West Coast. Housing 100 patients along with major services, it had expanded to 250 beds by 1974. A new wing provided for extended-care patients. In 1976 St. Vincent's was asked to operate an existing Extended-Care Hospital of seventy-five beds on another site. In 1984 the Board was asked to build and operate a new 225-bed institution. With the closing of a nearby Veteran's Hospital, St. Vincent's was asked to administer the extended-care unit of an additional 100 beds.

As religious communities realized their increasingly limited ability to staff and maintain their hospitals, a new organization called CHARA was set up in 1993 by the local Bishop and major superiors of three Vancouver communities to continue Catholic operation of the institutions. The B.C. government requested two remaining Catholic hospitals to unite with CHARA. Another organization called CARIM, Irish for "caring with love," is being established to operate all Catholic health-care institutions in Vancouver, with a Board consisting of the Bishop, the religious owners, laypeople appointed by each institution, and the government. St. Vincent's Hospital continues to have medical and surgical patients, but the emphasis is on treating the elderly.

Mary's Home in Moncton, New Brunswick, was opened by the sisters in 1926 and remained a viable home for the care of the elderly until it closed in 1971. Tobique Hospital was established in 1928 for the native Indians on the Maliseet Reserve. It closed in 1958 when Provincial Health Insurance came into effect and native people were cared for in a nearby hospital. St. Joseph's Hospital was opened by the sisters in Radway, 1926, to serve a large farming community. When the hospital needed to be replaced in 1976, the government decided on a Health-Care Center for the area, and the sisters withdrew in 1980.

Rocmaura Nursing Home was built by the Sisters of Charity in Saint John, New Brunswick, in 1972. There are accommodations for 150 residents, including relief beds for short-term care. As with hospitals, the provincial government now pays the operating costs on the basis of an approved budget. The Sisters of Charity of the Immaculate Conception's initial health ministry was to the elderly, and now their emphasis is again on geriatrics. "The old order changes, giving way to the new, and God fulfills himself in many ways." With the number of sisters rapidly diminishing in every congregation, sisters do not know how long they will be able to maintain even a presence in their health-care institutions, but they do know that "for everything there is a season."

LES RELIGIEUSES DE NOTRE-DAME-DU-SACRÉ-COEUR[7]

Les Religieuses de Notre-Dame-du-Sacré-Coeur of Moncton, New Brunswick, an offshoot of the SCIC, has always had care of the sick in hospitals and hospices as one of their major works. It was this calling that led Mère Marie-Jeanne-de-Valois to answer the need of the Stella-Maris Hospital in Kent County, responding thus to an urgent demand of the Acadian people that they undertake this charity. In 1955 Dr. Robert Marcoux resigned as Director of this small private hospital, which he had opened in Bouctouche. Mère Marie-Jeanne-de-Valois, Superior General, was invited to assume direction. The construction of a new and larger hospital was necessary. It was built between Richibouctou and Bouctouche. The congregation bore most of the expenses, but in the course of construction the provincial government became the main beneficiary. During Premier McKenna's second term in office, the government made more and more demands to suit ever-changing regulations of the Department of Health. As a result Stella Maris Hospital has become a purely government-controlled institution. Sixteen sisters served there in the early years, but with time they were gradually replaced. What is important to the sisters is that their mission is still alive. The spirit of loving and compassionate charity handed down from St. Vincent de Paul through St. Elizabeth Ann Seton has influenced the personnel in their care of the sick. Les Religieuses de Notre-Dame-du-Sacré-Coeur continue to serve in this Catholic hospital deeply involved in its spirit of charity.

THE SISTERS OF CHARITY OF LEAVENWORTH[8]

The Health Ministry of the Sisters of Charity of Leavenworth, Kansas, began with the opening of St. John's Hospital in Leavenworth on March 15, 1864, about five years after the sisters' arrival in Leavenworth. The first civilian hospital in Kansas, it was built to meet the needs of a growing population, especially the sick poor. Sister Johanna Bruner, a qualified and experienced nurse, and an astute businesswoman, was appointed the first Administrator. She opened a Training School for Nurses, also the first in Kansas, and was indefatigable in seeing that the patients received good care, a hallmark of the Leavenworth Charity's hospitals.

In 1869 some sisters were sent to Helena, Montana, to build St. John's Hospital (1870-1975). Montana was a rugged, untamed territory, with numerous mining towns. The sisters' services were requested in other mining towns in Montana, so they built several hospitals, including St. Joseph's Hospital (1873-1963) in Deer Lodge, St. Mary's Hospital (1875-1879) in Virginia City, St. James Hospital (1881) in Butte, St. Ann's Hospital (1889-1969) transferred ownership to local community in Anaconda, and St. Vincent's Hospital (1899) in Billings. In all of these Montana frontier areas the sisters had to go begging for money to build the hospitals, but the miners were very generous contributors. For the amount they were unable to collect the sisters went into debt.

In 1873 sisters were sent to Denver, Colorado, to open a hospital in a cottage, then a larger house, and finally a newly constructed hospital named St. Joseph's. Again Sister Johanna supervised the construction and was appointed Administrator. It was the first private hospital in Denver. The sisters found Denver of the 1870s much less civilized than Leavenworth. In 1875 Sister Johanna was sent to Laramie, Wyoming, to establish a hospital for the county poor and for the sick and disabled members of Union Pacific Railroad. A twenty-four-bed hospital was opened in 1878, called St. Joseph's. Elected Treasurer of the Sisters of Charity of Leavenworth (1877-1885), Sister Johanna had to return to Kansas. More than 100 years later, Sister Johanna Bruner was recognized by the Laramie people as part of its history when in 1981 the County Commissioners named a street in Laramie "Bruner Drive." A resident remarked, "This is the first street in Wyoming named for a woman, let alone a nun!"

Two other hospitals were opened by the sisters in Colorado: St. Vincent's (1879-1972) in Leadville and St. Mary's (1896) in Grand Junction. They also opened hospitals in other states, including St. Anthony's Hospital (1897-1955) in Las Vegas, New Mexico; St. Francis Hospital (1909) in Topeka, Kansas; Providence Hospital (1920) in Kansas City, Kansas; Our Lady of Perpetual Help Hospital (1940-1955) in Falls City, Nebraska; Saint John's Hospital (1942) in Santa Monica, California. The very last hospital built by the Sisters of Charity of Leavenworth was DePaul Hospital (1952-1992) in Cheyenne, Wyoming.

The establishment of all these hospitals from 1864 to 1952 enveloped considerable and ongoing expansion over the years. Sister Cornelia Donnelly was on the Council in charge of hospitals (1950-1968) and was instrumental in their expansion and development. Until 1940 the sisters were totally responsible for securing and financing any building projects. The Hill-Burton Federal Grants Program became an available source of funds in the late 1940s, and many of the SCL's hospitals took advantage of it. The utilization by the public of hospitals increased tremendously following World War II, as many participated in voluntary health-care insurance. The Medicare Program was established in 1965 under the Social Security Act, for people sixty-five and over. It also provided a medical-care program, Medicaid, for those in need of financial assistance. As a result of a study and evaluation of the Sisters of Charity of Leavenworth health-care ministry, they formed the Sisters of Charity of Leavenworth Health Services Corporation (SCLHSC). The Articles of Incorporation were filed with the Kansas Secretary of State on December 12, 1972. It was formed as a means to develop their numerous hospitals into a more unified system bound together by the same common philosophy of health care: make more secure the assets of the Motherhouse, especially the funds required for education, retirement, and other community purposes; continue the financial advantages to individual hospitals, especially the corporate borrowing capability that results from all hospital assets being held by the corporation. Sister Mary Dennis (Mary Margaret Shea) was the Council member in charge of hospitals at the time. A period of retrenchment was inaugurated as noted by the closing dates of some hospitals, following the recommendations of the Cresap, McCormick, and Paget study, as well as other valuable data. Sister Mildred Irwin, second President of the Health Services Corporation, was instrumental in its implementation and development of a multihospital system and corporate programs. Sister Marie Damian Glatt became the fourth and current President of the Health Services Corporation, her staff coping with continuing structural changes in hospital marketing, including hospital networking, managed care, vertical integration, capitation, and other hospital strategies.

A primary concern is how to provide care for the poor. In 1986 a freestanding primary care clinic was opened in Leavenworth, financially supported by the SCL's, the local community, and a few grants. The uninsured poor, and those under 150% of the poverty level government formula were admitted. This clinic became a model for other clinics. Marian Clinic, Topeka, Kansas, and Marillac Clinic in Grand Junction, Colorado, were incorporated in 1988. Duchesne Clinic, Kansas City, Kansas, was dedicated in 1989 as an affiliate of St. Vincent's Clinic Corporation (changed to Caritas Clinics, Inc.).

The major responsibility of Catholic hospitals today is to incorporate the principles of Christ in the midst of the ever-expanding and often overwhelming scientific knowledge and technology. The Sisters of Charity of Leavenworth are in a position and have the potential to be advocates for the welfare of the sick and suffering, the poor, and their neighbor in need, whoever that may be.

THE SISTERS OF CHARITY OF SAINT ELIZABETH, CONVENT STATION, N.J.[9]

The Sisters of Charity of Saint Elizabeth, Convent Station, New Jersey, trace their involvement in health care to their first foundation in the Ward mansion, Newark, New Jersey, where they had a young ladies' Academy, an orphanage, a novitiate, and a hospital. Within the first five years of their founding in 1859, they continued their healing mission, nursing the Civil War wounded soldiers (1861-1865) in a temporary hospital set up near the Center Street railroad station, Newark.

After the closure of their infant hospital in Newark and the transfer of its patients to newly established St. Michael's Hospital, and the involvement in governmental hospitals and havens during the Civil War, the first foundation in health care sponsored by the Sisters of Charity of Saint Elizabeth was St. Joseph's Hospital in Paterson, N.J., in 1867, now called St. Joseph Hospital and Medical Center. During Mother Xavier's lifetime four more hospitals were founded: St. Mary's Hospital (1895) in Passaic, N.J.; St. Elizabeth's Hospital (1904) in Elizabeth, N.J.; Good Samaritan Hospital (1904) in Suffern, N.Y.; the Hospital of Saint Raphael (1907) in New Haven, Connecticut. In 1913 they took over the management of All Souls Hospital in Morristown, N.J. This was a parish hospital with a lay and clerical Board of Trustees previously staffed by the Grey Nuns of Montreal. In the mid-fifties it was transferred to the Sisters of Charity and reincorporated. In 1970 it was relinquished by the Sisters of Charity and finally closed as an acute-care facility around 1976.

St. Vincent's was opened as a foundling hospital in 1875 in Montclair, N.J. It became a Nursery and Baby Hospital and then a general hospital. In 1981 it merged with St. Joseph Hospital and Medical Center, and it was eventually converted to a nursing home. Another health-care institution, called the House of Divine Providence for Incurables, was opened in Ridgewood, N.J. by Mother Xavier in 1891. It was destroyed by fire in 1925, and rebuilt as a residence for the elderly, Mount Saint Andrew, still in existence and open to all, regardless of religion, nationality or color. Sisters of Charity have the option of retiring there.

The establishment of Schools of Nursing is another contribution of the New Jersey Sisters of Charity to Catholic health care. Three-year nursing education programs were established in New Jersey in Paterson, Passaic, Elizabeth, and Morristown, and in Connecticut in New Haven. A school for baby technicians was opened in Montclair, N.J. As baccalaureate (4-year) and community college (2-year) programs began to flourish, the three year programs were phased out. The College of Saint Elizabeth, sponsored by the Sisters of Charity of Saint Elizabeth, currently offers an undergraduate program for registered nurses who wish to obtain a bachelor's degree in Nursing. Other contributions in education in health care are schools for medical technologists, radiological technologists, pulmonary technologists, nutritionists, and others.

During the past thirty years the New Jersey Sisters of Charity hospitals have developed Outreach programs in inner city locations, homes for the elderly, AIDS clinics, residences for children with AIDS, mental health centers with day-care centers, halfway houses, sheltered workshops, a day-care center for those with Alzheimer's disease, mobile neighborhood vans, home-care programs, nursing homes, physician-hospital organizations, and a host of others. One of the more recent contributions to health care is the involvement of sisters at the trustee level. Programs for persons interested in becoming trustees have been conducted by Sisters of Charity since the 1970s. Currently they have about forty sisters serving in this capacity.

Individual sisters are extending their competence in a variety of less structured health-care situations. They care for the health of migrant workers in rural areas; serve as midwives and educate midwives in underserved areas; work in small public health clinics in the rural south and on Indian reservations. The sisters established a hospital in Yuangling, China, and staffed it until they were expelled and their property was confiscated. They also staff a government hospital in Bolivia and work in a public hospital in St. Thomas in the Virgin Islands. Sisters have become physicians, medical technologists, nutritionists, patient representatives, patient visitors, therapists, mental health service directors, medical record librarians, comptrollers, computer programmers, lawyers, chaplains, teacher of dance therapy in a mental institution, and other positions. The faith-filled dynamic vision of the Sisters of Charity of Saint Elizabeth has consistently responded to the needs of the times. This readiness to adapt has gained for them the trust and admiration of those whom they have treated as well as those with whom they work in the field of health care.

THE SISTERS OF CHARITY OF SETON HILL, GREENSBURG, PENNSYLVANIA[10]

The Sisters of Charity of Seton Hill, Greensburg, Pennsylvania, have been involved in health care since 1897, but it has never been the primary work of the Congregation. Some of the sisters currently involved in writing the congregation's history heard the stories of the early days from the sisters who pioneered in each of the health care institutions. Unlike the sisters assigned to teaching, those in health care had a continuous assignment, and changes were made any time in the calendar year. Sisters were missioned to Pittsburgh Hospital, Roselia Foundling and Maternity Hospital, McGuire Memorial Nursing Home, and to Jeannette District Memorial Hospital.

Sister Electa Boyle is quoted in *Mother Seton's Sisters of Charity in Western Pennsylvania* as saying that Pittsburgh Hospital was the first general hospital undertaken by the congregation. Two physicians bought a nine-room house and opened an emergency hospital. They immediately appealed to the Sisters of Charity for assistance, and three sisters were assigned to manage the hospital and care for its two patients. Two months later a twenty-two-room house was rented and plans were made to open a new Charity Hospital. The name was changed to Pittsburgh Hospital. The sisters and their secular classmates were graduated from the School of Nursing; the Hospital continued to enlarge and serve the community until 1972 when a long-term lease was signed with Forbes Health System, and the sisters withdrew. They retain Board representation. The Health System currently encompasses two Acute-Care Hospitals, a Hospice, Skilled and Intermediate Care Facilities, and a Personal Care Home.

The second hospital, Providence Hospital in Beaver Falls, Pennsylvania, opened in 1909 in response to a request by the clergy for a Catholic hospital. It too operated a School of Nursing and continued to serve the area until a merger in 1966 made it impossible to continue as a Catholic facility. It still functions as an active part of a Health Care System in the community.

Roselia Foundling and Maternity Hospital offered shelter to unmarried mothers and their babies, and was an adoption agency in the Pittsburgh Diocese from 1891 until 1971, when the need no longer existed for unmarried mothers to withdraw from society, and the Diocesan Social Services took over adoptions. The sisters continued to staff the facility, which now offers shelter to homeless men and women.

McGuire Memorial was named for Eliza McGuire who donated eighty acres of land to the Sisters of Charity on which a nursing home was built in 1952. Despite an excellent reputation, financial problems led to its closure. The eighty patients were relocated, and Bishop John Wright turned the facility over to the Felician Sisters for care of retarded children in 1963. It has continued to enjoy a well-earned reputation for providing outstanding care.

In 1955 the Council of the Sisters of Charity responded to a plea from the Catholic community in Jeannette, Pennsylvania, to manage a new general hospital in the Greensburg Diocese. The Board turned the hospital over to the Sisters of Charity, who operated it successfully for almost thirty years. In 1984 the sisters relinquished ownership because the hospital became part of a Health System where the philosophy was in question. The sisters retain the right to have representation on the Jeannette District Memorial Board.

The Sisters of Charity sent almost all their sisters to the Pittsburgh Hospital School of Nursing. Specialization and advanced education in nursing was eventually acquired at Duquesne University and the University of Pittsburgh for the Baccalaureate and Master's degrees. Trends in nursing have moved from generalization in institutions to specialization in Obstetrics, Pediatrics, and Gerontology, to Home Care, Hospice Care, and the emerging Certified Nurse Practitioner. Specialization in Administration, Social Services, Dietetics, Anesthesia, and later Clinical Nursing came about slowly with sisters attending programs that required brief but full-time attendance, generally in St. Louis, Cincinnati, Springfield, and Washington, D.C. Since the late 1950s some of the sisters have also received doctoral degrees. The sisters have been innovative in finding fields of practice, since the Congregation no longer owns or staffs hospitals. They have become Certified Nurse Practitioners, Specialists in Gerontology, Oncology, Hospice, Supervision, Higher Education, and Freelance Consultors. They are employed by various state and county agencies, by universities, and by Schools of Nursing. Sister Rosemary Donley was a Robert Wood Johnson Fellow with the Senate and House of Representatives in Washington, D.C. This position led to her appointment as Dean of the School of Nursing at

Catholic University in Washington, D.C. Sister is now Executive Vice President of Catholic University, the first woman to hold that office. Sister Mary Jean Flaherty succeeded her as Dean of the School of Nursing. Another sister has been equally successful as initial faculty member of the Graduate School of Public Health at the University of Pittsburgh; still another sister is Director of Planning at a large Catholic Hospital; also a sister pharmacist is employed by the Veterans Administration.

In 1988 two sisters, a physician, and a medical technologist established a clinic in an underserved section of New Orleans, developing it into a self-sufficient center for the uninsured. The Sisters of Charity of Seton Hill, Greensburg, Pennsylvania, have sisters serving as hospital chaplains, attorneys in health care, Directors of Nursing in care for the aging, the blind, and the aging and the handicapped in Korea. Their ministry in health-care embraces every field.

THE VINCENTIAN SISTERS OF CHARITY OF PITTSBURGH, PENNSYLVANIA[11]

The Vincentian Sisters of Charity of Pittsburgh arrived in the United States from Szatmar, Rumania, in 1902 to work among the Slovak immigrant families in Pennsylvania. For the first twenty years their contribution to health care was simply that of visiting the sick in their homes, taking care of their simple health needs, and conversing with them in their native tongue, thus gaining their confidence and trust. Their treatment of the parishioners was thus more psychological than physical, although one is dependent on the other. During the 1918 influenza epidemic the Vincentian Sisters certainly came to the fore. It was the vision of their leader, Mother Emerentiana, that the Vincentian Sisters would someday minister to the sick poor.

In 1922 the Diocese of Pittsburgh purchased property with the intention of building a home for incurable patients. It was paid for in nickels and quarters, the offerings of the poor Slovak immigrants. Father Lawrence A. Carroll and his poor people of St. William Parish in East Pittsburgh were the benefactors and prime movers. They built the first unit for twenty-four patients of what he hoped would eventually be fifteen such cottages. The Vincentian Sisters were asked to operate this facility. Apparently the Diocese gave the sisters utter freedom to administer the Home as they felt best. They therefore added two wings to the original cottage, and the number of patients rose to seventy. All were indigent, too poor to pay, so survival depended on the sisters who worked without pay and depended on the generosity of a group called Friends of the Home. To provide food for the patients the sisters planted vegetable gardens and begged in the Strip District of Pittsburgh, where food for the city was auctioned and sold. In 1959 a new Vincentian Home was built and the original building razed. This new facility accommodated 100 women and fifty men. Although the sisters continued to staff it, they also had to hire lay help. Until 1967 the sisters' services had been donated. From 1967 they began to receive a salary. In 1980 a two-million-dollar addition to the Home was completed. Now care can be given to 220 patients, among them infirm, retired priests. The ownership of the Vincentian Home has passed from the Diocese to the Vincentian Sisters.

With her eyes on possible missionary work, Mother Ignatia Butka responded to Father Harold Purcell's invitation to minister to African-Americans at Holy Ghost Mission in Marbury, Alabama, and at Mother Mary Mission in Phenix City, Alabama, in the 1940s. Segregation had prevented black people from receiving proper health care, so a sister nurse was sent with the other sisters. Sister Clarence conducted the nursing home for four patients, their hygiene, food, and medicine. Eventually a new twenty-patient nursing home was built. The sisters were in charge until 1987, when the mission was given over to the Resurrection Fathers.

Mother Mary Mission, located in the middle of Phenix City, treated black people denied hospitalization and medical care. A clinic was set up in the school. Tonsilectomies were performed at the clinic with the nurse, Sister Celine, as anesthetist and postoperative nurse. A dentist took care of the students' dental problems during school hours one day a week, and a doctor of internal medicine was available on a weekly basis also. Medicines were provided by the Catholic Medical Association. After integration the number of patients mercifully declined as proper health care in hospitals became available to black people and their children.

By 1943 the congregation's health care ministry had expanded into another nursing home. Mother Gregory Kolesar was concerned for middle-class people who were not poor enough to be accepted into the Vincentian Home. Therefore the Vincentian sisters purchased the Donahoe Estate and converted the mansion into a nursing home for those who could afford to pay. Villa de Marillac Nursing Home was deluged with patients, necessitating a new building completed in 1965, which accommodates fifty-two patients. Presently the building of a larger facility is being discussed, with a special section to accommodate Alzheimer's patients.

Also in 1943 the congregation's health care ministry expanded to Monett, Missouri. Dr. William H. West made an outright gift of West Hospital to the Vincentian Sisters. They renamed it St. Vincent Hospital and made extensive renovations, but it was still too small to accommodate all who sought help there. Hence they launched in 1947 a fund-raising campaign and a wing was added in 1952. By 1963 the original building was razed and the new St. Vincent Hospital dedicated. Because of the dearth of doctors, the census was alarmingly low. Sister Mary Clement therefore hired several Filipino doctors and built for them a physicians' building to set up a group practice, thus allowing for the survival of the hospital for the next twenty years. In 1993 it was sold to Cox Medical Systems.

A new call for help came in 1951 from Montgomery, Alabama, for the sisters to staff St. Jude Hospital, one of the first in the South to accommodate both African-American and Caucasian patients. The hospital was a success until 1965 when integration became the law of the land. Because of the sisters' support for African-Americans, the Caucasian doctors staged an exodus from St. Jude's Hospital. To make matters worse, some more affluent African-Americans, who could now go to the hospital of their choice, no longer supported St. Jude's. Despite these trying conditions the sisters remained working at St. Jude's until 1976, when the hospital was transferred to a group of doctors who favored abortion on demand. From a moral/ethical standpoint the sisters had to withdraw. However the Vincentian Sisters had, since 1958, been staffing Purcell Memorial, a facility for severely handicapped children in Montgomery, and they continued their service and loving care of these children.

In the 1960s the congregation had taken over two more nursing homes: Assumption, a diocesan facility in Youngstown, Ohio, now being administered by another congregation, although a few Vincentians still work there; and Regency Hall Nursing Home near the Motherhouse in Pittsburgh, the latter a congregational facility serving 143 patients. Today they are both very viable facilities.

The history of the Vincentian Health Care Ministry would not be complete without including the Motherhouse Infirmary, opened in 1924, and housed in Pioneer Hall, until 1954. Presently it occupied the second floor of Marian Hall, where the environment has been enhanced by bright rooms and attractive furniture. There a twenty-four-hour-a-day staff of nine serve the physical needs of the elderly sisters as well as offering health care to any sick sisters. Their spiritual and psychological needs are taken care of by an additional staff.

Without sisters imbued with the spirit of St. Vincent de Paul and St. Louise de Marillac, the Congregation could never have accomplished what it did in health care ministry. It was the sisters who were registered nurses, practical nurses, nurse's aides, dieticians, laundresses, secretaries, lab technicians, X-ray technicians, and administrators who created the standards of excellence in the congregation's facilities. Over the ninety-four years of its existence, the Congregation has had 115 sisters ministering in health care. Of that number, fifty-six are in eternity and fifty-nine are still making the effort to keep the Vincentian Sisters of Charity's standards of health care high, according to the true Vincentian spirit.

THE SISTERS OF CHARITY OF NAZARETH, KENTUCKY[12]

The origin of the health care ministry of the Sisters of Charity of Nazareth, Kentucky, can be traced to 1812 in a log cabin in Kentucky. The first members came together to teach and to care for the sick, the poor, and the orphaned. Although their first apostolic work was the education of young girls, the sisters visited the sick in their homes and in 1821 began a health ministry in the infirmary of Saint Joseph College and Seminary in Bardstown.

In the early days, when there were epidemics of cholera, yellow fever, typhoid or influenza, the sisters often cared for the patients at the risk of their own lives. During the Civil War the sisters nursed soldiers on both sides of the conflict. Abraham Lincoln called them "Angels of Mercy." The sisters also planned for a long-term presence in health care by the foundation of institutions. In 1836 they set some rooms aside in their orphanage for the care of sick children. Over the years this developed into St. Joseph Infirmary, the first of many hospitals owned and operated by the Sisters of Charity of Nazareth. Three hospitals that were founded in the nineteenth century continue to offer services under the sisters' sponsorship today: Saints Mary and Elizabeth Hospital (now Caritas Medical Center), founded in 1874 in Louisville, Kentucky; Saint Joseph Hospital in Lexington where the sisters began to serve in 1877; and St. Vincent Infirmary Medical Center, Little Rock, Arkansas, which opened in 1888.

True to their pioneer spirit and charism, the sisters were open to meeting needs in a variety of places and in response to multiple needs. They opened a clinic in 1941 in Ensley, Alabama, where the majority of people were African-American. As needs expanded, this facility grew into Holy Family Hospital. In 1969 ownership of the hospital was transferred to members of the civic community.

The sisters ventured into the mountains of eastern Kentucky and became engaged in rural health ministry when they purchased a hospital in London, Kentucky. They renamed it Marymount Medical Center, greatly respected today as it responds to the needs of the surrounding communities.

In 1947 the Sisters of Charity of Nazareth went to India as missionaries. The following year they opened

Nazareth Hospital in the Diocese of Patna, Bihar. This institution continued to grow, and today the 250-bed hospital offers services in internal medicine, surgery, obstetrics, gynecology, and pediatrics. There are also departments for physical therapy and public health and for the treatment of leprosy and tuberculosis. The hospital's School of Nursing and Midwifery continues to educate young women in the health field and has many graduates serving the health-care needs of people all over India and around the world.

In the United States the sisters continued to expand their institutional health ministry. In 1948 they broke ground for Our Lady of Peace Hospital (now known as Caritas Peace Center). This facility was built to meet a need that the sisters had begun to address in 1913 when they developed Mount Saint Agnes Sanatorium to care for persons with psychiatric illnesses. By opening Flaget Hospital in Bardstown in 1951, the sisters formalized their ministry to the sick in an area they had served since their foundation in 1812. A call from Chattanooga took the sisters back to eastern Tennessee to open a hospital in 1952; they had staffed a hospital there in the 1890s but had withdrawn after the Spanish-American War.

Home health was another pioneering venture. In 1971 two sisters founded a home health agency (now known as Caritas Home Health) to provide in-home services to the rural poor and elderly of Kentucky. With its main office in Bardstown the agency also has offices in Elizabethtown, Louisville, and Shepherdsville, and presently serves eight counties.

In the early 1980s another pioneering effort saw the Sisters of Charity of Nazareth as the first to admit people with AIDS into their nursing home in Louisville. The sisters had previously lobbied the State of Kentucky to change a law to allow this to happen.

From 1976 to 1986 the Sisters were in health care ministry in San Antonio, Toledo District of Belize, Central America, and were involved in public-health nursing and a midwifery primary-care clinic in collaboration with the Government of Belize.

In 1984 the hospitals and home health agency were formed into the Sisters of Charity of Nazareth Health Corporation (later the Sisters of Charity of Nazareth Health System), a three-state network of health services through nine facilities – six in Kentucky, one in Tennessee, and two in Arkansas. A nonprofit company, its corporate offices are located in Nazareth, Kentucky, home of the SCN Congregation. In partnership with more than 11,000 employees, volunteers, board members and physicians, it was founded for the purpose of greater efficiency, better service, and the protection of assets for both the Congregation and the health care entities. The System's core values of quality, justice, collaboration, compassion, and stewardship continue to be its driving force. In fiscal year 1995 SCN Health System facilities had 64,019 patient discharges.

In the rapidly changing health care world, there is the ongoing challenge to live out the Mission Statement by which the SCN Health System commits itself to the healing ministry of Jesus in the pioneer tradition of the Sisters of Charity of Nazareth. Some SCNs work within the SCN Health System; some are active in other areas of health ministry. Wherever they are, whatever they do, they attempt to continue the pioneering spirit of Catherine Spalding.

THE VINCENTIAN SISTERS OF CHARITY OF BEDFORD, OHIO[13]

The Vincentian Sisters of Charity of Bedford, Ohio, from the very beginning were encouraged by Mother Mary

John Berchmans, General Superior, to study nursing. It was her dream to have several registered nurses working in hospitals and nursing homes and eventually to establish health institutions owned and staffed by the Congregation. Mother Berchmans selected sisters for nursing who were already teaching or preparing to teach. She consistently held that sisters should be flexible enough to do both.

In 1951 the community had five nurses who had been trained at St. Alexis Hospital School of Nursing and St. John's School of Nursing in Cleveland. One sister specialized in surgical nursing, another in obstetrics/maternity nursing. The sister nurses were on staff at St. Alexis Hospital, Marymount Hospital, and Bedford Municipal Hospital. For some years the nurses served part-time as they continued to teach in elementary schools on weekdays. In the late 1970s the last nurse completed her training at Ursuline College School of Nursing and served at Marymount Hospital for seven years, and at Isaiah Home for terminally ill patients, including those with AIDS, in Rochester, New York. She was a founding member of that Home. Another nurse who completed her training before entering the Vincentian community in 1978 continued working at Brentwood Hospital in Greater Cleveland. In 1996 she began working at a nursing home in Pineville, Kentucky.

Several sisters worked as nurse's aides and home health-care aides throughout the 1970s and 1980s. As some sisters retired from teaching, they became full-time aides in the homes of the sick and elderly. One nurse became a full-time nanny for a family who needed care for their three children. In the 1960s many sisters volunteered their summers to assist at two nursing homes administered by one sister's family. In 1978 one sister was asked to study for licensure as a nursing home administrator. After completing her studies, she was appointed Administrator of Villa Sancta Anna, a nursing home sponsored by the First Catholic Slovak Ladies Association.

Presently three sisters minister at the home in Beachwood, Ohio. More recently the community extended ministry to the elderly by renovating its former high school into a ninety-resident capacity for senior adults ranging from independent to assisted living. A Vincentian Sister has been administrator since 1989, when the Center opened, and five serve as members of the staff. Several retired Sisters also volunteer their time and ministry. The Center employs members from other communities in all phases of its work. This undertaking was extremely challenging, as it meant a total refurbishing of a school into living quarters and health facilities for the elderly as well as a change of mission to meet the needs of the Church today, given the resources at hand.

In 1979 the congregation began a home ministry to the terminally ill. The ministry was purely voluntary and focused on families unable to pay for care for a loved one. Most of the volunteers were laywomen with a range of professional health care experience. Two sisters were R.N.'s and administered the program, while a number of volunteer sisters provided prayer and pastoral support to the families. The ministry is still going strong today.

Notes

1. *Daughters of Charity*: Sister Eleanor Casey, DC, Southeast Province, Emmitsburg, MD; Sister Genevieve Keusenkothen, DC, West Central Province, St. Louis, MO; Jim Shadoan and Sister Catherine Madigan, DC, East Central Province, Evansville, IN; Sister Patricia Coughlin, DC, Northeast Province, Albany, NY; Sister Mary Ann Baez, DC, West Province, Los Altos Hills, CA.

2. Sister Anne Francis Campbell, OLM, archivist and General Superior, Charleston, South Carolina.
3. Sisters Patrice Murphy, SC, and Madeleine Mahoney, SC, New York, NY.
4. Sister Eleanor Barbour, SC, Halifax, Nova Scotia, Canada.
5. Sister Judith Metz, SC, Cincinnati, Ohio.
6. Sister Marion MacDonald, SCIC, Saint John, New Brunswick, Canada.
7. Sister Imelda Guignard, NDSC, Moncton, New Brunswick, Canada.
8. Sister Mildred M. Irwin, SCL, Leavenworth, Kansas.
9. Sister Angelica Doris, SC, Convent Station, New Jersey.
10. Sister Paul Gabriel Wilhere, SC, Greensburg, Pennsylvania.
11. Sister Mary Vincent O'Neill, VSC, Pittsburg, Pennsylvania.
12. Sister Dorothy MacDougall, SCN, and Mary Elise Biegert, SCN, Nazareth, Kentucky.
13. Sister Margaret Mach, VSC, Bedford, Ohio.

Chapter Three

Social Services

The variety of ministries that have evolved since Mother Seton established the Congregation of Sisters of Charity of St. Joseph in 1809 illustrates the need to adapt service of the poor to changing times. St. Vincent pointed the way in 1646 when he told the sisters that as the community in the beginning "was not then what it is now, there is reason to think that it is not now what it will be later when God brings it to the state on which He has decided"(February 13, 1646).

Mother Seton's Sisters of Charity of St. Joseph were incorporated in 1817 for "works of piety, charity and usefulness, and especially for the care of the sick, the succor of aged, infirm and necessitous persons, and the education of young females." The Daughters of Charity, founded by St. Vincent de Paul and his colaborer, St. Louise de Marillac, were dedicated to honor Christ as the source and model of all charity by serving Him in the person of the poor. In 1814 Mother Seton's sisters answered the call from Philadelphia to establish an orphanage there. Three years later Mother Seton sent sisters to New York to care for orphans. As part of their social work program, these early Sisters of Charity visited almshouses and prisons and continued to establish orphanages. They began to work for the poor in New York State: Albany in 1828, Brooklyn in 1831, Utica in 1834, Fordham (which was a seminary in 1841), and Rochester in 1845. They initiated social work in Cincinnati in 1829 at St. Peter's Orphanage and in New Orleans at New Orleans

Female Orphan Asylum and St. Vincent's Infant Asylum. In Boston in 1832 they helped to establish St. Aloysius Orphan Asylum and school. Between 1840 and 1860 the community opened twenty-four more orphanages, some of which included or were exclusively but temporarily for boys in Mobile, Alabama, in Baltimore, Cincinnati, and in San Rafael, California. The orphanage in New York City included boys as well.

THE DAUGHTERS OF CHARITY OF ST. VINCENT DE PAUL, UNITED STATES[1]

After 1850 when the Emmitsburg Sisters of Charity joined the international Congregation of Daughters of Charity in France, they continued to multiply in American vocations and to dedicate themselves to a vast array of social services throughout the United States. Over the next 150 years they adapted their social service ministries to meet changing needs. St. Ann's Infant and Maternity Home founded in Washington during the Civil War to care for single pregnant women and to act as an adoption agency for their children, is now a multiservice facility including high school education, adoption, classes in parenting for those who wish to keep their children, job training, and homes for one year, on the same grounds for those who need support. St. Anne's has a day-care center for residents and neighborhood children. It is also a refuge for children who have been abused or need temporary care.

The Daughters of the Emmitsburg Province since 1969 have worked in many areas at a variety of ministries. At Nazareth House in Macon, Georgia, two sisters and their lay collaborators provide assistance to pregnant women and short term aftercare. At St. Pius X in Greensboro, North Carolina, sisters serve in Catholic Social Services and in Hispanic ministry. A new venture has just begun in Roanoke Rapids, N.C., where three sisters are exploring needs in one of the poorest counties in the province. In Baltimore sisters serve in two soup kitchens – Beans and Bread, and My Brother's Keeper. They provide counseling and help as well as food for their clients. Many have problems with substance abuse; others are employed but homeless.

The West Central Province with Provincialate in St. Louis, Missouri, has a long history of social service. Around 1910, at the time of the division into two provinces, East Emmitsburg and West St. Louis, a surge of new immigrants from different national groups led to the formation of settlement houses to assist in the functions carried out by parishes in their neighborhoods: home visiting, classes in religion, clubs, sodalities, emergency relief for the poor, help in finding jobs, and homemaking classes for immigrants. The focus of the sisters had been on the individual family, sometimes taking children into half-orphan asylums, or technical schools. The settlement houses in which the Daughters worked took on these functions and focused on cooperation among families to help them work out social, economic, and moral problems. One new work was day-care for children, allowing older siblings the chance to continue schooling, the mother to work outside the home, and the family to stay together. Outreach social services were begun, occasioned by follow-up of former hospital patients, or the visiting of students' families when overwhelming needs were discovered.

Infant and maternity homes were numerous and increased in occupancy during the Depression. Orphanages became centralized under Catholic Charities, attempting to keep children in families by adoption or foster home placement. To create more homelike environments, homes were rebuilt on the cottage plan. In 1923, a new mission was opened in Poyang, Kiangsi, China. An orphanage, a technical school for girls and women, and a home for the aged were a part of the ministry. After World War II, children placed in homes were often court placements, the children of disastrous marriages, or victims of abuse. Residential and outpatient treatment programs for emotionally disturbed and educationally handicapped children were begun, and orphanages were closed.

In the 1960s, homes for unmarried mothers introduced outreach programs for unmarried fathers, realizing that they too had needs and problems. As more single parents opted to keep their babies, parenting classes were added to existing programs. They were also a part of the service of settlement houses and day-care centers. "Day nursery" designated care for infants, and preschoolers had educational programs termed "nursery schools." The focus of settlement programs shifted from recreation to development of individual potential, job placement, skill and leadership development, and group action for neighborhood improvement. Also in the 1950s and 1960s, sisters began accepting positions in Catholic Charities. One group of sisters in California operated from a mobile home, bringing services to people in several districts.

After the division of the two provinces into five, the sisters went to territories where the Church was underrepresented, taking on works such as homes for abused women, prison ministry, and laying the groundwork for a home for retarded adults. Work was expanded to include Native Americans in North and South Dakota, and outreach to the Mexican Americans in Oklahoma, Arkansas, and Texas. Among these services were elderly day care, emergency assistance, family counseling, home nursing, supplementary aid to families caring for older members at home, and a diocesan teen-pregnancy program.

In the 1990s, sisters are inserted in social ministries for dioceses, parishes, and other groups with similar values as administrators, directors, coordinators, school social workers, counselors, and case managers. They serve abused women, unwed mothers, AIDS patients, school children, emotionally disturbed children, the elderly, the homeless, housing projects, food pantries, thrift shops, emergency assistance, and in advocacy.

The Daughters of Charity in the East Central Province with Provincial House in Evansville, Indiana, proved themselves very adaptable in moving into new modes of service when their province was newly formed in 1969. They recognized the necessity of meeting the needs of the 1970s, characterized by mergers, withdrawals, and adaptations to respond to changing concerns. In 1970 St. Vincent Group Home in Milwaukee merged with St. Mary's Hill Psychiatric Hospital. Placement in foster homes had considerably decreased the number of children. The lack of sisters to care for them and the trend toward lay involvement prompted the withdrawal of the sisters. Instead the Daughters responded to new needs. Individual sisters began parish visiting of the sick and elderly in nursing homes, hospitals, and private homes. One sister was named Chaplain to the Catholic jail ministry in Saginaw, Michigan.

In 1979 St. Vincent-Sarah & Fisher Center for Children in Farmington Hills, Michigan, merged with Marillac Hall, a single-parent program. The Allen Memorial Home's single-parent program in Mobile, Alabama, was assumed by Catholic Charities of Mobile. The long-established day-care centers in Chicago and Evansville developed into multiservice centers, with new programs and services to meet the needs of the poor such as child abuse, outreach to the elderly, family counseling, young moms and babies, and assistance to the poor. The trend of ministry away from the corporate community setting to individual positions of insertion and presence is seen also in the area of social ministry. Sisters are collaborating with members of the laity, clergy, and religious as peers or are working under their leadership or in administrative positions. This has resulted in new and fruitful relationships in the service of the poor and the Vincentian spirit.

In 1981 the Catholic Charities of Effingham, Illinois, was opened with a Daughter of Charity as Director. A second sister administers a community outreach program that serves five counties of the diocese. In Nashville the Assumption/St.Vincent Outreach Program offers a variety of services for the poor under the umbrella of Catholic Charities directed by a Daughter of Charity, and Daughters direct Catholic Charities in Natchez and, in the past, Evansville.

With the increase in the life span of the elderly, the ministry to this age-group assumes a greater priority. In 1975 two sisters were requested by the Bishop of Mobile to be a presence of Christ-like love at Cathedral Place, an apartment complex for the elderly, by visiting, coordinating activities, taking them to the doctor's office and so forth.

St. John's Mission in Charleston was the first of three missions in rural Mississippi serving the poor. Home visiting, advocacy, and social justice issues resulted in government funds in 1993 for a GED program for AGDC parents. In Hernando and in Walls the sisters provided like services, and in 1995 a sister was asked to develop a similar program in Olive Branch.

Since 1985 the Daughters have ministered to African-Americans in the Belleville Diocese in East St. Louis, Illinois. At present three sisters work in public housing settings at the Griffin Center and the Roosevelt Center for after-school recreation and homework assistance programs with children from inner-city public housing. Advocacy, family counseling, and community organization are a few of the many activities of the sisters in this very low income area. From 1976 to 1992 Daughters of Charity have served in parish ministry in African-American parishes in Gulfport, Mississippi, in rural Alabama and in Huntingburg, Indiana, creating new areas of service and leadership roles.

The Daughters of Charity in the Province of the West continue the care of abused and abandoned children, which characterized their beginnings there. Three residential homes are serving children and adolescents from dysfunctional families characterized by physical, sexual, and/or psychological abuse, abandonment, and neglect. The sisters and lay staff provide a structured living situation, individual counseling, and therapy to heal the family and return the person to a healthy environment. Innovative and comprehensive services have been developed to meet new needs of teen mothers, girls on probation, and drug-impaired infants, children, and adolescents.

The Daughters of Charity Senior Citizen Nutrition Program started on Thanksgiving Day 1976, after a study revealed the need for hot, nutritious meals for the elderly in the service area of St. Vincent Medical Center. Initially meals were provided for 200 seniors on every major holiday, when other food programs were closed. Then on July 7, 1977, a regular dinner program for senior citizens was implemented at nearby Precious Blood Parish Hall. Dinner was served five afternoons a week to 140-200 seniors a day, and on holidays to about 250 seniors.

The homebound seniors, however, were still in need. Their plight prompted the development of the Meals-on-Wheels Program. Since this expansion required a larger facility, St. Vincent Medical Center offered the kitchen at

DePaul Pavilion, which could accommodate the preparation of about 2,300 meals a day. Currently, Meals-on-Wheels provides a hot meal to approximately 1,500 clients each day. A cold supper, which is also available, is delivered to about 800 of these clients as well. At present this is the largest Meals-on-Wheels Program in Los Angeles.

The Senior Citizen Nutrition Program continues to expand and improve. Meals are now being prepared every evening for the residents of the Cardinal Manning Homeless Men's Shelter. A sister nurse who attends to the medical needs of the clients has been added to the Meals-on-Wheels staff. A house cleaning service is also available for those seniors who are no longer able to take care of this task on their own. These services enable the clients to continue living independently for as long as possible.

In response to the needy, the sisters provide emergency assistance in various locations. They have also developed programs for lonely and isolated elderly people in low-income housing and in neighborhood and parish centers. The needs of refugees and immigrants are being served with special tenderness by sisters who speak Vietnamese and Spanish.

The Daughters of Charity in the Northeast Province with provincial house in Albany, New York, are witnessing, in the closing years of the twentieth century, different trends in both community living and modes of serving others. Within the scope of professional ministry in one field is combined in fact many different disciplines. The change to deinstitutionalized service in the 1980s became evident. Institutions founded by the Daughters in Buffalo, Albany, Philadelphia, and Boston either closed or began different forms of outreach, including emergency shelters, food kitchens, thrift shops, adult and child day-care centers, day treatment facilities, addiction, AIDS, and other health-care programs. The Daughters are now managing Catholic Charities organizations, senior housing units, specialized group homes, and outreach programs for the elderly. Several sisters organize social services in parishes and collaborate on parish teams. All members of the community are encouraged by the Peace and Justice Commission to become advocates within the religious, political, and economic systems.

Although the provinces of the Daughters of Charity in the United States are completely autonomous with Motherhouse in France, the five provinces have explored interprovincial ministries, particularly in the Gallup, New Mexico, Diocese, one of the most needy in the United States. In 1996 three Daughters of Charity have done pastoral work in Tuba City, Arizona, and two in the administration of Catholic Charities in Gallup. Their goal is to establish a ministry capable of responding to the needs of the people while remaining open to further development in future.

Early in 1995, the five provinces and their National Health System began plans for collaboration with Catholic Relief Services and the Angolan government to restaff and rehabilitate the hospital in Balombo, Angola, which serves 40,000 people. Goals include providing equipment, supplies, and medical staff to the hospital, and training the Angola medical and nursing staff to provide quality health care. Because of thirty years of war, ending in 1994, Angola is one of the countries with the most serious health problems in the world. In August 1995 four Daughters of Charity from different U.S. provinces were flown to Angola to begin a three-year mission aided by an American volunteer doctor. The sisters teach the nursing staff in the 60-bed hospital and the outpatient clinic serving 150 patients a day. As of June 1996 the hospital now has beds and mattresses in all wards, a laboratory, a Tuberculosis Unit, and key leaders have been identified in all hospital departments. A leadership training program is also in place. The pharmacy is now fully equipped and operational.

Another interprovincial activity took place in Guatemala in 1992 when Daughters from all five provinces were asked to volunteer in the refugee camps in Mexico to accompany refugees back to Guatemala at the end of the Civil War. In Guatemala the Daughters minister to the people, providing them with basic health care, training catechists, preparing liturgies, and adapting service of the poor to changing times. Declining numbers of sisters have resulted in serious discernment to make choices for the poor.

THE NEW YORK SISTERS OF CHARITY[2]

On August 20, 1817, a weary trio of black-capped Sisters of Charity from Emmitsburg, Maryland, arrived in lower Manhattan, sent by Mother Elizabeth Ann Seton to care for the orphans of her native city. In a small house near old St. Patrick's Cathedral, Prince and Mott Streets, the sisters soon welcomed five orphans – the first of thousands to be cared for in what later became the Roman Catholic Orphan Asylum. The seed had been sown for a social apostolate still flourishing today.

In 1831, three more sisters arrived from Emmitsburg to care for orphans in Brooklyn. This fledgling venture also developed rapidly. By 1873, a spacious residence, St. Joseph's Hall, was home to hundreds of needy children. During the Civil War a new need arose with the increase of juvenile delinquency in New York City. Thus, in 1863, the Sisters of Charity of New York began guiding young girls assigned to the Catholic Protectory.

The New York Foundling Hospital came into existence in 1869, when Sister Mary Irene Fitzgibbon placed a bassinet in front of a brownstone house on East 12th Street and received the first of many thousands of abandoned infants. In 1884, a two-story frame house, donated by Mr. John Reid to the congregation, became a haven for children in family crisis – St. Agatha's Home in Nanuet.

Today the social apostolate of the Sisters of Charity of New York continues, adapted to changing circumstances and consistent with a tradition of excellence. In Brooklyn, St. Joseph's Hall has been replaced by a well-organized system of child care that sponsors foster and group homes: St. Joseph Services for Children and Families. St. Agatha's today is a community in which developmentally delayed and physically-impaired children and young adults are cared for in family style cottages and apartments. St. Agatha's sponsors group and boarding homes for more than 400 teens, an Intermediate Care Facility for handicapped persons of all ages, a Respite Care program on weekends, and services for unaccompanied refugee youth.

The New York Foundling Hospital now sponsors forty-four diverse programs, including a maternity shelter, a crisis nursery for children and parents in times of stress, a skilled nursing facility, adoption and day-care services, and head-start programs in Puerto Rico. Other assistance includes Pathway, a substance abuse recovery program for women that allows the family to remain united, and collaborative programs that provide housing and other community outreach services.

Another important priority is to address homelessness. Seton House, a renovated building in Manhattan that opened in 1993, provides permanent apartments for sixteen formerly homeless families. Counseling and support services are available to tenants who are required to be free of substance abuse for at least a year. This project of the Elizabeth Seton Housing Development Fund Corporation remains today under the direction of Sister Claire Regan, SC.

Fox Memorial Shelter in East Harlem, completed in 1989, provides temporary housing to pregnant women and women with children. A variety of social services is offered to help these single-parent families find permanent housing and employment. Sister Florence Speth, SC, has overseen this project since its inception and is the director of Fox House today.

Battered women and their children receive safe temporary housing, counseling, legal services, and referrals at Sanctuary for Families. Sister Theresa Courtney, SC, has ministered here as an advocate/counselor since 1985. Sisters of Charity of New York work in city homeless shelters, in hospitals and courtrooms, in peace and justice centers, and on campuses in direct service to the poor and in bringing others to awareness of the poor. St. Elizabeth Seton's dream of having Sisters of Charity serve the poor of New York is alive today, different from anything she could have foreseen, but true to her spirit – the spirit of the Gospel.

THE SISTERS OF CHARITY OF CINCINNATI[3]

From their first days as a diocesan congregation, the Sisters of Charity of Cincinnati were engaged in social service. Care of orphans was their initial work in Cincinnati, beginning in 1829, and they continued to render service in this ministry for nearly 150 years. The sisters opened St. Peter's Orphan Asylum for girls in Cincinnati in 1829, which continued in operation until its merger in 1854 with St. Joseph's Boys Orphanage immediately after the sisters became a diocesan congregation in 1852. When the sisters went to New Mexico in 1865, they accepted the care of eighteen orphan girls. With few resources the sisters relied on army rations to feed their charges. They soon organized St. Vincent Home for Girls, serving the Santa Fe Diocese for the next 100 years.

The Cincinnati Sisters of Charity conducted successful missions in East Asia. In Wuchang, China, they again found themselves called upon to care for orphans. St. Vincent Boys' Orphanage was opened at the hospital compound in 1931 and moved to a new facility six years later. Japanese occupation during World War II resulted in the destruction of the Orphanage, which was not reopened after the war. Another overseas venture was undertaken in 1951 when Cardinal Domenico Tardini invited the community to send sisters to Rome to conduct Villa Nazareth Orphanage, established for exceptional boys ages six to thirteen who were being prepared for leadership in the post-war Italian Church.

Conducting St. Joseph Infant and Maternity Home in Cincinnati was a major social-service work assumed by the community. Begun at Good Samaritan Hospital to serve unwed mothers and their babies, St. Joseph's became a separate institution in 1873. It operated a maternity hospital for a time and provided services for unadopted children until they were transferred to St. Joseph's Orphanage. In 1976, in response to changing needs, the maternity home was discontinued and a resident program for profoundly retarded nonambulatory children was established. A second infant home, St. Anthony's in Kansas City, was operated by the sisters for a short time in the early twentieth century.

Margaret Reed Day Nursery in Denver, the first day nursery operated under Catholic auspices in Colorado, became the responsibility of the Cincinnati Sisters of

Charity in 1944. For thirty years the Margaret Reed Day Nursery served close to one hundred children per day.

Elder Care has long been included in the works of this Congregation. In Santa Fe, New Mexico, a Home for the Aged was begun as a service of St. Vincent Hospital, with twenty beds set aside for aged infirm, most of whom were charity patients. The sisters also administered and worked in St. Theresa Home in Cincinnati for a short time. They cared for aged residents at St. Joseph Infant Home in Cincinnati and St. Joseph Hospital in Wuchang, China. More recently in the 1980s the community has been sponsoring Eldermount, an adult day program at the Motherhouse. In 1990 a retirement center, Bayley Place, was constructed on the Motherhouse property.

Response to medical needs of the underserved is another of the community's social-service endeavors. Before there was a hospital in Albuquerque, New Mexico, the sisters were operating a Wayfarers Home in addition to their school duties. Sponsored hospitals operated clinics and dispensaries for the poor as part of their outreach program. Villa Therese Clinic in Santa Fe was opened in 1937, staffed by the Sisters of Charity of Cincinnati. For a time in the 1960s the sisters operated the Madres de Caridad Clinic and Center in Huancane, Peru.

Direct social outreach was begun as early as 1836, when the sisters became involved with the Martha and Mary Society in Cincinnati. Unstructured outreach programs conducted by the sisters out of hospitals and schools are too numerous to mention, but in 1897 the community initiated the Santa Maria Institute in Cincinnati, the first Catholic Settlement House in the United States. Originally established for religious social work among Italian immigrants in the downtown area, Santa Maria soon had outreach centers in several locations throughout the city. The flexible program established by the sisters was frequently modified to meet changing needs. For instance, it shifted its emphasis in the early 1940s to the city's growing Appalachian population. It also served as a base for sisters who were case workers employed by diocesan Catholic Charities for many years.

Another type of social response permeating the Cincinnati Sisters of Charity history is disaster relief. Nearly one-third of the sisters nursed on Civil War battlefields. Major floods in the Ohio Valley have been occasions for outreach, as was the 1918 flu epidemic when sisters from many missions responded to needs in their local areas. Mining towns were another center for the sisters' social work activities during the flu epidemic. In eastern Kentucky medical and social services were practically nonexistent until the sisters moved in to help the poor.

Since the Second Vatican Council individual sisters and the congregation as a whole have continued to respond to social-service needs through community development organizations and neighborhood outreach efforts as well as through more traditional channels. Congregational support of SET of Colorado (Service, Empowerment, Transformation) has led to an involvement of a number of sisters. With the changing needs of society, the Sisters of Charity continue to respond both through commitment of personnel resources and financial support to assist the most needy.

THE SISTERS OF CHARITY OF HALIFAX[4]

Social services began in the city of Halifax in 1849 after school hours. The sister teachers would set off with food, clothing, and medical supplies for the homes of the poor. Well into the next century, they organized breakfasts for poor children, homes for working girls, and shelters for aged men and women. St. Joseph's Orphanage was established in 1863 by Archbishop Cornelius O'Brien with the financial help of generous friends, and he also established the Home of the Guardian Angel for infants and unmarried mothers in 1888. Sisters Mary Clare Flanagan and John Elizabeth Joyce were responsible for competely updating the loving care and services offered to unmarried mothers, and the opening of a diocesan adoption agency. A Single Parents Center in Spryfield today provides counseling, education, and support for single parents and limited day care for children. Beginning in 1887 the sisters provided rooms at St. Mary's Convent and St. Theresa's retreat for working girls, and Seton Hall (1928-1963), a hostel in Truro for girls studying at the Provincial Normal School.

In 1938 with the request of Senator William H. Dennis and through his financial help, the Sisters opened Star of the Sea Convent and Community Center in Terence Bay, a poverty-stricken village where women were taught weaving, and men carpentry. The weaving industry continued for decades, becoming famous for its scarves, table mats, and other items sold at Department stores in Halifax and other cities under the label "Star of the Sea." Adsum House, a short-term shelter for homeless women or those subjected to violence at home, was opened by Sister Evelyn Pollard and the sisters in 1983. Sisters continue to remain on its Board and as volunteer workers. Individual sisters opened homes for young girls in the Halifax area. The elderly were provided for at the Flinn Memorial Home, the Vincentian Home, and in 1966, St. Vincent Guest House, owned by the Halifax Archdiocese with two sisters on staff as nurses, an administrator, and volunteer workers. DePaul Centre was opened at the Motherhouse in Halifax in 1994 by Sister Marie McPherson. It provides rooms and meals at a minimal cost for families from a distance whose relatives are in hospital in

Halifax and for those with transplants required to remain for further aid after surgery.

In Cape Breton social service has always been the sisters' priority. Clothing and food was offered from the sisters' own supplies long before there was a St. Vincent de Paul Society or any government agencies on which to call. Recess and noontime nutrition snacks were given freely to the school children. The sisters did advocacy work with civic and church governance on behalf of the unemployed and needy families. In each convent one nonschool sister was designated for visiting, providing for and advocating on behalf of sick and needy people. It would be no exaggeration to credit those ministries of the sisters dating back to the early 1900s to the formation later on of church and government social services as we know them today. In 1969 several social agency groups were amalgamated as Family Services of Eastern Nova Scotia where social workers, Sisters Louise Bray, Joan Connell and Rose McNeil, offered counseling, therapeutic services, advocacy, family life education, and home visiting. There was also active engagement by Sister Joan with the Young Christian Workers. Community development begun at Seton Centre by Sister Louise Bray and her group of priests and sisters, offered "Houses for People," new houses built for the poor, fostering a tremendous change in the improvement and development of hundreds of Cape Bretoners. Other services included the opening of DePaul House for the poor and Project Uplift working with low-income people in Glace Bay. Sister Lousie and Sister Joan Connell received the equivalent remuneration of any qualified professional in the field. The congregation returned an amount equivalent to Sister Louise's salary to Family Services of Eastern Nova Scotia to help support the work done for the needy.

Projects were initiated by individual sisters in Cape Breton. Sister Joan Dawson, with the help of Sisters Christene Forbes and Therese O'Malley, opened DePaul House in 1983 as a center for helping the poor, a place where depressed and needy women could drop in for a cup of tea and a chat. From this center the sisters did networking with social justice groups, brought Communion to shut-ins, and drove people to church on weekends.

"Project Uplift" was begun in 1989 by Sister Grace Hackett in the Glace Bay area with a congregational grant of $25,000. It was a plan of meeting, working, and affirming the value of low-income people covering spiritual, social and physical needs. An average of nine women attended the sessions on a weekly basis.

Sister Mary Carmelina MacLellan was asked by Father John Webb of Boisdale, Nova Scotia, to assist him in opening Gillis House for men with substance abuse problems. Sister oversaw maintenance, listened to their stories, drove them to appointments, and cooked special desserts for them. "Carm," as they called her, established a warm, compassionate relationship with those men. After seven years Sister Cleta McMullin took over.

In the Province of Boston in 1887 the sisters created after-school projects and activities, as well as providing for those suffering from hunger and illness. Young girls working in convents were given room, board, and time to attend local high schools. The top floor of St. Peter's Convent, Dorchester, was opened in 1984 by Sister Anna Donovan to abused adolescent girls in need of temporary housing, serving in five years sixty-seven girls. WAITT House (We're All In This Together) in St. Patrick's Parish in Roxbury was established in 1979 with a $50,000 grant from the Congregation, providing an after-school drop-in center for children, an advocacy program for welfare recipients, a clothing store, a day-care program, and an adult-education component. Former sisters Mary Kay Brady and Pauline O'Leary were the leaders in this project. The Elizabeth Seton Asian Center in Lawrence, Massachusetts, with a grant from the Congregation assists Asian refugees with resettlement in the Merrimack Valley. The center's concerns quickly broadened to include issues of food, clothing, housing, and advocacy. Numerous other social service enterprises of the sisters include serving the homeless in shelters, staffing alcohol recovery programs, serving as counselors, helping the elderly, infants, and adults who have contracted AIDS or are HIV positive. The retired sisters at Wellesley Hills have entered into a number of these projects, including addressing elected officials with their concerns on social justice issues.

The sisters went to Quebec in 1934 specifically for the education of English-speaking Catholic girls. But ten years later their ministry took an unexpected turn into social work when the Redemptorist Fathers asked them to take over the administration and care of St. Brigid's Home for the elderly and orphans. On July 27, 1944, sixteen Sisters of Charity arrived from Halifax for this purpose, and in 1994 Quebec celebrated the fiftieth anniversary of that event. The sisters continue there today as volunteers. The Welfare Office of St. Patrick's Parish in Quebec City with Sister George Francis as overseer for twenty-five years, made every effort to support the elderly through the painful stages of aging, sickness, and death. In Dorval, Quebec, Sister Carmelita Currie set up a foster home for six boys in 1974, which eventually opened up for girls. By 1994 she and her assistant had served sixty-six children. In the inner city of Montreal Sister Frances McLoughlin and other sisters were involved in a day shelter for women, Chez Doris, and have helped at Nazareth House for those with AIDS. Other sisters have worked with illiterate immigrants and physically and mentally disadvantaged adults at Monsignor Fraser School; at the Toronto Catholic Children's Aid for abused children, and at the Ministry of Communications and Social Services of the Government of Ontario.

The sisters came to Bathurst, New Brunswick, in 1867 to open schools, but immediately reached out discreetly to the poor. Several children came daily to the convent kitchen for their lunch. Over the years the sisters continued this ministry for the poor in Bathurst and today through combining the sisters' efforts with laypeople's community services, it has become a very rewarding endeavor.

It was not until after Vatican II that many sisters in the New York Province freely gave up the apostolate of teaching for full involvement in social services. By 1988 almost half of the sisters studying in the New York Province were pursuing social work degrees. Sister Frances Gritte's ministry since 1971 has been with the poor in the Brownsville and Bushwick sections of Brooklyn, in Chiclayo, Peru, and currently with immigrants in Glen Cove, Long Island. In Chiclayo there was a total absence of government social services and resources, with people living in cardboard boxes and straw shacks. Baby Antonio's death introduced Sister Frances to real poverty. Sister took the mother to the hospital to recover the little body and she watched her bring the child's body out, wrapped in rags. A carpenter made a pine box and a four-hour wake took place. Afterward the mother removed the rags from the body to use for her one-year-old child before Antonio was buried.

In 1981 the Sisters of Charity residence in Flushing became a shelter for abused women and their children. WHW (Women Helping Women) was initiated by Sisters Catherine O'Leary, Joan Holmberg, and Elaine Narus.

They offered food, clothing, counseling, educational, medical, and public assistance. That first year twenty-nine women and thirty-five children were helped. WHW has been an ongoing, fully active venture ever since.

Individual sisters are employed in various social service clinics. Sisters Kathleen Kull and Barbara Buxton, clinical social workers, with Sister Barbara Petty as leader, are at Glendale Mental Health Clinic, serving the vulnerable who range in age from preschool to senior citizens of African-American, Hispanic, Eastern European and Afghanistani backgrounds. Clients suffer from serious pathologies, abuse, AIDS, addictions, suicidal tendencies, and are offered therapy, advocacy, referrals, and concrete services to help them become aware of their giftedness, to empower them to transform their lives. Sister Frances Fahey, Supervisor of Jamaica Family and Youth Center in South Ozone Park, with clients who represent a racial, economic, and ethnic mix of working class African-American families, and immigrants, primarily Guyanese. A range of services are provided to 208 families per year. In 1996 the Federal Government provided money to computerize the child welfare system in New York. The impact of the Welfare Reform Bill with its lump sum federal grants to states, has yet to be felt. Sister Clare Romeo has been working since 1988 as House Manager in a community residence with nine developmentally disabled adults. Bishop Ryan Residence in Copiague, Long Island, state-funded and inspected, is home to nine men and women, ages twenty-two to fifty-two years, who have become a tightly-knit family. She and her companion provide a home-like atmosphere aimed at independent living, and try to develop happy and fulfilled adults with healthy self-esteem. Sister Mary McGowan specializes in mental health. She is certified by the State of Maryland, licensed by the District of Columbia, and works with a psychiatrist to whom she sends referrals. She helps couples with marital problems and families in crisis. Sister Marie Sorenson is currently employed at Housing Works Inc. in the Bedford-Stuyvessant section of Brooklyn, a community-based, minority-controlled, not-for-profit organization incorporated in 1990 to provide housing, supportive services, and advocacy for homeless families and individuals living with AIDS and HIV-related illness. A certified Social Worker, Sister Marie provides clinical supervision to staff in the Scattered Site Housing Program, the only provider of supportive housing in New York City for people with AIDS who are chronically mentally ill, and the only organization in the United States to provide housing with supportive services for drug addicts. Sister Joan Connell is a social worker ministering to individuals tortured by obsessive thoughts, incest survivors, abused elderly parents, young adults in suffocating relationships, married couples trying to preserve a marriage scarred by infidelity, or separated couples questioning marriage itself. Therapy and healing are her goals. Sister Ann Woodford is Supervisor of a Therapeutic Foster Boarding Home program with children who have severe emotional and mental problems. Sister oversees case workers and children to ensure that services are provided to families and court orders are implemented. She helps the workers to fine-tune their social work and teaching skills in handling family crises. Several Sisters of Charity of Hailfax are engaged in prison ministry in both Canada and the United States.

THE SISTERS OF CHARITY OF THE IMMACULATE CONCEPTION[5]

The Sisters of Charity of the Immaculate Conception in Saint John, New Brunswick, Canada, established their first mission in 1857 in the township of Portland, N.B., which later merged with Saint John to become Saint John City. Portland was the center of a large Irish immigrant population. Poverty was rampant. After school hours at St. Peter's School, the sisters spent many hours among the poor, ministering to their hunger and sickness as they went from home to home. Thus began the social service ministry of the SCICs.

In 1932 a more formalized social-service program was begun in the city's Cathedral Parish by the sisters in conjunction with the Catholic Women's League and the St. Vincent de Paul Society. Since that time the sisters have been actively engaged at the St. Vincent de Paul Center, supplying food, clothing, and sometimes the means to obtain shelter according to the needs presented. Recently a drop-in service for women has been added to the center. Here women who live alone or feel lonely and isolated have an opportunity to relax and enjoy some refreshment as they socialize with each other in an environment that is warm, friendly, and accepting.

The care of orphaned children was the primary ministry of this congregation when it was founded in 1854 in eastern Canada, but in 1906 the sisters were invited to add to this ministry western Canada as well. The call to staff an already established orphanage for boys and girls, St. Patrick's Orphanage in Prince Albert, Saskatchewan, was accepted by the SCICs. This provided further opportunity to collaborate with the existing social-service agencies of the wider area served by this institution, as well as the chance to offer support and aid to the children's relatives and especially those of Native origin.

Along with orphanages, and with formal and informal ministry to the poor and sick in their homes, the Congregation has also been involved in ministry to single mothers and their infants through the establishment of St. Vincent's Infants Home (1915-1954) in Saint John,

N.B., and Our Lady of Mercy Home (1929-1966) in Vancouver, British Columbia. In both these institutions care and guidance was provided for expectant mothers along with their medical needs. After the birth of the infant, further help was offered until the mother and child were returned to customary living conditions. Those infants left for adoption were cared for until placed in foster homes or transferred to orphanages.

With the closing of institutional forms of social services such as orphanages and infants' homes, the sisters continued with informal types of social ministry, becoming even more involved in individual work for the poor and disadvantaged. They are working for social justice issues, advocacy and support for immigrants and women's groups; housing for the marginalized and underprivileged; food banks, soup kitchens, crisis centers, and the many other social concerns of the present era.

THE SISTERS OF CHARITY OF SAINT ELIZABETH, CONVENT STATION, N.J.[6]

The Sisters of Charity of St. Elizabeth in Convent Station, New Jersey, have, from the time of their foundation, made social service one of their major apostolic works. Their beginnings, though modest, saw them responding promptly to the needs of the less fortunate. When their community came into existence in 1859, several orphanages had already been founded by the New York Sisters of Charity. Therefore the New Jersey Sisters gradually assumed charge of three of these existing orphanages: in 1861 both St. Mary's Orphanage, Newark (1852-1973) and Saint Joseph's Orphanage, later in Totowa (1853-1974); in 1906 Saint Mary's Orphanage, Jersey City (1860s-1928). The New Jersey Sisters of Charity under the leadership of Mother Xavier founded Saint Michael's Orphanage in Jersey City (1876-1912) and Our Lady of Grace in

Hoboken (1902-1963). Many older sisters, now deceased, told of their efforts to provide those children with educational training for decent jobs and a sense of self-worth. No uniform stamped them as orphans; no distinction was made between them and the other students in the parochial schools they attended.

Today child-care centers are practically a necessity, but over a century ago Mother Xavier opened the Orange Day Nursery, called familiarly "The Creche" (1880-1942), where the sisters cared for as many as fifty small children at a time. Another of the sisters' early day-care centers was Saint Mary Day Nursery (1904-1925) in Waterbury, Connecticut. The original enrollment was forty, but increased to ninety within a few years. Both nurseries sent the children, when they were old enough, to the nearby parochial schools, returning for hot dinners and regular care until their mothers returned from work to pick them up. The sisters discreetly inquired of parents if they needed coal or food, which the local St. Vincent de Paul Society would then provide long before the time of government relief.

Now in the last decade of the twentieth century the Sisters of Charity of New Jersey continue to maintain their proud tradition of human services. Their apostolate has become less structured, but their ministry to the poor goes on through an amazing number of services, for example, child-care centers in parishes, hospitals, institutions; day-care centers for adults; care of elderly shut-ins through home visitations; management of senior citizen apartment houses; administration of homes for the elderly. The sisters also visit homes, minister in rural areas, assist troubled youth, the deaf, those in need of nursing services, those in need of legal services through sister lawyers, and the urban poor in need of housing. They help prisoners, immigrants, those in need of family counseling through sister counselors. They administer a haven for addicted religious; participate in Project Children, hosting children from Northern Ireland for the summer; they are Directors of Civic Community Resources, Catholic Charity Resources, and Senior Citizen Centers. Sisters in some parish schools extend their care beyond formal education by conversion of an area to a day-care center in their convents. And in practically every one of their convents there are sisters who continue to hear the cry of the poor beyond corporate commitment, devoting their energies and "free time" to individual charities within their compass, like the woman of whom St. Paul wrote: "We commend to you, Phoebe, our sister, who is in the ministry of the Church . . . for she has assisted many."

All of the thirteen congregations of Sisters and Daughters of Charity in the Federation conduct missions in lands far from North America; many answered the call in the 1960s after Vatican II beckoned them to this service. The New Jersey Sisters of Charity were no exception. In 1963 four idealistic, lighthearted sisters sailed for Bolivia, spending the next six months studying Spanish and preparing for their future mission. During the next twenty-eight years fifteen sisters worked in education and health care in Bolivia, training lectors, Eucharistic ministers, catechists; organizing cursillos, cooperatives, parish centers; teaching cooking, sewing, and hygiene to the women and crafts to the children. They worked side-by-side with the poorest of the poor, most of them Indians.

Seventeen Sisters of Charity of New Jersey served as missionaries in Hunan, China (1924-1951), following China's struggle for democracy in 1911 to the triumph of communism in 1949 to the expulsion of foreign missionaries in 1951. The sisters conducted a catechumenate for women, two accredited schools, both elementary and secondary; an orphanage, a hospital, nurses' training school and dispensary.

Since the black and white races did not become integrated in the United States until 1954, Pensacola, Florida, was considered a Domestic Mission Territory until 1954. Therefore from 1939, forty-one Sisters of Charity from Convent Station, New Jersey, served in schools for Creole and black children. The children loved to sing and were full of melody. By 1955 the sisters were teaching 300 children. Saint Joseph's School turned out a generation of leaders in Escambia County, Florida, by 1968. At the present time only one Sister of Charity is in Pensacola, Sister Maureen Joseph Kirwin, who is involved in the resettlement of immigrants and has been granted a distinguished service award from the National Office of Migration and Refugee Services "in recognition of a decade of humanitarian commitment to welcoming the world's homeless."

From 1933 to 1948 twenty-three New Jersey Sisters of Charity served in Puerto Rico, opening the first Catholic elementary and high school in Guyana and an academy in Santurce. After school they went in pairs to the outlying missions teaching catechetics, and sharing space with chickens and goats. They successfully taught the Puerto Ricans academic and business courses until called home in 1948.

Still another mission was opened in the Virgin Islands by the New Jersey Sisters of Charity in 1933, eighty-two of whom served there. Some sisters continue to do so today. They administered and taught in elementary and high schools, accredited by the Middle States. They engaged in a wide variety of missionary activities such as visiting the poor and sick, conducting catechetical classes, serving as nurses and midwives, and as Associate

Pastors. Sister Louis Marie Bryan is now Diocesan Chancellor and Director of the Family Life Apostolate.

THE SISTERS OF CHARITY OF LEAVENWORTH, KANSAS[7]

The Sisters of Charity of Leavenworth, Kansas, have, from 1858 to 1996, served thousands of children in orphanages in Montana, Colorado, and Kansas. They have extended their treatment to the families and have prepared children for foster and adoptive homes. The sisters serve as administrators, social workers, support staff. They direct the projects of the Development Office and work with local business and professional individuals on the Board. They worked with troubled young people at the Boys Industrial Home in Topeka and at the Jackson County Juvenile Court in Kansas City, Missouri, as Deputy Juvenile Officers. One sister was Director of Hilltop Home for Girls, and the first woman Director of McCune Home for Boys.

Because Leavenworth is surrounded by prisons, the sisters have always been involved in prison ministries, visiting inmates, supporting prison families, providing educational and spiritual programs at the three prisons: Leavenworth Federal, the Disciplinary Barracks, and the State Prisons for Men and Women. "Outside Connection" was a special program planned and directed by one of the sisters to be an outside connection for inmates and a support system for families. Another program, Victim Offender Reconciliation Service, was directed by a sister who trained volunteers to mediate face-to-face meetings between victim and offender for making restitution to the victim and achieving reconciliation. One sister has been a Chaplain at the State Hospital and affiliated services at the local inmate treatment center. Two sisters have educated the sisters regarding the death penalty so that the congregation was able to take a corporate stance against this inhuman punishment. A related program is Visit by Mail, which matches inmates and volunteers who correspond with one another by mail, thus creating for some inmates the only contact with the world outside.

The Sisters of Charity of Leavenworth do not neglect the needs of the people outside the confines of prison life. Some sisters are licensed family therapists employed through agencies. Others are dedicated to the needs of women – young, homeless, battered women; women with children in need of care; women who need support and who have the opportunity to be partnered with a caring adult in a Mother-to-Mother Ministry. The sisters' Emergency Assistance Centers assist anyone in need of food, rental assistance, utilities, prescriptions, or shelter.

Sisters have become "pros" in approaching local governmental agencies for grants to assist with housing for homeless families, in inspecting substandard housing and recommending changes, in teaching individuals to become independent and achieve specific goals. The Sisters of Charity of Leavenworth are most generous in assisting with financial grants and volunteers. In the 1950s and 1960s they would load up boxes with fresh produce from the farms and go into Leavenworth to needy families.

The elderly are served by sisters who act as directors of recreation and activity programs, as social workers and receptionists in the Denver high-rise apartment areas for seniors on fixed incomes. The sisters work on Boards of the Gray Panthers and as Ombudsmen of the State of Kansas Department of Aging. St. Joseph Care Center is a residential facility serving the elderly who do not have financial resources. Here the sisters serve as skilled nurses, switchboard operators, receptionists, assisting "The Friends of St. Joseph's," sponsoring social activities.

At the Motherhouse the sisters serve their own aging members in many ways: as Director of Ross Hall, as helpers of personal needs, as chauffeurs, as directors of recreation and activity programs.

Recently the sisters have been invited to join the Foster Grandparents Program and spend time tutoring the children in Leavenworth. The mission to meeting the needs of the time continues and the sisters are ready to respond.

THE SISTERS OF CHARITY OF SETON HILL, GREENSBURG, PA.[8]

The social-service ministry of the Sisters of Charity of Seton Hill, Greensburg, Pennsylvania, was begun on July 16, 1891, when they initiated a home for foundlings. Within a month eighteen infants had arrived. The institution soon opened a maternity ward for shelter and prenatal care. From that time until 1971 the Sisters of Charity at Roselia Foundling and Maternity Hospital welcomed abandoned infants and unmarried mothers in need, transforming the social stigma into a restored image and a new life. As this ministry continued, a changing medical scene and shifting societal values affected the program so that by 1970 fewer pregnant unmarried women sought the protection and privacy of Roselia. Those who came to deliver their babies decided to keep them. The sisters partnered with Catholic Charities of the Pittsburgh Diocese to move the program to a large private home, Roselia Manor. The work continues under the direction of Catholic Charities in a building now known as Roselia Center. It is now St. Joseph House of Hospitality for the homeless and persons of low income under the combined management of Catholic Charities and the Sisters of Charity.

Again through Catholic Charities of Greensburg the sisters sponsored the Hoang family from Vietnam for the year 1975-76 when they moved to Texas. From 1985 to 1993 the sisters were comanagers of Maryhouse, a residence for low-income women. In 1974 they established the Elizabeth Seton Care Fund to provide financial assistance for the poor and to aid charitable works. In 1990 they established a Ministry Fund to supplement the needs of some ministries.

Among their ministries for the young and the elderly is Seton Hill day care sponsored by Seton Hill College and funded through Westmoreland County Conference for Economic Opportunity. Another program founded by the same Sister of Charity, a Professor at Seton Hill College, was PACT, or Pregnant Adolescent Childcare Program, operating out of Seton Hill College, an in-school program for pregnant and parenting teenagers. The sisters also established Elizabeth Seton Center, a multigenerational Center responding to the needs of a changing society. This nonprofit organization focuses on the Children's Center and the Senior Center, providing programs for both. Its initial project in 1985 was for "Latchkey Kids." That same year a sister established the Suzuki School of Music. In 1986, a Preschool Program benefited children aged three through kindergarten. In 1992 another sister began the Infant/Toddler Program for children six weeks to three years. Presently there are two hundred children enrolled in Children's Center programs with an additional 180 in the Suzuki School of Music. Through the activities of the Senior Center, at two Senior Citizen Centers and three Adult Care Centers, seniors are assisted in obtaining supportive services that are necessary for independent living and continued interpersonal growth.

The Sisters of Charity of Seton Hill have been a vital part of the Stephen Foster Community Center covering an enormous area of Pittsburgh that has the largest concentration of elderly in the U.S. With six senior citizen high-rises, the center enables the elderly to stay in their homes as active and involved seniors in their community. Sisters have served them in capacity of nurse and secretary of the Board, Site Manager, Coordinator of Senior Programs, and Office Manager. The Center provides multi-services for Pittsburgh folks aged four to ninety-four.

From 1982 Sisters of Charity have managed five Christian Housing Association high-rise apartments for the elderly and handicapped subsidized by HUD or the U.S. Department of Housing and Urban Development in various sections of Pittsburgh. Two sisters serve with VISTE or Volunteers in Service to the Elderly, in Lakeland, Florida, guided by an interfaith Board of Directors whose goal is to help the handicapped and elderly to live independently at home as long as possible.

In parishes Sisters of Charity organize and administer social service departments, minister to the needs of the elderly, coordinate parish outreach programs, organize telephone ministries for the grieving, meeting with Eucharistic ministers to the homebound, give care and nonjudgmental compassion, are liaisons with civic, ecumenical, and Catholic agencies. They are employed as Catholic Community Services Pregnancy and Parenting Programs, and "Right from the Start" coordinators, emergency assistance case workers, Ombudsman Coordinators, Directors of Bureaus for Services to the Aging. They have a long history of ministry to prisoners as tutors, liturgical music directors, and court advocates. One sister initiated Prison Network, connecting women inmates with family, friends, legal persons, rehabilitation facilities. They have ministered to minorities since the early part of the twentieth century, to African-Americans, Mexican-Americans and Native Americans, living and working with them on reservations. Their ministry has brought them to South Korea, where they have very successfully aided the people and inspired numerous South Korean young women to become Sisters of Charity of Seton Hill while remaining and forming their own province in Korea.

THE VINCENTIAN SISTERS OF CHARITY OF PITTSBURGH, PENNSYLVANIA[9]

The Vincentian Sisters of Charity, ever since coming to Pittsburgh in 1902, have followed the example of St. Louise de Marillac, the patroness of social service, by ministering to the poor sick in their homes, in hospitals, and in the streets. They also went south to Alabama to continue this ministry to the African-American people. They visited their homes in order to come to know them as persons and to assess their needs. As a result they were able to open a school, a rummage center, a nursing home.

Another mission was established in Phenix City, Alabama, where they were confronted with a seething cauldron of filth, poverty, and neglect. Broken-down shacks served as homes for these black families. The immediate reaction of the sisters was horror and dread quickly turning into love and compassion for human beings subjected to such misery. During the Selma march the sisters gave refuge to those who came to enlighten the minds of the white people. But the white people who rejected integration turned against the sisters, greatly affecting their service, especially at St. Jude's Hospital. In 1971 Sister Julian Griffin, a black Vincentian Sister of Charity, began a needy ministry to black people in the Savannah Diocese. Sister Carmelita Alvero joined her. Their ministry included crisis intervention, community action programs in rural and urban areas, the establishment of a diocesan social apostolate, summer camps for poor children, housing for the poor, raising the social consciousness of sisters serving in the South and elsewhere. Today the Vincentian Sisters of Charity of Pittsburgh continue to minister and act as advocates for poor black people in the South.

In Pittsburgh in the 1970s the sisters became involved in the Information and Referral Service, ministering in parishes in order to seek out those in need, the unattended sick in their homes, the powerless in need of advocates to correct injustices. They were referred to a diocesan office and action was taken. Sister Ernestine Macko was the first Vincentian to serve in this ministry. Today this program has become Parish Social Ministry with many more sisters involved. The sisters act as advocates in raising the standards of housing, utilities and health care. They serve in soup kitchens; they coordinate food banks; they organize clothing centers.

In the late 1970s Sister Rachel Sarosi, after working for some years with the poor in Mexico, went to the poor in Negritos, Peru, and then to Talara Alta, where the congregation established a house. Vincentian Sisters joined her full-time. Others gave their summers to this ministry. Vincent de Paul and Louise de Marillac taught the Daughters and eventually the Sisters of Charity that they had "for their monastery only the houses of the sick, . . . for their cell a rented room, for their chapel the parish church, for their cloister the streets of the city, for their enclosure obedience . . ." This teaching has been the guiding force of the Vincentian Sisters of Charity since their foundation in 1902 and continues to inspire them on their journey of charity.

THE VINCENTIAN SISTERS OF CHARITY OF BEDFORD, OHIO[10]

The Vincentian Sisters of Charity of Bedford, Ohio, have practiced social service voluntarily, along with their primary mission of teaching and nursing. Every summer between 1957 and 1965 the sisters organized and ran summer camps for poor children in Lorain, Ohio. They also worked with migrant workers in Michigan and western Ohio during the summers. In 1974, three sisters spent the summer with Cesar Chavez in California organizing marches for the grape pickers union and running a day-care center for the children of union organizers. Many sisters volunteered to work in nursing homes every summer in Cleveland.

Social service became more formalized in the late 1970s and early 1980s as sisters began to retrain and enter this field on a professional basis. In 1974 one sister was appointed to work with the mentally handicapped under the auspices of Jean Vanier's L'Arche Homes Foundation. The sisters opened a home for the handicapped poor on Cleveland's East Side, a very depressed part of the city, and a few years later opened another home nearby. Several sisters have been active on local, national, and international L'Arche Boards.

In 1982 the community joined an interfaith organization serving the physical and educational needs of what Robert Kennedy once referred to as "the poorest area of the United States," Pineville, Bell County, Kentucky. In this county less than 3% of the population of several hundred thousand have graduated from high school. One sister was appointed to serve in Pineville and to help Claire Daley, Interfaith's foundress, build the organization into a major social service offering full-time adult education to the many illiterate people there, clothing and food dispensation, counseling on money management, home improvement, and property ownership assistance, to name only a few of the group's services. The Vincentian Sisters of Bedford, Ohio, are still active in Pineville with at least two sisters serving full-time and others volunteering in the summer.

In the early 1980s the community took full administration and staffing of Villa Sancta Ana Nursing Home in Beachwood, Ohio, a home supported by the First Catholic Slovak Ladies Association, the wealthiest fraternal insurance company in the United States. In the late 1980s a sister was released from the social service staff of Villa Sancta Ana to join the Diocese of Cleveland's Department of Refugee Services. This sister welcomes and places families from all over the world. She assists in getting children into schools and parents into training programs. By 1987 the community began the project of refurbishing their all-girls high school into a senior citizens' living complex, a service more needed in the area than the service of education. Enrollment had been decreasing in the years leading to this change while the elderly population had been increasing. In the new Light of Hearts Villa, sisters serve as administrators, activity directors of activities, nurses' aides, and program organizers. In a variety of ways the Vincentian Sisters of Bedford, Ohio, are contributing successfully to social services for those in need.

THE SISTERS OF CHARITY OF NAZARETH, KENTUCKY[11]

In Mother Catherine Spalding's day the immediate social problem was the care of orphans. Her initial response, which led to the establishment of a home, was to provide shelter for two destitute children from the Louisville wharf and a baby whose German immigrant parents had died in Portland. Soon seventeen children, whose parents were victims of cholera, joined the growing family and

St. Vincent Orphanage was established. In a brochure entitled *The 90th Year* published in April, 1921, by the welfare League of Louisville, Kentucky, a vivid description of the foundation of St. Vincent's is given:

> When one of the river packets which then flourished upon the Ohio steamed noisily away, leaving upon the Louisville wharf two friendless and destitute children whose parents had died on the way from New Orleans, Mother Catherine was called on as being the person most likely to be able to do something for them. With characteristic sympathy and resourcefulness, she took them to live with the Sisters in the school building, and secured contributions for their maintenance from a number of interested women.

The St. Thomas Orphan Asylum for boys grew out of an appeal in the pages of the *Catholic Telegraph and Advocate* for the support of the projected home on St. Thomas farm in Nelson County. When the orphanage was destroyed by fire, the boys were moved to Louisville, then to Bardstown and back to Louisville in 1938 when St. Thomas Home, Anchorage, Kentucky, was completed.

In 1952 the St. Vincent Orphanage for girls on Payne Street in Louisville, Kentucky, was merged with St. Thomas Home to become St. Thomas-St.Vincent Home. The Home was no longer an orphanage, but a residential home for children. Catholic Charities of Louisville supplied counselors, and the children were prepared for transition to a foster or adoptive home or returned to their reestablished natural family.

As the number of children receiving short-term care decreased, the spacious buildings of St. Thomas-St. Vincent Home were not being fully utilized. In November 1982 the Sisters and children moved to Residence One on Preston Highway, Louisville, Kentucky, and to Residence Two on Outer Loop, Louisville, Kentucky. Each residence accommodated twelve children. This arrangement lasted until June 4, 1983, when St. Thomas-St. Vincent Home was officially closed.

The O'Leary Home for Men in Louisville was staffed by Sisters of Charity of Nazareth from 1898 until 1942 when it was destroyed by fire. In 1946 the Sisters were in ministry at Our Lady's Home for Infants in Louisville, a home for prospective mothers, infants, and children awaiting adoption. After thirty-nine years of service the Sisters withdrew from the Home in 1985.

SCN involvement in social services in the city of Louisville continues today with the Sister Visitor Program, St. John Center, and the House of Ruth. The Sister Visitor Program serves the emergency needs of the population in the West End of Louisville. Founded in 1969, it is now one of the services of Catholic Charities of the Archdiocese of Louisville. St. John Center opened in 1986 as part of the services of Jefferson County and is located in the former St. John Church near downtown Louisville. This is a day shelter for homeless people, providing them with a place to shower, enjoy tea and coffee, leisure and recreational activities and to avail themselves of routine medical and dental care. The House of Ruth, which opened in 1993, provides food, housing, medication, and other services for women and families with AIDS. All three entities have Sisters of Charity of Nazareth as Directors.

In 1886 the Sisters of Charity of Nazareth took over St. Peter Home, Memphis, Tennessee, from the Dominican Sisters who were unable to continue in ministry at St. Peter Home due to an insufficient number of Sisters. An interesting part of the history of the St. Peter Home is the fact that the Chaplains and Marines of the Memphis Navy Base volunteered their services working on the buildings and grounds and providing companionship to the children. As trends in child care changed, the need for a residential facility was no longer felt and in 1964 St. Peter Home closed.

The Bishop of Nashville, Tennessee, invited SCNs to take charge of St. Mary Villa, a residential care program for children in the city of Nashville. The Villa was more a home than an orphanage. The children attended schools in the neighborhood, participated in athletic programs beyond the home, and engaged in local youth activities. In 1977 the residential care program was gradually phased out, and children were either returned to their homes or placed in foster homes. When the SCNs left Nashville, the *Tennessee Register* paid tribute to the SCNs in the words, "The history of the Nashville Diocese and the Charities from Nazareth is a tapestry that spans the years with an indelible weave."

The social-services ministry of the Sisters of Charity of Nazareth began in Massachusetts in 1887 with the opening of St. Peter Orphanage, Lowell, Massachusetts. SCNs were also in ministry at two other locations in Massachusetts – St. Mary Infant Home, Dorchester (1890-1892) and Newburyport, Home for Destitute Children (1890-1892). St. Peter's was functioning at far below its capacity and on February 1, 1956, the children were transferred to another institution. Social services in the state of Massachusetts continue today with Sisters of Charity ministering in soup kitchens, shelters for the homeless, and with immigrants.

In February 1893 six SCNs went to Roanoke, Virginia, to open St. Vincent orphanage, which was conducted in connection with St. Andrew's School. In 1931, the two institutions began to function separately and the orphanage became the new St. Vincent's Home.

In India and Nepal SCNs are involved in a variety of social services including rehabilitation of women prisoners and prostitutes, tailoring and skills development programs, formation of cooperatives, ministry in the inner city of East Delhi, organization of domestic workers and of women's groups to fight against social evils, awareness programs and conscientization, which often result in protest marches against illiteracy, corruption, the sale of alcohol and the demand for just wages for women. Sisters are also involved in local, state, and national movements against environmental degradation and the displacement of people by development projects.

Social services in Belize, Central America, began with the first Sisters visiting the villages in the summer of 1974. Since then social services continued among the Maya and Ketchi Indian Villages in the Cayo, Stann Creek and Toledo Districts of Belize. Today the Sisters of Charity are in Independence, ministering in the surrounding villages. They have taken particular interest in the plight of the banana workers and are striving to bring about justice in their working and living situations.

Whether in the United States, India, Nepal or Belize, the Sisters of Charity of Nazareth endeavor in all their ministries "*to work for justice in solidarity with oppressed peoples, especially the economically poor and women and to care for the earth.*"[12]

THE SISTERS OF CHARITY OF OUR LADY OF MERCY, CHARLESTON, S.C.[13]

The involvement of the Sisters of Charity of Our Lady of Mercy in social-service ministry can be divided into care of orphans, establishment of outreach facilities, and parish-based services. The yellow fever and cholera epidemics of the nineteenth century left in their wake numbers of orphans and half-orphans, many of whom were children of Catholic immigrants. As early as 1830 a few orphan girls were living with the sisters in their first home, a small rented building on Friend Street (now Legare Street) in Charleston. In March 1841, when the sisters moved into their newly built Motherhouse on Queen Street, there were seventy orphan girls under their care. They were supported, in part, by donations solicited by an organization known as the St. Vincent's Orphan Society composed of charitable men and women interested in the care of the needy. The sisters taught the children and prepared the older girls for apprenticeship in the dressmaking and millinery trades. The disastrous fire that swept Charleston in December 1861, the bombardment of the city in 1863, and the earthquake of 1886 forced the sisters to move the orphans to other quarters temporarily. After each disaster the sisters managed to find the means to repair their Queen Street Home. In 1870, the U.S. Congress appropriated $12,000, which enabled them to rebuild the orphanage. In 1875, a contract was made with the Mayor and City Council of Charleston appropriating $6,000 annually for the support of not less than seventy-five orphans. Following the earthquake of 1886, contributions from all over the country enabled the Community to build a new brick structure adjoining the Motherhouse.

In 1901 the City appropriation was challenged on the grounds that public funds could not be used for sectarian purposes. Consequently, new legislation was passed by the City Legislature creating the *City Orphan Asylum.* Put simply, the Sisters' Motherhouse and the girls' orphanage, Queen Street, became a city institution governed by a board of seven commissioners chosen annually by City Council. All religious emblems were removed from the buildings, and only those sisters caring for the orphans continued to live on the premises. All others had to move to other convents in the city or elsewhere in the state. Under this arrangement the orphan boys, who were cared for in a diocesan home established by Bishop Lynch after the Civil War, were moved into what was formerly the Motherhouse on Queen Street. The girls continued to live in the wing added in 1887. Records indicate that about one hundred children were in the orphanage at that time. The city allotment of $350 a month had to go a long way, even though a loaf of bread cost only a bit more than two cents. The Duke Endowment's eighth Annual Report, published in 1933, listed the City Orphan Asylum as the third oldest institution for the care of children in the Carolinas and praised the sisters for their dedicated service. The money provided by the Endowment, along with that from the City of Charleston and charitable donations, enabled the sisters to operate the orphanage until 1965. In that year the Diocese of Charleston assumed responsibility for the care of the orphans. The old Queen Street buildings were sold and a new facility, The Charleston Home for Children, was built west of the Ashley River in Charleston. The Diocesan Office of Catholic Charities operated the Home with Sisters of Charity of Our Lady of Mercy constituting the staff until the Diocese closed the facility in 1991.

The Neighborhood House was opened in April 1915 by Sister Michael Leary, OLM, RN. A medical-social service center at 90½ Columbus Street, Charleston, SC, its aims were twofold: to provide home nursing care for the sick poor and to assist the needy. The Administrator of St. Francis Xavier Infirmary, Mary McKenna, supervised the health-care portion of the program. Doctors reported patients needing care, and she provided the nurses and supplies free. Sister Michael Leary took charge of the social-service aspects of the program. Originally called "St. Francis Neighborhood House," people soon referred to it as "The Neighborhood House." The deteriorated area of the city in which the center was located was peopled by Italian, Austrian, German, and Syrian immigrants of whom many were Roman Catholic. Sister Michael and a corps of dedicated laywomen provided a vacation school for children and classes in sewing, home nursing, and cooking for the older girls and young mothers. A well-baby clinic helped poor families obtain needed prenatal care. The Neighborhood House also was the base from which the sisters visited the prisoners in the nearby County Jail and the residents of the Old Folks Home on Columbus Street. When Sister Michael died in 1932, other members of the Congregation took over the work. However, during the 1940s the population of the area was changing. By the 1950s the Catholic immigrants had been replaced by predominantly Protestant African-Americans. Instead of closing the Neighborhood House, the General Superior and Council of the Sisters of Charity of Our Lady of Mercy opened it to the black population (mostly non-Catholic), many of whom were no more assimilated into the greater Charleston community than were the earlier immigrants.

In 1953 the Council appointed Sister Anthony Monahan, RN, as Director of the center. Sister Anthony soon decided that what the people really needed were programs to enhance their self-esteem and to assist them to attain social and economic mobility. She went to Catholic University of America, obtained a Master's Degree in Social Work and returned, determined to implement her convictions. Starting at the grass roots she formed block organizations involving black women as well as men. These groups met to discuss common concerns, listen to experts, and pursue solutions. The meetings resulted in a plan to combat juvenile delinquency and illegitimacy that focused upon young black males. A grant of $100,000 was obtained from Washington to finance the project. Sister Anthony also brought together leaders of nine religious denominations, white and African-American, to form the Charleston Council of Concern for the Poor. The group was invited to Washington, D.C., by the Office of Economic Opportunity to a briefing on antipoverty strategies. She was also instrumental in inaugurating a Charleston Chapter of the Human Relations Council. Many of the programs begun under her leadership are still in place at the Neighborhood House. In 1968 or 1969 the Neighborhood House became an agency of Catholic Charities under the Diocese of Charleston. The OLMs were replaced by the Franciscan Sisters from Rochester, Minnesota, who continue the good work to this day.

On September 11, 1989, Our Lady of Mercy Community Outreach Services opened as a nonprofit organization, addressing the needs of the economically poor and disadvantaged on James, Johns, and Wadmalaw Islands in Charleston County, South Carolina. Sponsored by the Sisters of Charity of Our Lady of Mercy, the Outreach became separately incorporated on July 24, 1991, with a nine-member Board of Directors. The Sea Islands, as the three Islands served are called, have a long history of poverty and racial discrimination. This area was selected because of the tremendous need of the population for the tools to enable them to break the burdensome cycle of poverty. The mission of Our Lady of Mercy Community Outreach Services is to offer human services to the people of the islands to bring resources that will enable them to help themselves. Making a difference in the lives of persons who are at risk due to the damaging effects of persistent poverty constantly challenges the staff. Many of the elderly live in homes whose structural disrepair and lack of water and sewer facilities make their dwellings unsafe and unhealthy. Making minor home repairs continues to be part of their mission. Migrant farm workers and their families come to the Islands needing the basics of food, clothing, medicines, and shelter. Young adults lack appropriate education and skills for employment, and children are deprived of healthy family systems. The Outreach Staff strives to develop programs and strategies with the communities served to facilitate creative and effective responses to their situations. Designed with an emphasis on self-improvement and personal responsibility for their community, the project focuses on overcoming isolation and broadening interests and skills for improving the quality of life for all segments of the population. Daily services of goods, clothing, utility assistance, medicine costs, and housing needs are a consistent part of the mission. Outreach home visits alert the staff to a family's many needs. The agency acts as a distribution center for USDA Commodity Foods, serving about 400 families four times a year. They sponsor a Parenting Program, Project H.O.P.E. (Helping Ourselves Parent Effectively), which includes child development activities for the children of those attending. The staff regularly visit the Head Start Centers and offer supportive services to them. Job Training Partnership Act (JTPA) approved their grant request for two consecutive summers to conduct a summer enrichment program at the Outreach for At-Risk students on the Islands. Last summer they sponsored, along with talented volunteers, an Arts and Music Camp for the neighborhood children. The Center welcomes young students who need tutoring or a quiet place to study. Each year they organize and support a health-screening event in the camps for the seasonal farm workers and their families. Volunteer health professionals from the Charleston area collaborate to make this effort possible. The Prenatal Mission Project, a program that assists pregnant women with receiving proper prenatal care and lessons in parenting skills, meets regularly at the Outreach. Throughout the year they network with the local schools in offering mentoring programs, especially for at-risk students. Presently one of their staff directs a Drum and Dance class at the Haut Gap Middle School to foster self-discipline and respect for cultural diversity. They sponsor a Migrant Task Force and a Housing Task Force, both of which bring agencies together to address issues of concern for the people of the Islands. Networking and collaborating are an integral part of their ministry of service.

The Sisters of Charity of Our Lady of Mercy have always been involved in parish-based service. Currently two sisters work in Senior Adult Ministry designed to support the parish in reaching out to members aged fifty-five and older. The direct services include working with the homebound elderly and residents in the local nursing homes and retirement villages through visiting programs, pastoral visits, liturgical celebrations, telephone contacts, transportation for doctor and/or hospital appointments, and, when possible, providing temporary care for caregivers. The services also include providing families with information on services available to senior citizens and how to access them. Sister M. Cyril Murray, OLM, is the Director of Senior Ministry in Christ Our King Parish, Mt. Pleasant St., S.C. Sister M. Carmelita Boyd, OLM, is a Pastoral Associate with responsibility for this ministry at St. Mary Magdalene Parish, Simpsonville, SC. Sister Marcella Zwingmann, Director of OLM Associates, is also active in visiting the sick and elderly in their homes and health-care facilities. She and the Associates have held programs for the elderly at the Motherhouse. The Associates also visit and plan programs for the retired sisters.

Notes

1. Sister Eleanor Casey, DC, Southeast Province, Emmitsburg, MD; Sister Patricia Coughlin, DC, Northeast Province, Albany, NY.; Sister Catherine Madigan, DC, East Central Province, Evansville, IN.; Sister Genevieve Kensenkothen, DC, West Central Province, St. Louis, MO.; Sister Mary Anne Baez, DC, West, Los Altos Hills, CA.
2. Sisters Georgette Dircks, SC, Jane Iannucelli, SC, and Madeleine Mahoney, SC, New York, NY.
3. Sister Judith Metz, SC, Cincinnati, Ohio.
4. Sister Anne Mantin, SC, Halifax, Nova Scotia, Canada. Sisters Cecilia Catherine, SC and Viola Cameron, SC, Cape Breton, Nova Scotia. Sister Mary Sweeney, SC, Boston, Massachusetts. Sister Joan Conway, Sillery, Quebec; Sisters Kathleen Kull, SC, Barbara Buxton, SC, Frances Fahey, SC, Frances Gritte, SC, Clare Romeo, SC, New York.
5. Sister Marion Murray, SCIC, Saint John, New Brunswick, Canada.
6. Sisters Mary Carita Pendergast, SC, and Anne Gertrude Coleman, SC, Convent Station, New Jersey.
7. Sister Margaret Mary Driscoll, SCL, Leavenworth, Kansas.
8. Sister Mary Catherine Seli, SC, Greensburg, Pennsylvania.
9. Sister Mary Judith Seman, VSC, Pittsburgh, Pennsylvania.
10. Sister Margaret Mach, VSC, Bedford, Ohio.
11. Sister Agnes Geraldine McGann, SCN, *SCNs Serving Since 1812* (St. Meinrad, IN: Abbey Press, 1986).
12. *SCN Mission Statement*, General Assembly, 1995.
13. Sister M. Anne Francis Campbell, OLM, Charleston, South Carolina.

Chapter Four

Education

Elizabeth Ann Seton was an experienced teacher, eminently qualified as an educator. She received assistance, encouragement, and guidance from the Sulpician priests who provided a dwelling for her and her children adjacent to their seminary. As the idea of forming a religious community evolved in 1809, one of Mother Seton's goals was to educate the poor. The new community of Sisters of Charity of St. Joseph was founded in Emmitsburg on July 31, 1809, and six months later in February 1810 a day school for children of the neighborhood was begun. This is considered the origin of the parochial school system in the United States. Teaching was the sisters' principal service until 1814, when they added social service and health care. Throughout the years the growth of thirteen congregations of Sisters of Charity, members of the Federation, contributed enormously to education on every level.

After Mother Seton's untimely death in 1821, the Council's first major decision was to respond favorably to a request for sisters to teach at Saint Mary's Free School in Baltimore. There followed more requests for sister teachers: to open Saint Paul's Academy on Capitol Hill in Washington, D.C., and an orphanage and school in Georgetown – both short-lived missions. In Virginia, schools were opened by the sisters in Alexandria, Richmond, Norfolk, and several schools in the states of Pennsylvania, New York, Massachusetts, and Ohio. By 1840, due to an ever-increasing number of immigrants to the United

States, the Catholic population had risen enormously. More than 300,000 Catholic immigrants had poured into the U.S. during the 1830s. The need for more and more Catholic schools was evident. Between 1840 and 1860 the community opened twenty-eight schools and twenty-four orphanages in sixteen states. In the midst of this the Emmitsburg community had joined the Daughters of Charity with Motherhouse in France. Those sisters who preferred that the Sisters of Charity form diocesan communities branched off from Emmitsburg. These sisters taught in numerous parochial schools in an ever-widening area of education throughout the United States.

THE DAUGHTERS OF ST. VINCENT DE PAUL, UNITED STATES[1]

Beginning in the 1840s the Daughters of Charity opened technical or industrial schools for girls twelve to eighteen years of age where they could both live and be educated to sew, cook, launder, and keep house for independent employment later on. The earliest of these were in the cities of St. Louis, Utica, New Orleans, and Baltimore. During the Civil War the Daughters concentrated on nursing. After the war until the turn of the century the sisters in the South opened only a few schools, as people were separately in need of food, clothing, housing, and the sisters made every effort to meet these needs.

Changing patterns in education made the responsibility for Catholic education that of the parishes and dioceses. From 1910 to 1948 schools accepted by the sisters were all parochial and mainly elementary. There were increasing demands for teacher certification, and the sisters began working towards their degrees. With the end of World War II a new era had begun. The Daughters of Charity were part of the postwar boom in Catholic education. The growth of diocesan high schools, the integration of schools and the sister-formation program were pivotal points in providing quality education for Catholics. With the division of the congregation into five provinces in 1969, Emmitsburg became the center for the Southeast Province, which served the states of Maryland, Virginia, West Virginia, Florida, North and South Carolina, Georgia, and the District of Columbia.

During the next twenty-five years the thrust was social service in the South and the inner city, which deeply affected education as did the declining number of sisters. Daughters of Charity withdrew from four schools as qualified lay personnel took over. Seton High School and Keough High School have become the Seton Keough High School. Daughters of Charity collaborate with administrators of Seton Keough High School. An important innovation was the establishment, in conjunction with several other communities, of Mother Seton Academy which opened in 1993. With a total registration of sixty students in grades six, seven, and eight, it attempts to provide free education for academically promising, low-income, at-risk students. The Catholic high schools of the city have agreed to provide scholarships to those eligible.

The Southeast Province continues to sponsor Mother Seton School in Emmitsburg, Elizabeth Seton High School in Bladensburg, and to staff two elementary schools in Washington, one with a large Hispanic population, the other 100% African-American. In the South the Daughters remain in schools in Richmond, Petersburg, Fayetteville, North Carolina, and Martinsburg, West Virginia.

The same history of education in the Southeast province followed in the West Central Province with center in St. Louis, Missouri. There an important step was taken in the education of sisters with the opening of Marillac College in 1954 at the provincial house, which provided quality college education by sister professors from established colleges and universities, particularly those who were members of the Federation. For twenty years it continued to give young sisters from all congregations the opportunity to obtain college degrees.

A decision was made to deploy 10% of the sisters in short-term missions among the disadvantaged and in areas where the Church was not represented. As a result sisters were withdrawn from schools for the middle class or in areas where the Church was strongly established. The sisters involved the laity to take over their work. Besides being teachers on every level, librarians, principals, school superintendents, new positions were accepted by the Daughters such as Director of Diocesan Communications, seminary professor, pastoral evangelization, teachers of English as a second language, GED teachers, parish and diocesan directors of religious education, and directors of mission effectiveness in the West Central Daughters of Charity Health System. Sisters have diversified their services to become parish administrators, pastoral associates, and parish ministers. In 1996 twenty-seven schools have one or more Daughters of Charity on the staff.

The East Central Province of the Daughters of Charity includes nine states east of the Mississippi, with provincial house in Evansville, Indiana. Since 1844 their schools have had a continuous impact on Catholic education. As in the other two provinces, the sisters have been forced to withdraw from many of their schools in the 1970s and 1980s as new trends in the education ministry initiated a response to special needs, one of which was to serve the black community in poverty areas. In East St. Louis the Daughters have been working in an inner-city African-American school, and at Vincent Gray Alternative School as administrator and teacher for African-American students unsuccessful in the traditional school. In schools in Illinois, Mississippi, and Indiana, Daughters of Charity serve as principals, teachers, chaplains for both African-Americans and white students in poverty areas, and as teacher of the handicapped at Our Lady of Roses in Chicago. They participate in religious programs in the parishes, in summer vacation schools, and in leadership roles such as campus ministers, Superintendent of Schools, and Director of the Diocesan Office of the Deaf and Disabled in Biloxi, Michigan. A Daughter is Program Chair for Human Services and Counseling at De Paul University in Chicago, and another is Associate Director of Big Shoulders Fund for Catholic School grants in Chicago. The presence of the Daughters in schools and other educational ministries has been marked by flexibility and adaptability in short-term ministries today.

In the Daughters of Charity Province in the West with its center in California, the sisters currently staff six elementary schools and one high school there, one in Arizona, and two in Utah as well as the Diocesan Office of Education in Utah. They also work in five parishes in those states. Many innovative programs have been established to meet the complex needs of children today, including providing assistance for the poor with special needs, computer-based education programming, mentoring programs by adult volunteers, tuition-assistance programs, obtaining grants. The sisters work on the staff of a number of parishes directing the Rite of Christian Initiation of Adults, developing parish liturgies, leading youth programs, supervising sacrament programs, and administrating parish outreach programs for the poor. Although Daughters of Charity in Parish Education currently serve in fewer locations and fill fewer positions than in the past, their desire to provide formation in the life of faith and to offer an excellent academic preparation remains strong. These convictions motivate them to continual updating and refining of the programs that they offer to children and others in the parish, especially the disadvantaged.

In the Northeast Province with its center in Albany, New York, sixty Daughters of Charity serve in educational or parish settings. This number includes those in religious education, campus and adult ministry, traditional school-related positions, early childhood programs, parish works and diocese-wide activities, as well as two universities and three college programs. With the marked changes in the trends of educational placement, diocesan superintendents and members of other religious communities assisted in the process of consolidation for parish elementary schools and smaller high schools. To concentrate on reaching underserved inner-city residents, the Daughters moved into two schools in Harlem and one school in Elizabeth, New Jersey. Participation in literacy programs, tutorial classes, and career training efforts for adult learners also increased.

Educational services continue to be provided for children with special needs through the Astor Home in Rhinebeck, N.Y., and through other programs associated with medical facilities or diocesan works such as St. Catherine's in Albany, N.Y. Since 1917 Daughters of Charity are still working in St. Mary's Cathedral School in Syracuse, and since 1830 in St. Peter's School, formerly an orphan asylum in Wilmington – two of the oldest schools staffed by them in the Northeast Province.

THE SISTERS OF CHARITY OF NAZARETH, KENTUCKY[2]

The Sisters of Charity of Nazareth have taught in over 200 schools in the past 180 years. Sister Ellen O'Connell was the principal founder of the Congregation's educational ministry. A trained teacher, she grew up in an intellectual environment as the only daughter of an eminent professor of languages and rhetoric at a Baltimore college. Just months after her arrival at Old St. Thomas, Nazareth Academy opened on 23 August 1814. This school, begun for girls and young women, grew rapidly during its long history.

Other schools started in the early 1800s include Bethlehem Academy, Bardstown, Kentucky (1819), now called Bethlehem High School, St. Vincent Academy, Union County, Kentucky (1820), and St. Catherine Academy, White Sulphur, Kentucky (1823), which moved to Lexington in 1829. In 1831 Presentation Academy, Louisville, Kentucky, was started. Sister teachers for these institutions were trained largely by Sister Ellen and Bishop David (cofounder of the Sisters of Charity of Nazareth). Another significant point in those early days was the Sisters' establishment of free schools near academies.

In the nineteenth century other schools were added: St. Francis Academy, Owensboro, Kentucky (1849), LaSalette Academy, Covington, Kentucky (1856), Immaculata Academy, Newport, Kentucky (1856), St. Mary Academy, Paducah, Kentucky (1858); St. Columba Academy, Bowling Green, Kentucky (1863); Bethlehem Academy, Holly Springs, Mississippi (1868); St. Clara Academy, Yazoo City, Mississippi (1872); Sacred Heart Academy, Helena, Arkansas (1879); Annunciation Academy, Bine Buff, Arkansas (1880); and St. Mary Academy, Leonardtown, Maryland (1885). Although these schools could not legally admit African-American students, SCNs began teaching them in 1871 at two elementary schools, St. Augustine in Louisville and St. Monica in Bardstown.

The Community opened three academies in the twentieth century: Sacred Heart Academy, Klamath Falls, Oregon, in 1917, Our Lady of Nazareth Academy, Wakefield, Massachusetts, in 1947, and Nazareth Academy, Gaya, India, in 1951. Sacred Heart closed in 1924; Our Lady of Nazareth is now the only academy that the Congregation owns in the United States. But Nazareth Academy, Gaya, remains vigorous. The Community owns other schools in India and Nepal, but these are not academies.

The first SCNs to attend summer school away from Nazareth enrolled at Creighton University, Omaha, Nebraska, in 1917. The following year Sisters Columba Fox and Mary de Lourdes Macklin received bachelor's degrees from St. Xavier College, now Xavier University, in Cincinnati, Ohio. In 1919 Sisters Marie Lane, Mary Eunice Rasin, Margaret Gertrude Murphy, and Columba Fox were allowed to study full-time. Another "first" in 1919 was Sister Mary Adeline O'Leary's attainment of her master's degree at Creighton. In the early 1920s several Sisters missioned at St. Catherine Academy, Lexington, Kentucky, took summer classes at the University of Kentucky, the first instance of SCN students at a secular college. In 1925 Sister Mary Adeline became the first Sister of Charity of Nazareth to receive her doctorate, a feat Sister accomplished at Fordham University. The Congregation established a senior college in Louisville in 1920 and a junior one at Nazareth the following year.

Music education always enjoyed a prominent place in schools taught by SCNs. From the time of Sister Scholastica O'Connor, some Sisters were assigned to full-time teaching of vocal and instrumental music. Recitals, choral singing, and musical plays demanded much time and energy in SCN schools.

The Congregation's educational ministry to African-Americans expanded from its 1871 beginnings at St. Augustine and St. Monica to include secondary schools in Louisville and Ensley, Alabama. Sisters also staffed additional parochial schools for African-American students in Kentucky, Maryland, and Alabama. In 1950 Spalding University, then Nazareth College, Louisville, enrolled its first African-American students following the repeal of Kentucky's Day Law, a measure which had previously ensured racial segregation. After 1954 separate schools were no longer needed as the Supreme Court finally permitted racially integrated schools throughout the country.

With the election of Sister Mary Ransom Burke to the Council in 1960, the Community acquired its first official Director of Education. From 1961 through 1969, she directed the SCN Education Association (SCNEA), a vehicle for all sisters to share needs and expertise. In 1968 the SCN Board of Education began its efforts on behalf of personnel placement and education for retirement. In response to the Church's call for Catholic educators to stress justice issues, Sister Dorothy MacDougall, appointed Director of Education in 1972, prepared a program called *Education for Justice: One Model* with assistance from Sisters Gwen McMahon and Phyllis Hannon. The Education Committee of the Leadership Conference of Women Religious published this material as a booklet in November 1974, identifying its purpose as involving all people in education in their obligations to justice.

The SCN General Assembly of 1971 led Sisters into types of ministry utterly different from formal classroom settings but involving SCNs in situations as vital as the Kentucky pioneers' need for literacy in 1814. A number of SCNs have pursued traditional apostolates in education consistently, and some have returned to this ministry. At present, approximately 151 Sisters out of a total membership of 814 work in formal education ministries. Increasingly, retired Sisters are tutoring children and adults who need individual help. For twenty-three years a Montessori school has functioned at Nazareth under Sister Patricia Marie Hill's direction. A few Sisters teach in public schools, and several hold positions in secular universities and in Catholic colleges not affiliated with the SCN Community. Some Sisters work full- or part-time in adult literacy programs, and many direct parochial religious education for children, youth, and adults.

In 1970 Sister Anne Rita Mauck founded the De Paul School in Louisville to address the special needs of dyslexic students. During its twenty-five year history, this institution has ministered to over 7,500 students. Another effort for students with special needs is Peace Academy, a classroom ministry cosponsored by Caritas Peace Center (formerly called Our Lady of Peace Hospital) and the Jefferson County Public Schools. This program supplies the instruction required by children and young people who are patients at Caritas Peace Center. These youth continue their education while they are hospitalized. Upon dismissal, they resume classes with their peers in a local school. Sister Margaret Albert Charlton began this ministry in 1971.

An event unique in the Congregation's 180 years of educational ministry occurred early in 1995. Because of grave difficulties, the Trustees of the Nazareth Literary and Benevolent Institution announced that Presentation Academy would close at the end of the current school year. Efforts had been underway to merge Presentation Academy and Spalding University. The merger could not take effect, however, without additional financial loss to the Congregation. When this news became public, there was an outpouring of support in the form of donations from individuals, groups, and corporations that exceeded the amount required. Spalding University assumed ownership and management of Presentation Academy on March 1, 1995.

One area of education where lay teachers have always outnumbered religious is the foreign missions. At Nazareth Academy, Gaya, India, there has always been a Sister principal, but most of the faculty are and have been laypeople. All of these efforts are relatively new, since the Congregation first sent Sisters to India in 1947 and to Belize in 1975. SCN ministry in education in India began in 1951 when a high school, Nazareth Academy, and a parish school, Creane Memorial School, in Gaya were administered by the Sisters of Charity of Nazareth. Today the Nazareth Academy campus includes a coeducational preschool, elementary school, high school, and a junior college. Educational efforts in India have reached out to the poor and marginalized people of society. A school for the children of leprosy patients was started in Gaya in 1976 and SCNs teach at De Britto School, Gomoh, also a school for children of leprosy patients. The Sisters in India administer and teach in several parish-owned schools. In Kathmandu, Nepal, SCNs provide education for mentally disabled children and in Dharan, East Nepal, the Sisters own and administer an elementary school where the medium of instruction is English.

In Belize, Central America, the ministry of education has been through individual ministries. Sisters have taught at both grade and high school levels. A Sister served as Assistant Manager of Catholic schools for the Stann Creek District. The primary focus of the parish Directors of Religious Education was in the area of in-service training for teachers of religion in grade schools, providing them with skills in the use of religion books in the classroom. The Sisters of Charity of Nazareth continue in the ministry of education in Belize through the presence of a Sister who teaches religion at St. Catherine's High School, Belize City.

As Sisters of Charity of Nazareth look to the year 2000, the 188th year of the Congregation's life, it is appropriate to recall St. Vincent's plea that Sisters of Charity "honor Jesus Christ . . . by rendering Him every . . . service in their power in the person of the poor . . ." SCN professional educators honor Jesus Christ by alleviating intellectual poverty and complement various Community ministries that address problems of persons who are poor because of other deprivations. In all these efforts Jesus Christ is honored and his people are served; the Congregation was founded to pursue these goals, and they will propel it into the twenty-first century.

THE SISTERS OF CHARITY OF NEW YORK[3]

In 1817 shortly after three Sisters of Charity from Emmitsburg had founded St. Patrick's Orphan Asylum in New York City, they were asked to staff the girls' department of St. Patrick's Free School and start an academy for girls. The New York Sisters of Charity still run St. Patrick's Old Cathedral School on Mott Street in Lower Manhattan, 180 years later. A plaque has been installed inside the old cathedral, stating: "This marks the beginning of the ministry of the Sisters of Charity in the Archdiocese of New York. This plaque commemorates 175 years of dedicated service to the people of New York."

The Sisters of Charity in New York began their apostolate of education within walking distance of the two houses in which St. Elizabeth Ann Seton tried to support herself and her five children by taking in boarding students. From St. Patrick's School on Prince Street, New York's oldest parochial school and the Congregation's first mission in New York, this pioneer community of religious women in New York has instructed students in almost two hundred institutions of learning from preschool through college. Archdiocesan education history can virtually be traced by reading the history of this Congregation.

In education as in other ministries, the Sisters of Charity of New York undertook works for which there were few precedents. Schools such as the former Holy Cross Academy and St. Vincent de Paul Industrial School were established on the same "rural" West 42nd Street site, a risky venture in 1857. As Catholics migrated to the country village of Harlem, sisters from the Motherhouse in McGown's Pass, now part of Central Park, ministered to their needs in parishes such as St. Paul's. By 1900 the sisters had opened eighty-two schools and eighteen academies in New York City, Westchester, Pennsylvania, and Rhode Island. This long list expanded to Cathedral High School in 1905, the first archdiocesan high school, St. Barnabas in the Bronx, and St. Gabriel in New Rochelle. Toward the close of the nineteenth century they undertook educational initiatives in the Bahama Islands, where they still serve, as well as in Guatemala. In 1910 the College of Mount Saint Vincent evolved from a fifth year program of the Academy of Mount Saint Vincent. In 1996 the College is a large coeducational institute of higher learning noted for its advanced courses in the arts and science.

Throughout the history of the congregation's education apostolate, the one constant factor has been the ability to adapt to the times. The complexity of New York's mobile and multicultural population has resulted in corresponding changes in institutions begun by the Sisters of Charity. Some works have reluctantly been discontinued, such as Elizabeth Seton College in Yonkers, while others have been entrusted to other religious communities or to the laity. The latter had to be paid salaries commensurate with the demands of justice, and thus it was necessary to charge tuition in keeping with students' ability to pay. This placed a financial burden on families, and indeed on the archdiocese. With the passage of time, some students who transferred to public schools were replaced by a larger number who entered parochial schools from the public sector. There are now more non-Catholic students in Catholic schools, and creative initiatives have to be established to sustain strong Christian communities in the schools.

In the years following Vatican II, sisters have moved to a mode of personal discernment in the choice of ministry rather than being assigned to a particular apostolate. As a result, sisters who did not feel a gift for education ministry left it for other ways of serving the people of God. Together with the great drop in religious vocations in recent years, this has added to the loss of sisters in the classroom. At the threshold of the third millennium Sisters of Charity find themselves educating the poor as a means of alleviating poverty and of empowering as many as possible to acquire marketable skills. In keeping with the demands of the times, they are engaged in literacy programs geared particularly to the high immigrant population that yearly arrives on the shores of New York.

In educating others about a critical contemporary concern, which is ecology and the environment as it affects life on our planet, they are teaching for the survival of the species. This represents education in the broadest sense. Other areas of the sisters' concerns include being directors of religious education programs in a number of parishes where laypeople teach religion to elementary and high school students. Still a third area of education is that of feminist issues in a Women's Center where the sisters hope to awaken in women a consciousness of these issues that will significantly enrich their lives.

Having served the Archdiocese of New York since 1817, the Sisters of Charity strive to continue in the steps of St. Elizabeth Ann Seton, foundress of the parochial school system in the United States, by undertaking every educational challenge presented to them under the guidance of the Holy Spirit.

THE SISTERS OF CHARITY OF CINCINNATI[4]

The Sisters of Charity of Cincinnati have been involved in numerous aspects and types of education throughout their history. They have served as classroom teachers, tutors, principals, supervisors, and superintendents. Some have been involved in the education of the sisters themselves, striving always to provide competent and professional personnel in the schools staffed by the community. A few have written textbooks, and some have been involved in innovative programs that were adopted across the country.

Education has always been a principal ministry of the Sisters of Charity of Cincinnati. When they arrived in 1829, they opened a school that included three departments: orphans, pay pupils, and those unable to pay. After the community became diocesan in 1852, the sisters opened academies at Mount Saint Vincent in Cincinnati, St. Mary's in Dayton, Ohio, and St. Patrick's in Fayetteville, Ohio. In addition they began accepting responsibility for parish schools, staffing fifteen in Ohio by 1870. Special emphasis was always given to art and music education. By the turn of the century a number of additional academies as well as new parish schools in Ohio, Michigan, New Mexico, and Colorado were accepted. In 1873 sisters went to Bay City, Michigan, to teach at St.

James Elementary and High School, the first coeducational parochial high school in the United States. Other secondary schools soon followed as the movement for more education began sweeping the country. The sisters conducted a few specialized institutions such as commercial schools, Latin schools, and one industrial school as well as four-year high school programs. In 1915 the community began staffing St. Rita School for the Deaf, and in 1944 assumed responsibility for Springer Institute, a school for children with learning problems.

By 1927 the sisters were conducting four academies, one resident school for deaf children, twenty-two high schools, fifty-five parochial, and two orphanage grade schools – all totaling 23,560 pupils under the instruction of 670 sisters aided by forty lay teachers. This commitment continued to grow with the increasing demand for parochial schools through the pre-Vatican II period. By 1965 the Sisters of Charity of Cincinnati had 900 sisters in Catholic elementary and secondary schools: 587 in seventy-nine elementary schools and 313 in thirty-nine high schools.

The community has also been involved in post-secondary education. Beginning in the 1890s nursing schools were established in most sponsored hospitals. The earliest opened at Mount San Rafael Hospital in Trinidad, Colorado, in 1893, and offered the first nursing program under Catholic auspices west of the Mississippi River. The most distant conducted by the Sisters of Charity of Cincinnati was at Wuchang, China, in connection with St. Joseph's Hospital. Three sponsored nursing schools in Colorado combined in 1933 to become Seton School of Nursing. Eight years later this program was one of the first thirteen nursing programs in the country to be nationally accredited by the National League for Nursing Education.

Mount Saint Joseph Academy was begun in 1906 at the Sisters of Charity Motherhouse outside Cincinnati. Soon young women who completed their courses requested postgraduate work. From this beginning grew the College of Mount Saint Joseph. Chartered in 1920, the liberal arts college moved to an all new eleven-building campus in 1962. It continues to be sponsored by the Congregation and has a current enrollment (1996) exceeding 2,300 students.

An additional type of education in which the community has engaged is catechetical. The sisters always taught catechism or Sunday school classes, but beginning in 1935 with the establishment of the Confraternity of Christian Doctrine, a new emphasis was placed on religious education for children enrolled in public schools. The community's "summer letter" from this time on included assignments to summer CCD schools. In 1960 there were forty-one summer school programs run by the sisters.

Although there are fewer sisters in classrooms since the Second Vatican Council, the educational ministry of the community continues to be carried out in a wide variety of arenas. Through workshops, retreats, and public speaking, many sisters have turned their attention to the field of adult education. Sisters serve as Parish Directors of Religious Education, and in positions that focus on social justice education. In addition, the congregation reaches a large audience through its public statements, corporate stands, and publications. Meanwhile others remain in elementary, secondary, and college classrooms, carrying on the long and hallowed tradition of Catholic schools in the United States.

THE SISTERS OF CHARITY OF HALIFAX[5]

In Canada, where there is no separation of church and state, religious education in the schools is on a different level. When Bishop William Walsh was appointed Bishop of the Diocese of Halifax in 1842, he soon realized that Catholic religious education in Halifax was quite inadequate. He turned to the New York Sisters of Charity, and in 1849 they sent four sisters to take charge of a school for 200 girls located in the Cathedral parish. In 1857 they opened St. Patrick's School. In 1859 the Public School System of Nova Scotia was taking shape, an event that was to have an extraordinarily positive impact on the Sisters of Charity in the field of education. The Act for the Better Encouragement of Education became law on April 18, 1865. It provided that all existing free schools should rate as public schools, that no public money should be given to any but free schools. In October 1865 two priests met with the School Board to speak on behalf of the Catholic schools. These schools were accepted as public schools, embodied in another resolution that the teachers should be approved by the Board and subject to all tests and requirements set down in the provincial law relating to public schools. At the end of the school year all the teaching sisters passed the examinations set by the Council of Public Instruction.

When Normal School classes were held at Mount Saint Vincent Motherhouse in Halifax to prepare novices and young sisters for the teaching profession, the training was not recognized by law until the Council of Public Instruction appointed three prominent male educators to appraise the quality of instruction. They observed the sisters' teaching in the classrooms and visited the Mount Training School. On November 12, 1895, the Council recognized Mount Saint Vincent Training School as a Provincial Normal School for sisters, confirmed by an Act of Legislation in 1907 and 1947.

In the years between 1849 and 1900 the sisters, as a result of many urgent requests, staffed twenty-one schools: nine in Halifax, two in Cape Breton, four in the French area of western Nova Scotia, two in New Brunswick, a private academy in Bermuda, and three parochial schools in Massachusetts. In the twentieth century the schools extended from the Atlantic to the Pacific and northward to the Yukon and the Northwest Territories in Canada. In British Columbia and the State of Washington the sisters staffed parochial schools. From 1925 the sisters were asked to teach in the Separate School System of Alberta funded through the public tax system. Initially they provided commercial classes and staffed a small elementary school, but later they joined the staff, some as principals, of five more elementary schools and a large central high school. From 1936 to 1970 they staffed Kootenay Residential School in Cranbrook, British Columbia. This school was under the Department of Indian Affairs.

The sisters' teaching reputation had far-reaching effects. In Massachusetts alone from 1887 on, they staffed numerous elementary and high schools in Roxbury, Dorchester, Lowell, Lawrence, Medford, North Andover, and several other cities and towns. At Wellesley Hills they built in 1893 the Academy of the Assumption, a boarding school for elementary and high school girls, and St. Joseph's School for boys up to grade 8. These were successfully maintained until 1972.

On August 24, 1924 the Sisters of Charity of Halifax were brought back to their origin in New York at the request of Bishop Thomas E. Molloy of Brooklyn to staff a large elementary school, Our Lady of Angels, which soon ranked among the best in the Diocese. Through the dedicated work of Sister Mary Clarissa Conlan, appointed Supervisor, the Sisters of Charity's reputation as educators became widely known. In 1927 they were asked to staff an elementary and high school in Staten Island, in the 1930s a school in Canton, upstate New York, and two schools in New Jersey. From 1928 to 1950 ten more schools were staffed by the sisters, these on Long Island, including a new diocesan Bishop Reilly High School (now St. Francis Prep) in Fresh Meadows and a new coeducational high school in Patchogue.

Seton Hall was built and staffed by the Sisters of Charity of Halifax. According to an article in the *Brooklyn Tablet* in 1949, the sod was turned for the high school in that year. The article states, "It is singular and at the same time worthy of the Halifax Sisters of Charity that they wish to mark both the centenary and silver jubilee (in Brooklyn) by a gift to the Diocese of Brooklyn. Convinced that they have a real mission to the young of outer Long Island, they will break ground a week from tomorrow for the New Seton Hall High School in Patchogue." This coeducational high school in Suffolk County flourished, producing many scholarship students as well as athletes and future leaders in many fields. It was with great regret that parents and former students witnessed its closure in 1974 due to the decline in sister teachers and in financial resources. The Sisters of Charity transferred ownership to the Sisters of St. Joseph, who transformed it into St. Joseph College, Suffolk County.

In 1935 the Sisters of Charity of Halifax were asked to open the first English-speaking school for girls, St. Patrick's elementary and high school, in Quebec City. It began with a registration of 170. English-speaking Sisters of Charity increased in number. Soon they were teaching in Sillery, St. Foy, Arvida, Dorval, and Ville St. Michel – a total of seven elementary and six high schools.

In Nova Scotia from 1900 to 1950 a total of twenty-three schools were conducted by the sisters, an Indian Residential School in Shubenacadie, and in 1923 a degree-granting college for women with a Charter granted by the government of Nova Scotia making it the first degree-granting college for women in Canada and the Commonwealth. Today Mount Saint Vincent University is still developing with a peak period of enrollment of approximately 3,700 students and a faculty of full- and part-time women and men totaling 310, of whom 163 are full time. Since 1967 it has accepted male students into its degree-granting program. In 1988 the sisters transferred ownership to the Board of Governors.

Teaching was preeminent among the works of the Sisters of Charity of Halifax. They came to Halifax from New York as teachers, and as a teaching order they were established. One hundred years later, their Centennial Year in 1949, they had foundations in five provinces in Canada, four states, and Bermuda. The number of schools increased considerably in the next twenty years. The scope of their teaching ranged from preschool through elementary, junior, and senior high schools, and university. In all their schools besides the traditional subjects, they fostered the fine arts of vocal and instrumental music, art, and drama. In the "Catholic" public schools in which the sisters taught and received regular public school teachers' salaries in Canada, they taught religion on a daily basis in their classrooms to their own classes, adding one half-hour to their school day before or after the regular curriculum. The sisters have always been engaged as tutors, as instructors in adult education, remedial reading, English as a second language, religious summer schools in rural areas. Today they have added literacy for adults, homemaking for single parents, computer classes, and education in ecology. This new world of unprecedented speed and change, of advances in science and technology, the probing of outer space, keeps the Sisters of Charity alert and energized to change. Though fewer in numbers and in the field of traditional education, they are individually making their contributions as dedicated women.

THE SISTERS OF CHARITY OF THE IMMACULATE CONCEPTION, SAINT JOHN, N.B.[6]

The Sisters of Charity of the Immaculate Conception, Saint John, New Brunswick, note that "education, one of the SCIC's traditional ministries, appears to have been a lifeline of its mission in the Church. The history of the Congregation bears witness that with each new establishment the ministry of teaching was involved." Along with all the secular subjects, the teaching of religion was "not a fringe subject but an integral part of living the Gospel Values."

An SCIC had to be prepared to teach in any sector of the educational field ranging from kindergarten to university, including students with special needs or exceptional gifts. This wide spectrum of the teaching profession was recognized by the founding sisters. In 1855 the facilities of the first permanent house on Cliff Street (site of the Motherhouse) provided classrooms for the orphans and a Select School for the young ladies, children of wealthy immigrants. This high school was a forerunner of the establishment of academies to meet the needs of young girls in urban and rural areas.

The Academy of the Immaculate Conception (1857-1873) in St. Basile, New Brunswick, was opened to prepare young women for the teaching profession at the primary level. In 1873 Notre-Dame-du-Sacré-Coeur in Memramcook, New Brunswick, opened as a day and boarding school where academic classes included lessons in art, music, and business. Seven years later Immaculate Conception Convent, Bouctouche, New Brunswick, became a day and boarding school for the French Acadian girls. Three other convents were opened for the teaching ministry in the Acadian area: St. Anne's Convent (1888) in Shediac, N.B.; Our Lady of Lourdes (1916) in St. Anselme, N.B.; Our Lady of Good Counsel (1923) in Petit Rocher, N.B. Those five convents were given to the SCIC Acadian sisters when they were recognized by Rome as a separate community, Les Religieuses de Notre-Dame-du-Sacré-Coeur.

Mount Carmel Academy (1920-1956) in Saint John, N.B., a boarding and day school for girls, opened with high school courses preparatory to Provincial Matriculation and University Entrance. It also held classes in Business Education and Music. Commercial classes flourished in other areas too. Holy Rosary Convent (1930) in St. Stephen, N.B., attracted American students from Maine as well as the Canadians from surrounding areas; St. Joseph's School in Winnipeg, Manitoba, staffed by the SCICs from 1938 added commercial options in the high school in 1942; in Digby, Nova Scotia, a new school provided a section for business education; at Hanna, Alberta, a commercial school was set up at the Convent in 1946 with boarding facilities for young ladies at the convent, and for young men at the rectory.

Schools that began with parish support were known as parochial schools. As time and change demanded in Canada, many of these schools evolved as public schools. There being no separation of church and state as in the United States, many of these public schools became Catholic public schools and Protestant public schools. Parents could send their children to either, regardless of their religious affiliation or lack thereof. In some provinces the sisters remained as teachers in the Catholic public schools, remunerated with the same public school teachers' salaries and pensions as the lay teachers. The SCICs taught in numerous parochial schools in New Brunswick, in Saskatchewan, and in British Columbia. With the passing of the Equal Opportunity Act in New Brunswick in 1967 the government took away the need for the parish school in this province.

In 1967 the SCICs opened their first foreign mission in Peru, where they constructed their first parish school in San Filipe. Two of the sisters taught with the indigenous teachers, preparing them to take responsibility for the school as their own.

The history of Catholic students in the public school system in New Brunswick dates back to the Common School Act of 1871, which in 1873 and 1875 made concessions to Catholic students allowing them to enroll in their own Catholic schools. These were built by the Church and rented to the Common School Board and called by tradition "Catholic" schools but legally public. In these schools Catholic teachers and students met all the academic government standards and received the same financial assistance and wages allotted to the other public schools, the restrictions being that religion classes must be held outside the regular school hours and religious pictures be works of recognized art. The lived experience was that the Catholic schools had their special atmosphere, which permeated the whole day.

The SCIC community strove to have all their teachers licensed in some Canadian province and to obtain the Bachelor's degree in college, the Master's degree, and in some instances the Ph.D. In the late 1970s some of the sisters taught in colleges and universities as Professors at the University of New Brunswick and St. Thomas University in Fredericton, Newman College in Edmonton, Alberta, and at UNB Saint John Campus in Saint John, N.B.

The sisters in Quebec, Alberta, and Saskatchewan taught in public schools known there as Separate Schools. Under this system the Catholic School Board only received the education taxes from the Catholic population, making the financial situation difficult at times. In Alberta the sisters agreed to work for 70% of the regular teacher pay.

In 1924 the sisters went to Holdfast, Saskatchewan, to teach. This was a German settlement, its people engaged in farming. A convent was built large enough to board several girls who lived at a distance. The Minister of Education decreed that the sisters must doff their religious habits and wear secular clothes or leave. The sisters wisely chose to remain and wore secular clothes during school hours. Gradually with a change of government the sisters were permitted to wear their distinctive religious habit but without the rosary beads. In 1968 Schell High School was built and named to honor one of the teaching sisters.

In 1942 the sisters were requested by the Archbishop of Edmonton to staff Sacred Heart School in Wetaskiwin, Alberta. The pastor, a one-man school board, paid low salaries to the sisters in an effort to increase the building fund for a badly needed new school. It was truly the Sisters' school.

Unique was the situation in Powell River, British Columbia, where the kindergarten was public under the management of the Department of Education, Government of B.C., and the Pulp and Paper Company. It was nondenominational in character. The sisters opened this school in 1939 with fifty students and kept it in operation until 1960.

Another school system under which the sisters taught was the federally-funded reserve schools for native Canadians in New Brunswick from 1928 until the early

1980s. The mission to the prisoners at Matsqui Prison, Abbotsford, British Columbia was classified as a federal school. English and Art were taught by a gifted Sister of Charity of the Immaculate Conception. In all of these school settings, formal and informal, the ministry of teaching catechetics was primary not just for students in the sisters' schools but for all children in the surrounding areas. The Catechetical Center in West Saint John, New Brunswick, was opened for those who could not attend school. Lessons were mailed to all parts of the Diocese until 1983.

If this account of the Sisters of Charity of the Immaculate Conception's ministry of education sounds like a chronicle of past glories, the question is "What about now?" Because of the apparent lack of vocations to the religious life, only a remnant of sister teachers are left to carry on. These sisters are in public, Catholic, and separate schools in Saint John, New Brunswick, and Edmonton, Alberta, courageously carrying on the ministry of teaching, forging ahead on the Information Highway and reminding the world that compassion and love are more than ever needed by today's students. Retired sisters continue to tutor students. Several teach in the Literacy Program and give functional English lessons to immigrants. Running vertically through all ages is the ever present teaching in the R.C.I.A. parish programs wherever the sisters are missioned.

THE SISTERS OF CHARITY OF SAINT ELIZABETH, CONVENT STATION, N.J.[7]

The Sisters of Charity of Saint Elizabeth, Convent Station, New Jersey, though, like most religious congregations today, older and fewer than they once were, continue to honor their history as a community of educators. That history almost spans the history of the Church in New

Jersey. Its first Bishop, James Roosevelt Bayley, nephew of Mother Elizabeth Ann Bayley Seton, reported to the Propagation of the Faith that there was no educational institution under the care of religious in the entire state until he took possession of the diocese. After only forty years of the Sisters of Charity's collaboration with the Bishop and his priests, every level of Catholic education could be found in New Jersey, even to the founding of the first successfully established and continuing baccalaureate degree-granting women's college in the state, the College of Saint Elizabeth, founded by the Sisters of Charity, and shortly afterward the first Catholic parochial high school.

Sister Mary Pauline Kelligar was a key figure in furthering the realization of Bishop Bayley's dream of developing a Catholic-educated people. Formerly a small minority, New Jersey Catholics were subject to religious bigotry and discrimination. There were only 40,000 Catholics in the whole state, most of them poor, according to Bishop Bayley's report, and only thirty-five priests, of whom only eight were born in the U.S. There were but forty-one churches and chapels and twelve Mass stations. Mary Kelligar, an experienced teacher and administrator, entered the Congregation in 1868. She was assigned to the new St. Vincent Academy in Newark, then on to take charge of St. Agnes Institute, a "select school" for girls established in 1867 by Father William McNulty in Paterson under the direction of the Sisters of Charity. In 1877 Sister Mary Pauline became directress of the Academy of Saint Elizabeth, established in 1860 as the community's Motherhouse in Morris County. Responding to the growing demand for opportunities in higher education for women equal to those of men, which Rutgers College ignored and Princeton College heard but failed in its eight-year establishment of Evelyn College for Women

(1889-97), the Sisters of Charity of New Jersey, under the leadership of Sister Mary Pauline, succeeded with the founding of the College of Saint Elizabeth (1899-). It quickly attained recognition for meeting the highest academic standards. The College of Saint Elizabeth, Princeton, and Rutgers were the only New Jersey colleges on the Middle States Association's first list of accredited colleges, and, with Stevens College, the only colleges in New Jersey on the 1917 prestigious list of colleges approved by the Association of American Universities. A pioneer in Catholic higher education for women, it was one of three Catholic colleges in the United States whose quality was so recognized.

The extraordinary contribution of Sister Pauline to the field of education, especially Catholic higher education for women, was signalized by Fordham University's awarding her in June, 1917, the degree Doctor of Laws (*honoris causa*), the first to be conferred upon a woman by Fordham University.

The Sisters of Charity kept abreast of the exigencies of the times, generously sharing their gifts with one another, and resolving to truly educate, no matter the cost. Before 1920, the community had inaugurated a state-approved summer school for teacher training, and in 1926 had begun giving young women who planned to enter the community a good secondary education through the Saint Vincent Preparatory School (1928-60). Eventually sisters were sent abroad to study for special teaching assignments; sisters with one or two degrees were sent on for higher degrees, and at one point seven sisters were released to pursue doctoral degrees. Meanwhile baccalaureate courses were being intensified and broadened. In 1959 there were 1,324 sisters teaching on every level. As they approach the twenty-first century, the Sisters of Charity of Saint Elizabeth are still serving in the college, in five academies, and in many parish schools. Still holding the belief that Catholic education has been and continues to be a vital ministry, the sisters recognize that their commitment is affected by their personal resources. Since 1988, 50% fewer sisters are engaged in elementary education; part-time ministry has increased; approximately a 20% decline is noted in the numbers of sisters in secondary education, and a 33% decrease of sisters on the college level.

Paradoxically, though their numbers are now lower, their activities are more widely distributed. Currently they serve education in twelve states outside of New Jersey. They have found opportunities for pre-kindergarten and day-care education. As they collaborate with other congregations and the laity through their presence on their faculties, the sisters are urged to leadership in education. Above all they are encouraged to broaden and update their personal development through enrichment courses. The 137 years of the congregation's life and development marks an extraordinary dedication to education that even today is still exhibiting vital growth.

THE SISTERS OF CHARITY OF LEAVENWORTH, KANSAS[8]

In the Constitutions of the Sisters of Charity of Leavenworth, Kansas, their ministry of Christian education holds top priority as ". . . one of the great acts of charity: serving others . . . ministering to their need to know and come to the truth; to be opened to the good and the beautiful; to understand the past; to confront and help shape the future; to be called to justice; to be more fully and completely human and Christian."

The sisters began teaching in two small frame buildings, the girls on Kickapoo Street opposite the convent, the boys on Kiowa, north of the residence of Bishop J.B.

Miege, SJ. The great need of a boarding school became more apparent each day. The sisters secured a cottage on the corner of 6th and Kickapoo, opening their first school for boarders in the spring of 1860. The overflow of students led to the building of the first St. Mary's Academy on Kickapoo Street in 1860. A small house known as Ewing Cottage served as the first boarding school. That spring over 100 children enrolled in the boarding and day school. As membership grew, parish schools were built and the sisters began teaching in Lawrence, Topeka, and Wyandotte. By 1869 at the persistent requests of the famous Father De Smet, SJ, five sisters were on their way to Helena, Montana. At the time of their twenty-fifth anniversary (1883) the Sisters of Charity of Leavenworth had opened or staffed twenty-five parish schools and academies. The inevitable hardships of pioneer life, great poverty and unsuitable housing, necessitated the closing or withdrawal from ten of those schools.

Between 1884 and 1939 the sisters staffed elementary and high schools in Montana, Wyoming, Colorado, Missouri, and Kansas. In the years between 1940 and 1960 the community experienced phenomenal growth, as did most of the congregations of sisters in North America. This enabled the Leavenworth Sisters of Charity to staff three additional high schools and twenty-seven grade schools. Sister Mary Baptista Ward not only supervised these schools but was largely responsible for staffing and, on occasion, planning the construction of those schools. Her leadership and insistence on the sisters being truly professional teachers led to a great improvement in the quality and uniformity of curriculum provided for the students.

Although interest in education and self-improvement of members had been traditional, the professional aspect of teacher preparation developed slowly. By 1886 the

Leavenworth Diocesan School Board conducted examinations for Diocesan Teachers Certificates. Distinguished educators conducted summer classes; conventions, institutes and summer sessions furthered the sisters' professional competence. By 1913 the sisters were being sent to Catholic and state universities.

In 1923 Mother Mary Berchmans opened St. Mary's Junior College, becoming a four-year liberal arts college in 1930. The establishment of a graduate division in 1950 enabled many sisters to obtain a Master's degree in Elementary and Secondary Education as well as in Administration. Under the leadership of Sister Mary Janet McGilley, President from 1964 to 1989, Saint Mary's College expanded to include the "Two Plus Two" program with Donnelly College, the extension of its services to older women, and expanded offerings in evening classes. A Prison Education Program was offered at four sites, and became coed in 1988. A new college site for adult students in Johnson County was opened in 1990.

Perhaps no other events so greatly affected the education apostolate as did the Sister Formation Program and Vatican II. By 1980 over 90% of the sisters possessed Bachelor's, Master's or higher degrees. The implementation of the decrees of Vatican II provided far-reaching and radical changes in the lifestyle and ministries of the sisters. They moved away from education into ministries of social service, peace and justice, prayer houses, pastoral assistants, and many other areas. By the late 1980s the Sisters of Charity of Leavenworth had closed or withdrawn from twenty-seven schools, while in other schools only one, two, or three sisters remained on the faculty. The 1990s brought a renewed interest in Catholic schools. Catholic lay teachers took over the challenge of educating youth. The education apostolate now comprises 20% of the community.

However, the education ministry has taken on new forms, as evidenced by the sisters working as Religious Education Directors, in RCIA, parish adult classes, GED and other programs. After Vatican II the Leavenworth Sisters of Charity, as with all the other congregations, were requested for sisters to work full-time in religious education. The first request came from the Kansas Archdiocese in Kansas City in 1963. Sister Mary Pauline Degan was the first full-time ACL in parish work. She was assigned to work with a priest in the Confraternity of Christian Doctrine program, a national organization for establishing parish programs for adults and children. Religious education boards were organized, adult education classes were offered, preparation of lay people to become catechists was planned.

Sister Mary Pauline shared her expertise at workshops around the diocese while other sisters were gradually assigned to similar work. Bishop Raymond Hunthausen of the Diocese of Helena, Montana, in 1965 asked two SCLs to help establish a Diocesan Office of Religious Education and to devise a way to survey all the parishes of the diocese to ascertain the status of religious education. They did this by planning a four-part workshop on some of the Vatican II documents to present in the deaneries to teachers of religion. Sister Mary Catherine became editor of the diocesan newspaper in 1971. Other sisters became CCD Coordinators in Oklahoma City, in small towns near Leavenworth, in Topeka and Prairie Village, Kansas, and in Denver. One sister was asked to be Director of Religious Education in Evergreen, Colorado.

Pastoral Ministry also became a full-time ministry for the sisters. Currently a number of sisters are parish administrators and pastoral associates. SCLs serve in pastoral positions in Colorado, Kansas, Missouri, Nebraska,

Oklahoma, Texas and Wyoming, as well as in Latin America. The same can be said of all thirteen congregations in the Federation, and indeed of all sisters serving in North America, so that all the states and provinces have an enormous number of sisters serving in parish ministry as the number of priests declines.

THE SISTERS OF CHARITY OF SETON HILL, GREENSBURG, PENNSYLVANIA[9]

The Sisters of Charity of Seton Hill, Greensburg, Pennsylvania, initially were invited by Bishop Michael Domenec of the Diocese of Pittsburgh to staff a school in Altoona as well as begin a new foundation of Sisters of Charity. On September 5, 1870, three hundred children reported to Saint John School, the first of many thousands to receive their education in schools directed by the Sisters of Charity of Seton Hill.

The young congregation expanded its mission of teaching to seven schools in southwestern Pennsylvania, following the Pennsylvania Railroad from Altoona to Blairsville, to Johnstown, Sharpsburg, and Pittsburgh. Before the turn of the century the sisters had responded to requests from Irwin, Crafton, Wilkinsburg, Rochester, Scottdale, Hazelwood, Carnegie, and other areas of Pittsburgh as well as East Liverpool, Ohio. At St. Benedict in Greensburg the sisters lived above the school, moving eventually back to Seton Hill and their Motherhouse established by Mother Aloysia Lowe, the foundress, in 1882. They commuted to St. Benedict's until a convent was built in 1962.

One year after their arrival in Greensburg the sisters established St. Joseph Academy, which continued from 1883 until 1947. St. Mary's School for Boys continued from 1881 until 1927. In 1908 the sisters opened De Paul

Institute Oral School for Deaf Children, later including blind children. Many went on to higher education.

Throughout the first six decades of the twentieth century, as Catholic schools mushroomed all over the country, the Sisters of Charity of Seton Hill continued to extend themselves. They staffed more than eighty elementary schools in Pennsylvania, Arizona, Maryland, Louisiana, California, and West Virginia. With the opening of the Elizabeth Seton Montessori School in 1970, followed by numerous day-care centers, they demonstrated their commitment to young children. Beginning with Sacred Heart High School in Pittsburgh, the sisters staffed many parish high schools followed by central high schools in which they assumed responsibility for specific departments, accepting administrative posts in schools located in Pennsylvania and Arizona. Elizabeth Seton High School in Pittsburgh, owned and operated by the Sisters of Charity of Seton Hill, inspired many vocations to the congregation.

Seton Hill College, a four-year liberal arts college for women, received its charter in 1918, the first Catholic college for women in Western Pennsylvania. Besides Bachelor's degrees in Arts, Science, the Humanities, Fine Arts, Music, Management, and Marketing, it offers the Master's degree in Education and Art Therapy, accepting men in the School of Fine Arts. Through its Continuing Education Office, Seton Hill offers opportunities for the nontraditional student. It is the home of the National Educational Center for Women in Business. It also sponsors the National Catholic Center for Holocaust Studies in conjunction with a center at Yad Vashem, Tel Gamaliel, Israel, coordinated there by a Sister of Charity of Seton Hill. The sisters have also served on the faculties of other colleges and universities. One sister is Executive Vice-President of Catholic University of America, Washington, D.C.; another is Coordinator of Special Education at Duquesne University. A Seton Hill Sister of Charity is a teacher at Sogang University, Seoul, Korea; another has served as Director of the Greco Institute of Pastoral Studies in Shreveport, Louisiana.

Between 1954 and 1971, Seton Hill College and the Sisters of Charity financed the Undergraduate Teaching Plan enabling students to gain experience in teaching while easing the burden on parishes with overcrowded schools. Thus young women received financial assistance while participating in the work of the Sisters of Charity. Several of these young women entered the Congregation.

Another project (1921-57) was the establishment of a Summer Extension Program to educate African-American religious women (Sisters of the Holy Family) in New Orleans, who, because of their race, were not admitted to the segregated high schools and colleges in the South.

From 1921 until 1957 the Sisters of Charity conducted a Normal School for Sisters of the Holy Family at their Motherhouse in New Orleans. Because of Segregation Laws, these sisters were denied admission to many schools and colleges. In 1942 Seton Hill College established a scholarship program for the Sisters of the Holy Family, nineteen of whom received degrees by the early 1970s. They also initiated a teacher-exchange program involving two Seton Hill Sisters and two Holy Family Sisters exchanging teaching positions in New Orleans and Seton Hill.

Other ways of easing racial tensions included work with African-American people in Pittsburgh's Lower Hill District. They opened a kindergarten and primary school; they taught catechism to the children and Bible Studies to the adults. One sister taught the children to play the violin and developed a large string ensemble of African-

American children who received invitations from across the country to give concerts.

A further work with African-Americans was the staffing of a school for them in Abbeville, Louisiana, in 1956 until desegregation of the schools took place. The educational ministry of the Seton Hill Sisters in the southwest began in 1933 in Tucson, Arizona, and continued with the staffing of seven elementary schools and two high schools. They also teach the rudiments of the faith to the indigenous people of Mexican-American and Native American cultures.

In 1960 they opened their first foreign mission in Korea, assuming responsibility for Saint Joseph Middle School for Girls, which soon developed into a large high school. They staffed another high school and opened schools for the handicapped and the blind, and an early childhood center. Bible study groups furthered the Koreans' religious education. Not only leaders in the academic field, the sisters have been equally devoted to religious education, teaching, and preparing the children for the reception of the sacraments in many small parishes as well as in the schools where they taught. The Seton Hill Sisters also conducted classes for the Adult Religious Education Institute throughout the Diocese of Greensburg to educate lay adults in the faith and prepare them to become their coworkers in the ministry of religious education.

Many sisters have served as supervisors, consultants, superintendents in diocesan education offices; others have authored textbooks for the schools. One sister is a representative of an educational publishing firm. The educational ministry of Saint Elizabeth Ann Seton and of Mother Aloysia Lowe continues through their daughters, the Sisters of Charity of Seton Hill. Through education they feed Christ's people; they open eyes and ears and tongues; they bring Christ's love.

THE VINCENTIAN SISTERS OF CHARITY OF PITTSBURGH, PENNSYLVANIA[10]

The Vincentian Sisters of Charity came to America to educate the children of the Slovak immigrants. Five sisters volunteered, arriving in Braddock, Pennsylvania, from Rumania in 1902. St. Michael School in Braddock was turned over to the sisters. Their first duty was to learn the English language, which they mastered in a remarkably short time and proceeded to instruct the fifty-four children both in Slovak and in English. At the end of the first year the enrollment had increased to 150 and in the third year to 400. Four more sisters arrived from Rumania.

Pastors of numerous other Slovak parishes in Pennsylvania and Ohio, hearing of the good work of the Vincentian Sisters, asked for sisters to staff their parish schools. Between 1902 and 1953 the sisters were in charge of thirty-six elementary schools. After 1953 the sisters received requests from non-Slovak parishes, so widespread was their reputation in the field of education. Five large territorial parishes received the services of the sisters in the four years after 1953. Requests also came from parishes without schools, asking the sisters to instruct public school students in the Confraternity of Christian Doctrine. In 1932 the sisters opened Vincentian Academy on the Motherhouse grounds. Originally only for aspirants to religious life, in 1936 it was opened to all girls and in 1938 it became a boarding school. In 1971 it became the coeducational Vincentian High School. The sisters continued to take on teaching assignments in secondary schools in the Dioceses of Pittsburgh, Greensburg, Altoona-Johnstown, Youngstown in Ohio, and Welland in

Ontario, Canada, in 1958. They continued to staff schools in the province of Ontario. The call for sisters came also from Puerto Rico to serve at St. Miguel Parish in 1930, but because of the poor health of the sisters serving there for three years the congregation regretfully withdrew their sisters.

The Vincentian Sisters' special ministry to African-Americans began in 1940, when seven sister volunteers were sent to Marbury, Alabama, to open an elementary school for them. Shortly after, they were asked to staff a new school for black children in Phenix City, Alabama, and a high school and elementary school at the City of St. Jude in Montgomery. The sisters were also invited to teach at St. Mary's School in Pierce City, Missouri.

As enrollments began to dwindle in the late 1960s, the Vincentians took an active part in helping the dioceses consolidate schools, no longer known as Vincentian schools. Today there may be one Vincentian Sister as Principal or one sister teaching in a school of all lay teachers. Vincentian Sisters have also chosen to teach in schools not traditionally staffed by them. With the large number of working mothers today, the need arose for child-care centers in the area around the Motherhouse. Hence a child-care center was opened in 1972. The need expanded, and in 1995 a new building was constructed, Vincentian Child-care Center, licensed for 150 infants through kindergarten children.

In 1994 Vincentian High School was invited to be a partner with Duquesne University in a new educational program known as Vincentian Academy/Duquesne University. It offers an international baccalaureate program. The Vincentian Sisters of Charity continue to hold the educational ministry as one of their primary works. The sisters continue today to serve in the United States and Canada, caring for infants, teaching preschoolers, elementary, secondary, and college students, and administering a Montessori school. Retired sisters give private tutoring and small group adult instruction, even in the Slovak language. At the end of the twentieth century the sisters are faced with the new challenge of adapting to changing times and providing education in fields unthought of a century ago.

THE VINCENTIAN SISTERS OF CHARITY, BEDFORD, OHIO[11]

The Vincentian Sisters of Charity of Bedford, Ohio, founded by the Pittsburgh Vincentian Sisters in 1928, operated a total of eighteen elementary schools. While the first schools were predominantly for Slovak families, the community eventually broadened its efforts to serve in the newly emerging suburban schools. Whereas in the beginning the sisters taught not only the children but their parents, also providing food and clothing for the poor immigrant families, the picture changed rapidly in the late 1950s, when the Bishop of Cleveland organized a capital campaign to build more Catholic high schools in his Diocese. He asked the Vincentian Sisters to build a high school for girls in Bedford. Bishop Edward F. Hoban gave the school its name, Lumen Cordium, or Light of Hearts, from his own coat of arms. The sisters ran the school for twenty-three years before a dramatically changing cultural environment forced the school to close in 1987. The sisters decided to convert the building into a beautiful contemporary residence for senior citizens administered by the sisters.

The Vincentian Sisters have served on every level of education, with two sisters with doctorates now teaching at John Carroll University and Ursuline College, both in Cleveland. For the past thirty years the Vincentian Sisters have had to withdraw from schools that Pastors were closing due to diminished enrollments because Slovak families were moving to the suburbs. As this sociological shift in city culture began, the sisters were also beginning to age, making it unrealistic to expect them to operate the suburban schools. From a total of fifty-six teaching sisters in 1966, there remain fourteen teaching in elementary education. Since the 1970s when paradigmatic shifts became obvious in the ministries of women religious, the focus on elementary education has shifted to literacy programs and religious education for adults. The Vincentian Sisters of Charity continue to serve as new fields of education open up. As recent as 1976 to 1986 the Vincentian Sisters served in El Salvador, Central America, in a thrust that was based on education. Three sister teachers followed programs structured on teaching adults. Peace and Social Justice, as well as literacy programs and religious instruction, were the order of the day. With a very progressive agenda for the rights of others one of their sisters is cofounder of Cleveland's Central American Interreligious Task Force working for sanctuary for Central American refugees.

THE SISTERS OF CHARITY OF OUR LADY OF MERCY, CHARLESTON, S.C.[12]

The education of young girls from the poorer classes of society and of free African-Americans was among the purposes for which Bishop England founded the OLMs in Charleston in 1829. When England died in April, 1842, the Community was operating the Academy of Our Lady of Mercy, founded in 1830, as both a boarding and a day school offering a basic education with some frills (e.g., music, art, and embroidery) to those who could afford the minimal charges. Non-Catholics were welcome and assured that there would be no interference with their religious beliefs. In the early years religious instruction for

Catholics was given after school hours. The curriculum was broadened over the years. The school continued in existence until 1929. St. Mary's Free School was founded in 1838 or 1839 to educate girls who could not afford the Academy tuition. The OLMs provided the faculty and conducted it until 1906. It was situated at various locations in the city of Charleston throughout its long history. In 1835 Bishop England first established a school for free African-Americans, boys and girls, Catholics and non-Catholics, who wished to attend. Although this first school was closed within a matter of months due to pressure of influential white citizens who feared the efforts then being made by the abolitionists, it was reopened in 1841 and continued in existence until 1848. The sisters taught the girls; diocesan seminarians taught the boys. Its location changed over the years. At first it was located across the street from the Motherhouse on Queen Street, Charleston. Later, it was moved to King Street. The records do not indicate the reasons for its closing.

In 1854 at the request of Rev. Jeremiah, J. O'Connell, Pastor of St. Peter's Church in Columbia, S.C., the sisters opened the Academy of the Immaculate Conception in that city. Basically, the school was a duplicate of the Academy in Charleston. Four years later, Bishop Patrick N. Lynch asked the OLMs to return to Charleston to conduct an orphanage for boys. The Usuline Sisters replaced the OLMs in Columbia.

The bombardment of Charleston during the Civil War caused the sisters to move their Academy boarders as well as the orphan girls inland to Sumter, S.C., in 1863. There they established the Academy of St. Joseph, which remained in existence until 1929. Following the War, the Community struggled to rebuild and reopen their pre-war educational institutions. There is evidence that they applied to the Freedmen's Bureau for money to open a school for black children. However, the request was denied. The Third Plenary Council of Baltimore (1884) decreed that parochial schools be erected and maintained near every Catholic Church where there was not yet one. The first parish schools established in Charleston in the late 1880s were open to boys only and staffed by lay faculty. At the turn of the century, however, women religious began to replace lay faculty in the parochial schools. By 1905, the OLMs constituted the faculty in the parochial schools in the city of Charleston including the schools for African-American children: St. Peter's and Immaculate Conception. When the Community closed St. Mary's Free School in 1906, the parish schools became coeducational. The establishment of Bishop England High School, a coeducational diocesan Catholic high school, in Charleston in 1915, and the continued growth of parochial schools throughout the Diocese contributed to the Community's decision in 1929 to close Our Lady of Mercy Academy in Charleston, and St. Joseph's Academy in Sumter. St. Angela Academy, Aiken, S.C., which the Community had accepted after the Ursulines withdrew in 1907, continued to operate under the OLM auspices until 1988.

In 1929 Bishop Emmet Walsh established Religious Vacation Schools and camps throughout the Diocese to provide children who could not attend parochial schools with some Catholic education. The OLMs served with diocesan priests and seminarians as faculty in many of these schools from their establishment into the early 1960s. In one of these, St. Mary's, Bluffton, SC, religious instruction was given when the tide was out. When it was in, the children went swimming! (This was known as "religion by the tide.") The World War II years witnessed an influx of Catholics into South Carolina around the military bases, which led to the growth of new parishes and schools. The OLMs moved into some of these and taught Sunday School in areas without schools. By mid-century the Community was staffing schools in Aiken, Sumter, Greenville, Mt. Pleasant, Myrtle Beach, and Charleston. In 1963 the racial integration of all of these schools began and was completed by the end of that decade.

During the 1970s and 1980s, while the Catholic population in the diocese continued to increase, the number of women and men religious serving in parochial schools continued to decrease. Nonetheless, Catholic education remains a priority concern in the Diocese. At present, the Sisters of Charity of Our Lady of Mercy have three sisters serving as Principals of parochial schools, but no sisters on the faculties. Some of the sisters who formerly taught are now serving as Pastoral Associates or as members of Parish Staffs, or have moved into new ministries, e.g., the Outreach Program, spiritual direction, and visiting the sick in their homes and health-care facilities. It should also be mentioned that the Community established a Junior College in 1935, which later was affiliated with the Catholic University. One of the chief purposes in doing this was to provide higher education for the novices and junior sisters. The faculty was drawn from local colleges as well as from OLM qualified sisters. The Junior College closed in 1961 as sisters were sent away to study at institutions throughout the country in an effort to provide them with the best professional preparation possible. OLM Congregational leaders were very active in the Sister Formation Movement and in efforts to implement the Decrees of Vatican II.

LES RELIGIEUSES DE NOTRE-DAME-DU-SACRÉ-COEUR[13]

The Congregation of Les Religieuses de Notre-Dame-du-Sacré-Coeur was founded by the Acadian Sisters, whose sole purpose was to educate the Acadian people in their own language and culture. The small community rapidly grew and houses were open everywhere in Acadian parishes where the sisters were requested to teach, first in New Brunswick and then in Nova Scotia and Prince Edward Island. Where the Acadian people had been anglicized, the sisters worked to revive the French language. In certain areas where they did not succeed, they nevertheless bought about an understanding between the Protestant and French Catholic population. Goodwill and courage replaced money and comfort as they continued to open houses, take the direction of schools, give solid instruction to Acadian youth, and inculcate pride in their mother tongue. They say that people who lose their language also lose their faith; the sisters saved both.

In 1943 Mother Marie-Jeanne-de-Valois, a dynamic, clearsighted, audacious member of the Council and later General Superior initiated classical studies at the college level with a view to establishing a college. The first candidates in Cours classique were few indeed, but the sisters who were most discerning knew that a college had a future. In 1947 they built Notre-Dame d'Acadie College in Moncton. The future was assured and the college affiliated with St. Joseph University (later the University of Moncton) offered degrees through this affiliation. During its existence it educated Acadian women who became well-known in the arts, music, literature, and public life, exercising important roles in Acadian culture and Canadian society. Inspired by this initial college for women, other colleges were opened by English Canadians for women in New Brunswick, thus making considerable impact on the community as a whole.

From 1945 to 1960 the Congregation opened many other houses and schools throughout the Maritimes which contributed greatly to the field of education serving as a liaison between small village schools and large modern high schools. At that time only religious communities could, in the French milieu of Canada, occupy those strategic posts. In the Maritime provinces the education given to boys and girls in schools both public and parochial helped many villages to find and express their own identity. Thus the sisters in a way performed a missionary work in that respect.

In 1951 the Congregation made its first contact with Nova Scotia by establishing a convent in Weymouth which was to have a far-reaching consequences leading to the opening, by the 1970s, of eight more houses between Kentville and Pubnico, a distance of some 200 kilometers, taking root in Humphrey, Grande-Digue, and Sainte-Marie, and Saint Paul. They then accepted invitations to open two more in Prince Edward Island, which, like Nova Scotia, threatened to have its small population of Acadians assimilated into the English language and culture.

At the end of the 1950s the school consolidations, which had become very acceptable in the Maritimes, were not favored in Prince Edward Island. There the people preferred their small village schools to the centralized, the educational system being instituted by the Ministry of Education and its Board. But the Acadians, desirous of having their schools on the same level as those of the other provinces, decided, with permission of the government, to build a central school in the region of Egmont Bay. The government agreed because they saw it as a means of creating a precedent capable of conquering the prejudices of the rest of the province. At that point religious only could assume charge of such a project. Urged on by the Bishop of Charlottetown, Monsignor McEachern, the community answered the request of the Acadian people and in 1959 a few sisters began to teach in Mount Carmel. In 1960 a new sister was put in charge of organizing Evangeline School. The enterprise was a real success. The following year the sisters opened a second convent in Egmont Bay, judging it an opportune time to do this. The sisters had the work of preparing a group of men and women teachers to take up the teaching as soon as possible. By the end of a few years they had a competent teaching staff.

As the sisters aged and began to retire, they knew that their work of educating Acadian people to their language and culture would be carried on by lay educators. They had laid in the pieces contributing to the larger mosaic of Acadian culture.

After Vatican II the sister staff grew smaller and the works necessarily decreased. In 1965 Notre-Dame-d'Acadie College closed, and the high school followed shortly after. The success of Moncton university and modern high schools obliged its sister servants to retire. They immediately took up missionary work and education in foreign countries. Today the sisters' work has moved from education to pastoral ministry and service of the poor. They serve in Peru, Japan, Colombia, and Haiti. In 1996 the Haiti mission is still open and two of their missionary sisters continue to brave the conditions of this third-world country in quest of a dreamed liberation.

But from its foundation Les Religieuses de Notre-Dame-Du-Sacré Coeur's vision was more or less local, despite its continued availability to enlarge its field of action, particularly in nontraditional ministries. They walk with their sisters and brothers toward the end of the millennium, witness of a world in deep change, accepting this period of history with all its hazards. Tomorrow will be different from today; yet it will be the same as far as a deep engagement to serve God and the Church is concerned. It was the same in Elizabeth Seton's time in the birth of a new nation; in Monsignor Louis Thomas Conway's time in the epidemic; in Suzanne Cyr and her companions' time as they prepared to found a new congregation. Each time there was a challenge to face, a people to serve, a God and God's will to follow. It is God who gives the sign to new life and new ventures.

Notes

1. Sister Eleanor Casey, DC, Southeast Province, Emmitsburg, MD.; Sister Patricia Coughlin, DC, Northeast Province, Albany, NY.; Sister Catherine Madigan, DC, East Central Province, Evansville, IN.; Sister Genevieve Keusenkothen, DC, West Central Province, St. Louis, MO.; Sister Marjory Ann Baez, DC, West Province, Los Altos Hills, CA.
2. Sister Miriam Corcoran, SCN, Margaret Rodericks, SCN, Nazareth, Kentucky.
3. Sister Joan Marie Freer, SC, and Yolanda DeMola, SC, New York, NY.
4. Sister Judith Metz, SC, Cincinnati, Ohio.
5. Sister Madeleine Keating, SC, Halifax, Nova Scotia.
6. Sister Helen O'Neil, SCIC, Saint John, New Brunswick, Canada.
7. Sisters Mary Carita Pendergast,SC, Anne Gertrude Coleman,SC, Convent Station, N.J.
8. Sister Kathleen Coman, SCL, Education; Sister Mary Catherine Dougherty, SCL, Religious Education, Leavenworth, Kansas.
9. Sister Francis de Sales, Joyce, SC, Greensburg, Pennsylvania.
10. Sister M. Denise Hibel, VSC, Pittsburg, Pennsylvania.
11. Sister Margaret Mach, VSC, Bedford, Ohio.

12. Sister M. Anne Francis Campbell, OLM, Charleston, South Carolina.
13. Sister Imelda Guignard, Les Religieuses de Notre-Dame-du-Sacré-Coeur, Montcton, N.B., Canada.

Chapter Five

Nontraditional Ministries

The Federation of Sisters and Daughters of Charity sees its future in a radically open and changing religious life. Its resources of intellect, education, experience, insight, and expertise provide new ways of coping with present and future needs, not only with the needs of the deprived people of the world but also with those who have the resources but are not using them for the benefit of life on this planet.

Within each congregation there are many Sisters and Daughters of Charity now involved in individual ministries far removed from the institutional work of nuns in the past. So numerous are they and so far-reaching their influence on the present generation that it is difficult to make a selection. Some examples from each of the thirteen congregations will offer an insight into the work of sisters today. These examples are representative of similar ministries undertaken by countless sisters throughout the world. They embrace new ways of dealing with legislators in government, in big corporations, and in the Church, in social work, in third-world countries, in health care, education, ecology, and in the spiritual life.[1]

POLITICS AND THE GOVERNMENT

In politics, for example, the American political stance in El Salvador was challenged by a young Vincentian Sister of Charity from Bedford, Ohio, Sister Mary Ann Flannery. As cofounder of Cleveland's Central American Interreligious Task Force, organized to challenge President Reagan's policies on third-world nations, which whom he felt were procommunist and a threat to national security. Thousands of innocent people were slain as a result. Sister Mary Ann worked for the Sanctuary Movement for Central American refugees. With many other sisters she marched for social justice for the poor in El Salvador. Sister Mary Ann was part of the team that helped bring refugees to Canada. Her congregation, of which she was General Superior, have a very progressive agenda for the rights of others, especially on their mission in El Salvador. It was their sisters who were called upon to identify the sisters of other Roman Catholic congregations who were martyred in El Salvador a few years ago. Sister made three trips to El Salvador, the last one to a guerilla camp where she stayed for three weeks at the height of the country's civil war. She interviewed labor leaders, religious leaders, journalists – all of whom provided stories of the oppression there. She was heavily involved in this activity for twelve years. In 1989 their group was exposed on national television as one of fourteen American groups engaged in so-called anti-American activities. The FBI had been watching them for some years. Sister Mary Ann is a freelance writer for *The Cleveland Plain Dealer* and presently Assistant Professor of Communications at John Carroll University. Her doctoral dissertation is on the trial of eleven persons who provided sanctuary to illegal immigrants in Tucson, Arizona, in the mid-1980s.

The newspaper *Central America Education and Advocacy* gives its readers information on the realities of what is happening there and points out what social justice-minded Americans can do about it through legislation. Its editor is Sister Margaret Dowling, former President of the New York Sisters of Charity, Mount Saint Vincent-on-the-Hudson. Human rights is the central focus. Sister

Margaret is also the Lower New York State Coordinator of NETWORK, a National Catholic Social Justice lobby in Washington, D.C. Using every form of communication, she informs the district of major issues and what they must do in terms of legislation. An activist on health-care reform, housing, and welfare reform, she gets detailed updates that she shares with those interested in responding to the needs of the poor.

In Canada there are also sisters working through legislators to aid the poor and oppressed. One of these is Sister Virginia Turner, a Sister of Charity of Halifax and a social worker. She is Senior Adviser to the Attorney General of Ontario and thus in a position to recommend assistance for the victims of family violence and homelessness. She can introduce programs for children's aid, unemployed women, single parents, and for those needing occupational therapy. Her Master's degree in Social Welfare Policy and Administration is a suitable background for her work as senior adviser to government officials in such fields as defendent and appelate needs, support for victims of crime and for the vulnerable. She can monitor legal aid for women and children, and for the disabled and mentally incompetent whose estates are handled by the province. The effects of violence on women and children, and the neglect of children are also areas in which Sister Virginia can be effective.

Another area needing monitoring is that of the neglected deaf. A certified interpreter for the deaf is a Vincentian Sister of Charity in Pittsburgh, Pennsylvania, Sister Rita Gesu. She worked with the deaf, fighting the system, the courts, the social services, to get the law changed that claimed the defendant in court must pay for the interpreter. Eventually Sister and the group with whom she worked were successful. One of her lucky breaks was an occasion when she was in court interpreting for a deaf defendant. The judge was blind. It made the headlines of the newspapers and the TV national news. Sister Rita and Judge Leonard Staisey became good friends, and he became her powerful supporter and link with the system.

Advocacy against the death penalty is another political arena for the Sisters of Charity. Sister Therese Bangert of the Sisters of Charity of Leavenworth is just such an advocate. Her career in religious life has been spent mainly in a world of pain with the vulnerable, the abused, the abandoned, and young criminals. Realizing how important it is to become involved in the political process if she is to accomplish anything for those helpless people, she obtained a government appointment to the Kansas Sentencing Commission and to the Mental Health and Corrections Committee as the Court Appointed Special Advocate in the juvenile system. It was through her work in the Kansas Legislature that she realized how vital it is for Americans to be involved in the political process. She is presently Associate Coordinator of the Kansas Coalition Against the Death Penalty. Through her advocacy work she realizes how negative the so-called solutions can be. Violence is used to solve violence! Black people are less valued than white people in our society. The lives of the poor are expendable. Sister Therese points out that we have lost touch with the Jesus of the gospel who was cruelly executed but whose followers did not seek vengeance. Instead they told his story. She has met such like-minded people who have had a family member murdered but who are still against the death penalty. They have allowed her to glimpse the power of forgiveness in a whole new way.

Labor relations is another field in which the sisters are working. Probably the first Sister Personnel Director to sit on a Negotiating Committee (Holy Family Hospital,

Prince Albert, Saskatchewan, 1973) negotiating a contract with the Canadian Union of Public Employees (hospital workers) in the Socialist Province of Saskatchewan was Sister Laura Hughes of the New Brunswick-based Sisters of Charity of the Immaculate Conception. The majority of members on the Negotiating Committee were males, who, it was said, cleaned up their language that year! Sister Laura brought a totally different aspect to that job as a friend, a counselor, and a Religious. She tried to be fair to both sides and had the reputation of being a mediator with a very low grievance area. Much was solved in her office. The hospital employees were from the Ukraine, Poland, and eastern Europe. There were also Métis (mixture of French and native Indian) as well as pure Natives. It was and still is a male-dominated world and she is a woman in that ethos but a woman with a sense of her own dignity and worth. From 1990 to 1994 Sister Laura Hughes was Personnel Manager of St. Joseph's Hospital in Saint John, New Brunswick. In 1995 she was appointed member of Region 2 Hospital Corporation, a large secular corporation encompassing nine buildings, where she continues working as a negotiator.

The sisters have penetrated the legal field as well, many of them becoming first-rate lawyers. Sister Kathleen Gilbride, a Sister of Charity of New York, is a lawyer involved in social concerns and corporate responsibility. It is her job to keep her congregation informed of current social issues and of some corporations' indifference to those issues. The congregations of Sisters of Charity in the Federation have taken a similar public stance and can go on record for filing shareholders' resolutions in companies in which these congregations hold stock. For example the New York community has, in the recent past, filed resolutions against General Motors' foreign military sales, against City Corps' unfair criteria in lending to foreign countries, against Texaco Oil and Gas for their poor affirmative action and lack of equal employment opportunities for African-Americans and women, against New York State's death penalty. The sisters' positive activities involve influencing New York State legislation to pass laws curbing domestic and other violence against women; building Seton House in East Harlem in 1993 for sixteen homeless families with a loan from the Sisters of Charity and financial assistance from New York State; holding a large alternative Investment Portfolio in a local bank that makes small business and housing loans. They also have investments that lend to borrowers who have difficulty accessing money through normal channels such as banks and credit unions. They have investments specifically dedicated to building housing for the poor. The CEOs of large corporations have become very wary of what they consider the sisters' interference in affairs that the CEOs consider outside the field of their expertise, a comment made to this writer by a retired President of one of the largest companies in the United States.

After twenty years in hospital administration, Sister Marjorie Shelvy, a Daughter of Charity in the Western Province, felt called to another field in her service of the poor. She began the arduous task of preparing for and then attending law school in 1988. As a law student, she was accepted as a law clerk at the Legal Aid Foundation of Los Angeles in the Government Benefits Unit, taking calls from clients who did not receive their welfare benefits, e.g., General Relief, AFDC, and food stamps. After passing the California Bar Exam in 1992, Sister began work for Legal Aid and developed a specialty in Foster Care benefits. She found it very satisfying to obtain benefits for grandmothers, aunts, cousins raising a relative's children. Her favorite client was a grandmother raising six grandchildren, a woman of faith, patience, perseverance. In 1996 after three years of arguing with the county agency, going to court, winning the case, returning to the county for more confrontations, four of the six children were acknowledged as entitled to retroactive Foster Care. Grandmother used the money to buy a house for the children. Currently the favorable decision on the other two children is being appealed by the state, so Sister will be back in court again. Sister admires what the poor are trying to do for themselves and their families, with the state and county putting ever greater obstacles in their way. She feels blessed to be working with a number of wonderful attorneys who do public interest work. They give generously to promote justice for the poor.

The sisters inform the political positions they take with prayer. A British Peace Group (Gulf Peace Team) just before the Gulf War asked Sister Eileen Storey, a New York Sister of Charity and former Fulbright scholar, to join 100 activists representing almost every country to assemble on the border of Iraq (Baghdad, Mosul) at a campsite given them by Iraq as a "Peace Presence" trying by prayer to prevent the war. Sister Eileen led a meditation for the group each morning. They then spent the day together discussing their vision of a better world. Shortly before the war began, they had to return home. Yet they felt that their presence had been noted, their stance against war recorded. One of the few people admitted to Iraq today, Sister Eileen Storey travels there annually as a guest of the Ministry of Culture and Information.

The encouragement of prayer to bring warring factions to peaceful solutions is universal. The Roman Catholic Church has a history of inaugurating and supporting higher education in this effort. Pope Paul VI in 1965 founded, on the West Bank in Palestine, Bethlehem University where the majority of students are Muslim. Sister Mary Elizabeth Early of the New York Sisters of

Charity was invited there as Professor of English. She helped found at the University a House of Prayer to bring the three major faiths into dialogue – Muslims, Jews and Christians. One Muslim student, a young man, said to her, "Your God Jesus, my God Allah – same God!" The House of Prayer was a rarified atmosphere, but Sister Elizabeth, seeing the terrible oppression of the Palestinians, felt she had to become more involved with them. She visited their homes and refugee camps, made friends with them, and grew to love them. Her work today continues to be prayer-oriented to achieve peaceful solutions to oppression.

POLITICS AND THE CHURCH

The sisters' relationship with the institutional Church is today in a precarious position. Religious women in the Church are not recognized on an equal basis with male religious, nor are their requests for equality adequately addressed. They continue to be classed, whether consciously or not, by hierarchy and clergy as second-rate, despite the enormous influence they have had in the past two hundred years as educators, health-care givers, missionaries, and social workers. As they face a new century with its new demands they are highly sensitive and, at times, cynical of the politics in the Church. They realize the necessity of facing political intrigue with integrity, courage, and forthrightness.

As our culture changes rapidly, the sisters know they must learn to walk the fine line between challenging that culture where it needs to be challenged and simultaneously being in tune with it so that they can clearly see what the needs of the people are. The really big change, claims Sister Noreen Neary, a Sister of Charity of Convent

Station, New Jersey, is the sisters' relationship with the institutional Church:

> It is a Church that continues to see sisters as second-rate. Yet it has a long tradition of standing up for human rights. For everything good about it, one can also say the opposite: it has a history of pacifism, but wars were waged in its name; it promotes the dignity of the person, but denigrates some of its own members; it offers a critique of culture, but is co-opted by the leaders of culture; it has a long tradition of intellectualism, but sometimes stifles intellectual inquiry. Let us as sisters, not lose the vision of our founding mothers. Let us study how that vision can be lived out today.[2]

Sister Noreen maintains that the sisters today have much to learn from those early nineteenth-century sisters who initiated the congregations to which we belong today. They challenged the culture of their times, but they also fit into it.

The Director of Ecumenical and Interfaith Relations for the Canadian Conference of Catholic Bishops with an office in Ottawa, responsible for relations between the Catholic Church and other groups including Protestants, Hebrews, Buddhists, Hindus, is a Sister of Charity of Halifax. Sister Donna Geernaert has a Ph.D. in Theology with a dissertation on the Evolutionary Perspective of Teilhard de Chardin. She works with the Canadian Council of Churches, and was appointed by the Vatican in 1991 to the Plenary Assembly of the World Council of Churches Commission on Faith and Order. For all Dialogue groups between Catholic and non-Catholic churches, Sister Donna's task is to oversee the Dialogues. Her portfolio is women's concerns and ways of improving the role of women in the Church. She represented the congregation at the NGO (Non-Governmental Organization Forum on Women) being held in Bejing, China, at the same time as the United Nations Fourth World Conference on Women in 1995. Since her return, Sister Donna has spoken eloquently on the conference and on the role of women from an international perspective.

Sister Patricia Wilson of the Seton Hill, Greensburg, Pennsylvania, Sisters of Charity has for ten years been with the Marriage Tribunal of the Diocese of Raleigh, North Carolina, and, for the last six years its Director. It is her responsibility to oversee the administration of those Church Laws that are applicable to previously married individuals who petition for an annulment. Her day-to-day work involves the painful meeting with hurt petitioners, and, occasionally, with angry, vindictive respondents, as well as with anti-Catholic parties (peculiar to the South) who were named as witnesses. There is also tension between individuals who believe the Tribunal takes too long to process a case, and the Roman Rota who believe that American Tribunals expedite too many cases. Sister Patricia's work can be emotionally draining as she reads numerous cases of abusive marriages often entered into by individuals who themselves came from extremely dysfunctional families. But what encourages her are the many petitioners who speak positively of a nullity process enabling a healing and closure to the pains of a failed marriage, a healing that was not facilitated by the process of civil dissolution. The Tribunal's requirement to prepare a comprehensive history of self/former spouse and their relationship from courtship to final separation can be likened to a moral assessment of one's life and sharing it with a trusted other person, thus bringing about a healing far beyond a determination of one's freedom to marry.

Gradually as the number of priests diminish and parishes are left without a pastor, sisters have been invited to take over this ministry. Sister Patricia Godi, a New

Jersey Sister of Charity, is "Resident Pastoral Minister" of a small, rural parish in central Mississippi. The majority of her parishioners are rural African-Americans. The others are Caucasian, Choctaw Native American, Hispanic, and Filipino. About 70% of the parishioners live at or below the poverty line. Each culture is unique in its gifts as well as its needs. Sister's ministerial responsibilities include all pastoral, liturgical, educational, administrative, financial, and building and grounds maintenance aspects of parish life. They maintain a second-hand clothing shop on the parish grounds where the local poor may come for clothing. Their Liturgy Committee and Parish Pastoral Council are multicultural by design to represent the parish membership of good, dedicated folks, deeply interested in their parish community. Sister Patricia lives alone in the Parish House, which was formerly the Rectory. There is no doubt that Sister Patricia Godi finds her ministry richly fulfilling.

Sister Mary Beth Moore spent several years in Peru with the Halifax Sisters of Charity. The original 1968 group of four sisters and two priests from Halifax developed a methodology to gather a disparate group of poor people in a newly-formed squatter settlement near the city of Chiclayo known as Victoria Nueva. The seminal work, which would become famous first in Latin America and then within the whole Church, was *A Theology of Liberation* by a native Peruvian diocesan priest, Gustavo Gutierrez. Organizing work was based on a reading of the gospel that saw Jesus as liberator of the poor, spokesperson of the "God of life" who was scandalized by the subhuman conditions God's people had to endure. The missioners brought to the task their expertise in theology, pedagogy, social work, and health care. But a deliberate choice was made to spend every effort on empowering lay leadership. This meant the transfer of skills to unsophisticated people at a pace and in the style of the people themselves. The missioners strove to keep in mind the long-range goal of ownership of the mission by the people who lived there. By 1970, La Victoria, a settlement of 50,000 persons, boasted of three churches built with local volunteer labor symbolizing the bonding of the communities, and a fifty-fifty cost-sharing between the people and the Archdiocese of Halifax. The missioners facilitated the planning, negotiation, and communication skills necessary for a common project. Each church developed its own internal organization based on small group cells that studied the Gospel and reached out to the surrounding community. The people had little need to distinguish between pastoral and social work. They formed teams to hold the wake services in bereaved homes. They spoke up in the Teachers Union, dug ditches for the sewerage system block by block, learned to assume leadership in the high schools.

Committed Christians in La Victoria who name the Gospel as their "option for the poor," never comprised more than 1 or 2% of the population. Their influence is greatly disproportionate to their numbers. The government has pursued policies to please first-world creditors rather than attending to the basic needs of its people. The Church is still a trusted institution. For the poor majority "church" is experienced at the local level through civic leaders formed and influenced by the Christian community. For thirty years now the Sisters of Charity of Halifax have accompanied the Peruvian people, and service has evolved with the needs of the times. One of the most important developments is the explosive growth of communal kitchens run exclusively by women who cook and feed 150 children a day in each kitchen. The sisters act as moderators teaching the women accounting, crisis management, long-range planning, and other skills. In Lima a health cooperative draws on the gifts of doctors who volunteer twice a week while the women, under the sisters' guidance, do consultations and dispense medicines daily. In a southern city of Ilo a team of sisters, some of whom belong to the original band of 1968, are beginning again in a brand-new squatter settlement. The reality of the Latin American people, their gifts and the injustices they bear, seen in the light of the Gospel – that has been the focus of the work of the Sisters of Charity of Halifax in Latin America.

POLITICS AND SOCIAL WORK

From the seventeenth century to the present, Sisters and Daughters of Charity have been engaged in social work in countries throughout the world. Sister Jane Albert Mehrens, a Sister of Charity of Leavenworth, Kansas, is Program Director of Catholic Social Services. There are political ramifications to this position, as she is landlord/tenant advocate. She examines housing for improvements or condemnation. Her work also includes an Emergency Assistance Center dealing with the immediate needs of the poor – utilities, rent, medication, gas, transportation, shelter, school supplies, window fans for the elderly, sick, and children. Those who need housing may live from three to five months in one of two Hope Houses, which Catholic Social Services sponsor. Caseworkers are at the disposal of the families twenty-four hours a day. Financial support is provided by the people of Leavenworth in a fund. Sister Jane and her group also work in Leavenworth with disabled veterans just beginning to recover their health. The sisters offer them a transitional home until they are ready to move out into the community. The government paid $40,000 to remodel the house. Catholic Social Services offers professional counseling as well as financial help to those in need. Sister Jane's office is where the poor are, in the impoverished area of the city. Her work is politically oriented to achieve adequate and immediate help for the poor from government sources.

Some women were activists for the poor before they entered religious life; some entered and later returned to secular life as courageous activists for the destitute. Sister Mary Kay Bush was one of these. She entered the Sisters of Charity of Cincinnati in 1957 but left later on and married. She and her husband were activists in Detroit, initiating "Block Clubs" to promote neighborliness and safety against gangs. They put out a local newspaper for the civic community in Jefferson Chalmers, Detroit (70% African-American professionals and poor blacks). To prevent drug-dealing and vandalism, they and their associates boarded up vacant houses until occupied. Although Caucasian, they experienced the deep prejudice and hatred of the blacks by the white community. Mary Kay and her husband had three children who are today professionals in economy and communications. In 1976 she and her husband divorced but remained friends. From 1978 to 1988 Mary Kay was an Associate member of the Sisters of Charity of Cincinnati. In 1988 she obtained an annulment of her marriage and entered the congregation. Her former husband never remarried, but remains her friend and loving support. As a Sister of Charity, Mary Kay is a Grade School Principal continuing to dedicate her life to the needs of the poor in whatever way she can achieve her goals.

The founder of Outreach, a center to help the poor of any color or denomination, Sister Mary Albert Greer is a Sister of Charity of Our Lady of Mercy in Charleston, South Carolina. She located a house on John's Island that the sisters purchased in 1989, two weeks before Hurricane Hugo hit with devastating results to the house and to the homes of the poor. The sisters had already distributed brochures to try to overcome the bigotry among both the black and white community of poor people toward the Catholic Church. They had divided John's Island among team members, issuing invitations to Christian Hope House, but with little results. After Hugo hit they no longer needed to advertise. The poor came in droves for help, and the sisters were able to satisfy them. Donations of food, clothing, and monetary help poured in from people in Florida, Georgia, and California. They had a room for each type of donation, and on the porch 200 gallons of water. The needy lined up, and one of the sisters took their names, addresses, and number of family members. They were then directed to take whatever they needed. A new Christian Hope House was built by the sisters. Their reputation spread, and gifts continue to pour in. At Christmas two truckloads of toys and clothing were sent down from Fairfield, Connecticut, just one example of the generosity of people everywhere. Sister Mary Albert's project is continuing successfully on John's Island.

Sister Carol Wentworth, before entering the Sisters of Charity of Our Lady of Mercy in Charleston in 1985, was a teacher, a Physical Education and Athletic Director, winning two State Championships in Volley Ball; playing and coaching golf, softball, basketball and field hockey. Presently she is a staff member of Outreach in charge of Nails, a home repair program in which she assists the poor and teaches them the rudiments of repair work, a "Do-it-yourself" program. She is also involved in a senior literacy program for the elderly.

Another form of social work that is not new to the sisters is the care of the elderly. Sister Ann Margaret Boone, a Sister of Charity of Nazareth, Kentucky, a descendent of Daniel Boone's brother, Squire Boone, is currently Manager of HUD with two buildings of low-income housing for the elderly on the grounds of the Motherhouse in Nazareth, called Nazareth Village. It is devoted to the dignity of the elderly and their independent living. Sister Ann Margaret says that what we can do for the elderly when we unite our common efforts in ministry can be very challenging. Like her Boone ancestors, she has the energy, enthusiasm, fearless determination, and political know-how to move ahead for those in need.

A decade ago, Catholic Charities in the Diocese of San Jose, California, embarked on an ambitious program. Their goal was to attract fifty Vietnamese elders to the John XXIII Multi-Service Center to provide services to meet their needs. The idea was to break the cycle of depression, loneliness, and isolation, which many elderly Asians experience in a new country, by fostering their assimilation into the American culture. Sister Marie Christiane Nguyen, a Daughter of Charity of the Province of the West, formerly of the Vietnam Province, roamed the streets and grocery stores to find Asians in need. Today 700 Asian elders, including a growing Chinese population, participate in programs and services through the Asian Elderly Program (AEP). Comprehensive bilingual/bicultural English/Vietnamese case management, including outreach, counseling, monitoring, support groups, prayer services, and mainstream socialization and recreation programs are provided. For many it is their primary means of social, emotional, and spiritual support.

Covenant House in Manhattan, with its worldwide reputation of helping children and young people of the streets who have no place to sleep and no one to guide them, is now headed by a Daughter of Charity of the

Northeast Province, Sister Mary Rose McGeady. A clinical psychologist, Sister Mary Rose is CEO and President of the thirteen Covenant Houses in five countries – the United States, Canada, Mexico, Guatemala, and Honduras. 35,000 adolescents are provided with food, shelter, medical care, and counseling each year. Their communica-tions with the public bring in about 5,000 pieces of mail a day containing donations amounting to about $127,000 daily. They need at least that to survive. Sister Mary Rose received the Fifth Annual Bishop's Communication Award for "Excellence in overall achievement in communications." Money management is a modern apostolate if they are to help the poor. Sister Mary Rose visits every Covenant House once a year. She attends Board Meetings and directs the programs for fund-raising. She says, "The families are falling apart so fast and the kids are the fall-out."[3] Sister Mary Rose has the foundlings – the street kids of the end of the century. She understands the need to be politically aware of government sources for aid. Hillary Rodham Clinton, in her 1995 acceptance address on the occasion of receiving an Honorary Doctorate from Mount Saint Vincent University in Halifax, Nova Scotia, based that speech on the necessity of educating mothers if the children are to escape the perils of violence in today's society. The Sisters of Charity have a longstanding reputation for supporting women. Sister Mary Arthel Cline, a Leavenworth Sister of Charity, is a social worker with a Mother-to-Mother Ministry. She pairs mothers of the poor with volunteer mentors who are mothers of middle-income families. These well-to-do ladies are willing and eager to walk with and learn from the poor. It is a reciprocal arrangement. Sister Mary Arthel and her volunteer mothers set up activities for destitute mothers and their children. The middle-income mothers bring their children to mix with the children of the poor. Sister Mary encourages middle-income mothers to try to influence legislators to pass, for example, the Welfare Reform Act. This intentional friendship between two classes of mothers and legislators is creating community. It also encourages lower-class mothers to take advantage of free educational opportunities. It educates mothers that they may raise their standards of living and thus offer their children security against violence and crime.

A frequently unrecognized need in society today is that of women trying to deal with the loss of a spouse, whether through divorce, abandonment, or death. Sister Margaret Toner, General Superior of the Sisters of Charity of the Immaculate Conception in Saint John, New Brunswick, Canada, has been committed to this ministry. These women are the poor, the marginalized, those cut off from society. Their children are often looked down on by other children; their friends shun them. Sister Margaret with genuine compassion offers her loving support and help to many of these poor women. She has gradually become close friends with the women she helps. In the course of her work she watched women recover, develop, and get a sense of themselves, a belief in themselves. Again it became a reciprocal arrangement. The women she was helping kept her attuned to herself and to what sisters are called to be and to do today.

Women in general need, on occasion, peace and quiet to work out their problems. This unidentified group has, in Leavenworth, Kansas, been the object of Sister Anne Paula Loendorf's ministry. She is the founder of the House of Menuha (Hebrew "to rest"). Because she always worked with women's groups, she often heard them say, "If I only had a quiet place to go to and think!" She talked to such exhausted women. One lady asked her if she could stay at the home of a friend of Sister Ann's for two days while the friend was away. She needed to sort things out without the presence of her husband. It was that incident that caused Sister to found the House of Menuha, a nonprofit corporation from which no woman would be turned away. The Board purchased an eight-room house for $86,000 and furnished it. They planted a garden of reflection – trees, flowers, birdbaths, benches – in an elderly people's neighborhood, Shalom Plaza. The House of Menuha is never empty. Many female therapists send women there – women from ages thirty to seventy, women in transition, examining the values in their lives. The mission of the House of Menuha is to provide a comfortable and safe place for rest, reflection, and renewal for women.

Sister Linda Roth, a Sister of Charity of Leavenworth, Kansas, is Coordinator of Job-Training for the economically disadvantaged, with *El-Centro,* founded seventeen years ago by Father Ramon Gaitan for Spanish-speaking, people but currently for everyone in need of employment. Most of the applicants are women. In two years she has trained five men and fifty-five women in computer skills and other areas. Currently they are expanding their programs to include basic skills to gain entrance into college. Dedicated to improving family life, Sister Linda and her colleagues, employment specialists, also conduct a bilingual day care center and two tutoring programs, one for the children of migrants and the other for regular elementary school children. Sister Linda finds this work most rewarding, helping people develop skills so that they can come off welfare and obtain employment, health insurance, and other benefits to support their families.

The resettlement of refugees is also addressed by sisters of every congregation.

Sister Regina Tevis, a Vincentian Sister of Charity of Bedford, Ohio, resettles refugees in the Cleveland Diocese. In four years she has resettled 375 refugees by contacting churches or communities to sponsor a free case, for example, the Serbian and Croatian churches, the Iraqi community. Sister finds a family who will take them in, a hospital for health screening, food, clothes, job referrals, welfare, classes in English as a Second Language. Sister Regina has had the support of government in these endeavors.

Social work in "the hollers" of Kentucky with the Appalachian people is provided by many sisters and priests. Sister Liz Wendeln, President of the Sisters of Charity of Nazareth, Kentucky, worked in those rural areas for many years, helping the poor in various ways. She was Director of Parish Ministry Councils in the mountains and Director of RORE, the Rural Office of Religious Education. After Vatican II rural people were not as well ministered to by the Church as were city people, who were far better served. Sister therefore plunged into this work with thirteen counties under her jurisdiction. Sister Liz became known and loved by the Appalachian people for her genuine loving interest in them.

Sisters Christine Rody and Ruth Ann Rody, Vincentian Sisters of Bedford, Ohio, are sisters from the same family. They exemplify in their lives the many sisters of the same parents who have dedicated their lives to religion. One congregation alone had two sets of five sisters each, from two families in Boston. The Rody sisters entered the congregation in the early 1960s. Christine was the first Vincentian Sister to serve in El Salvador. She was Delegate for Religious appointed by the Bishop of the Cleveland Diocese. Elected General Superior (1983-1991), Sister Christine has been a courageous leader. Her sister, Sister Ruth Ann, is a nurse and chairperson of St. Joseph ministry for the terminally ill which she founded in 1979.

There are twelve volunteers of whom nine are laypersons. Four are registered nurses who train the others. They care for any terminally ill person who lives within a twenty-minute car drive of the Motherhouse. One of her first patients said she did not want to put days to her life but life to her days. Since 1979 Sister's group has cared for about 500 terminally ill patients who have experienced "life to their days."

Before Vatican II the sisters were often not in a position to help their elderly parents by providing nursing home care or senior citizen residences. Today that has become part of their dedicated service. Sister Lorraine d'Entremont of the Notre-Dame-du-Sacré-Coeur Sisters is the administrator of a residence for the sisters' elderly parents who need a place to live and/or nursing care at a very modest fee. Opened in January 1983, it is a beautiful and spacious residence in Dieppe, not far from Moncton. Everyone there has one thing in common – a daughter who is a nun. Although the parents say the nuns give them something special in their love and care, the sisters feel that they are really the recipients.

The Daughters of Charity see their mission to the poor as the central dedication of their lives. In the 1960s, their peak period, there were 45,000 Daughters of Charity in every country of the world with the exception of Norway and Sweden. Sister Maura Hobart, a Daughter of Charity and a social worker with the Daughters of Charity in Albany, spent fifteen years in the so-called hell hole of Bedford-Stuyvesant neighborhood in Brooklyn, New York. Sister says she would not trade it for anything. The poverty and violence spawned by it among the black and Puerto Rican families needed immediate attention. Sister Maura and the other sisters gained the trust and confidence of this neglected community.

Sister Joan Repka, a New Jersey Sister of Charity, is directing Seton Center, founded and funded by the Sisters of Charity of Saint Elizabeth, Convent Station, New Jersey. Seton Center was born in Jersey City to answer the needs of poor African-American, Hispanic, Central American, and Filipino families. The primary focus is a family-systems approach – making information available on prevention programs for alcohol, drug, smoking, and sexually transmitted diseases. There are programs for parenting: traditional parents, single parents, and teen parent groups. Women and young girls are helped to take control of their lives. The majority of these groups are facilitated by mental health professionals from agencies operating in Jersey City. The sisters have a program called Pro KIDS (Keeping Individual Decisions Smart). It consists of classroom modules and presentations by health professionals on sound health practices. Seton Center also provides programming for school faculties with special emphasis on multicultural understanding and on teaching techniques to meet the needs of diverse populations.

Prisoners and their welfare have also been the focus of many sisters' social work. Sister Alice Joseph Brady, a Sister of Charity of Our Lady of Mercy in Charleston, South Carolina, is an educator. One of her former students was arrested for murder. She therefore went into prison ministry and was most successful in helping male prisoners. She now conducts a Phone-assistance Ministry with sexually-abused men, having been asked to do this because of her background in the prisons. As she expresses it, she is merely a stop-gap to keep them from falling by the wayside. Basically she tells them it is not their fault; there is life after this; they have survived for a reason. She encourages them to get help from a psychiatrist. Sister Alice has found her real ministry with men to whom, as they put it, she comes across as a mother.

Prison Network, a ministry of the Sisters of Charity of Seton Hill, Greensburg, Pennsylvania, was initiated by Sister Eleanor Dillon as a service to the women inmates of the Westmoreland County Prison in Greensburg. It functions to connect the women inmates with the world outside – family, friends, legal persons, rehabilitation facilities. It is the first step to help the inmate prepare for release. It has had no predecessor in the county. Sister Eleanor volunteered to give Bible Study classes to the women inmates in 1994 and through this learned that the women did nothing but "time" in their new facility. Eventually Narcotics Anonymous, Alcoholics Anonymous, Parents Anonymous, and Women's Services for Abused Women offered weekly classes on a volunteer attendance basis. But there was no follow-up. Sister Eleanor therefore proposed her Prison Network plan to judges, Community Council members, the Warden, the Deputy Warden, and executives of substance abuse services, all of whom approved and encouraged. With a small grant from the Sisters of Charity Mission Fund, Prison Network was born on June 8, 1994. Sister Eleanor interviews women inmates who have given their signed permission. After two or three hours of hearing and recording information by the woman about her situation when she leaves prison, Sister then makes appropriate phone calls, obtains information for the inmate to whom she writes a letter giving her the information. This prepares the inmate for housing, job opportunities, counseling, services for children. It is interesting to note that Mother Seton's daughter, Catherine, was most successful in prison ministry which is not new to the Sisters of Charity of Elizabeth Seton. "Prison Network" is listed in *Directory of Programs Serving Families of Adult Offenders* published by

U.S. Department of Justice, National Institute of Corrections.

Sister Deborah Humphreys, a Sister of Charity of St. Elizabeth, Convent Station, New Jersey, is a poet and a social worker. Here we have "the passion of the poet tempered by the patience of the therapist."[4] Sister Deborah embraces these paradoxes as she works with the underprivileged in the Lincoln Park/South Broad Street neighborhood of Newark, New Jersey. A graduate in Sociology, she came to Saint Columba Parish and School in 1975 and, with another Sister, founded the Saint Columba Neighborhood Club/El Club del Barrio committed to neighborhood improvements by holding city and county political office-holders accountable for the quality of life of the immigrants from Central and South America, the Caribbean and Africa. They achieved concrete improvements in the area by including residents in city planning for the community. In this way they also strengthened the bonds of community among them. In 1989 Sister Deborah established the Saint Columba Family Life Center focusing on building community, family by family, who were deprived of education and meaningful employment in a city beset by crime and violence due to drugs and the HIV infection. The Saint Columba Collaboration (people of diverse races and ethnicities, including Muslims, Roman Catholics and other Christians, and men and women religious) build bridges and use the tools and law and politics to effect social changes to improve conditions in the neighborhood by providing an integrated delivery system of education, health care, and pastoral and social services. In the early days they banded together to fight city hall to shut down a bar, for example. Today they challenge state legislators to defend their voting records on housing and budget allocations to grass-roots lobbyists from Saint Columba who are connected with statewide efforts to promote social justice. Sister Deborah, who has had her poetry published in a wide range of social work journals and a national anthology of peace poems, uses the "stink tree" (a ten-foot tall weed that has grown up through the metal cyclone fence, its trunk surrounding and incorporating the mineral resistance in its push toward the sun) as a metaphor for her and her colleagues' challenge to politicians:

we are not just some trees
Look at the way we have grown
fast, along the concrete borders of the street
with red-clay rowhouses, the repetitious
sound of letters
escaping through kinderclass windows and
the left-behind-for-us
memories of other families who have known
what we now see for ourselves
look how strong, how fiercely we have
held on for our
just portions of simple elements – earth,
air, water, fire
so you can't keep us down, even this cold
weave of steel
chain cannot stop our stubborn push up from
tenacious roots, straight to the sun.[5]

POLITICS AND THE MISSIONS

The Sisters and Daughters of Charity have worked consistently in third-world countries as doctors, social workers, and religious missionaries. Sister Emily Lordon of the Sisters of Charity of the Immaculate Conception worked in the soup kitchens of Latin America. They had 145 in her parish sector, Villa El Salvador, with a population of 500,000 people. This pueblo was divided into six sectors.

She was in Sector 1 with a population of 35,000 people. Her main work was the organization of soup kitchens, especially when President Fujimuri took over. In Peru Sister Emily worked with the liturgy, youth groups, and refugees. Because of terrorism the refugees had to leave their pueblos. Caught between the military and the terrorists, they came in droves down from the mountains, arriving in Peru. Sister Emily was asked to help them. When she questioned what work they did, they replied "weaving." She purchased wool and they produced beautiful products that she sold for them in Canada. Sister Emily had showers built and places for them to wash their clothing, a doctor for the sick, and a full dinner at lunch time. She felt privileged to work for the underprivileged, to be for them the voice of the voiceless.

Sister Teresa Duncan, a member of the Sisters of Charity of the Immaculate Conception, also worked with the impoverished people in Peru. This experience changed her whole value system as she observed and contributed to the formation of lay leaders, building Christian communities, seeing strong leaders arise from those uneducated people – leaders with courage in a parish of a quarter of a million people. The sisters conducted prayer services, Bible studies, anything to bring the community together. Sister Teresa also worked with Native peoples in northern Canada – the Cree and the Chippewan. This was a contrast to the Latin American missions because Canada contributed to the social welfare of their Native peoples. The sisters empowered the Native peoples to raise their status and to give them a better sense of themselves. Sister Teresa joined them in their activities and went to their Sweat Lodges, which were very spiritual experiences. The Native peoples attended Catholic liturgies, and leaders were trained to preside.

Sister Barbara Thomas, former President of the Sisters of Charity of Nazareth, Kentucky, and for twelve years Vice President of their Missions, used her office responsibly for the education of sisters in India, Nepal, Belize, and Central America. Her vision empowered many to raise their standard of living. Asked what the Federation could do, she replied that she sees a common thread running through the Federation because of our shared history. Sister Barbara Thomas feels that from this will come our shared vision, particularly as a result of the sisters' work in third-world countries, where so much is yet to be accomplished.

POLITICS AND HEALTH CARE

Health care for the poor has been one of the most outstanding works of the sisters in the United States throughout the nineteenth and twentieth centuries, and it promises to be their continued focus in the twenty-first. The most affluent country in the world has still no universal health-care plan for its people. The sisters have therefore founded numerous hospitals, cared for the sick poor, and responded when government did not. They strongly supported Hillary Rodham Clinton and her committee's plans for universal health care and were deeply disappointed when political factions prevented it from being realized. Every congregation of Sisters and Daughters of Charity in the Federation have founded altogether an enormous number of Hospitals in the United States and some hospitals in Canada. Sister Gertrude Bastnagel, a Daughter of Charity, nurse and health-care worker, Provincial of the Southeast Province (1981-1990) with headquarters in Emmitsburg, spoke of the Daughters of Charity and the large number of hospitals they established in the United States during the nineteenth and twentieth centuries. Today their nurses have to work with the problems of the environment, with crime, with illiteracy in order to improve the health of their patients. She mentioned the fact that the census in hospitals is happily down because of preventative medicine. In a recent seminar that she attended in California the emphasis was on "Healthier Communities." The word *disease,* was not even mentioned, revealing how positive is the approach today. Sister Gertrude stressed the need for interdependency in the Federation's health-care programs. The thirteen congregations in the Federation must come together in solidarity if they are to achieve the maximum in health care.

Every congregation in the Federation has contributed its services to victims of AIDS. Sister Marilyn Spink of the Kentucky Sisters of Charity opened Glade House for men with AIDS. In the spring of 1993 she opened The House of Ruth for families with members touched by HIV/AIDS. Sister Marilyn is an Associate Professor of Medical and Surgical Nursing at Spalding University in Kentucky. She has had the help of Sister Julie Driscoll, who works for peace and social justice issues and has had third world experience in India, Belize, Nicaragua, Venezuela and Mexico. Together with three other sisters in the House of Ruth's Outreach Program, they serve forty families in their homes. They offer financial assistance in crisis, volunteers for child care, and help in homes under stress. They visit AIDS patients in hospitals. The sisters plan to offer art and massage therapy, programs on holistic health, and whatever else their people request.

Sister Dorothy MacDougall, General Superior of the Sisters of Charity of Nazareth, Kentucky (1980-1988), Professor and Director of Education, is a dedicated supporter of helping the victims of AIDS and educating young and old in the prevention of AIDS. Her support in this field and the work of her congregation earned for them a nomination in the 1994 Award for Organizations Assisting in the Care of Victims with AIDS. Her congregation has encouraged health institutions to help the victims of AIDS. The sisters dedicate beds in their nursing home for people afflicted with AIDS, and form support groups for those who are HIV-positive. They also stage concerts for World AIDS Day.

Many elderly sisters are still working full-time in varied programs, particularly programs for the elderly. Sister Frances Louise Mihalak entered the Vincentians of Pittsburgh in 1927 and today, at nearly ninety years of age, she is still working full-time as a parish minister and visitor to Lutheran Nursing Home, Passavant Hospital, and Allegheny General Hospital. She prays with the patients, brings them Bibles and prayer booklets, listens to their problems. When they ask for absolution, she must tell them the Church does not allow sisters to give absolution. She must notify a priest. Her elderly patients are mystified by this. They want Sister Frances. Sister said that ministry with the elderly is one of consolation, deepening her own spirituality.

Seton Family Center in Cincinnati is another source of consolation to the sisters. It is a place where sisters offer family therapy and play therapy for children working through their problems of emotional, physical, and sexual abuse through the use of toys, puppets, and art. Established by Sister Jackie Kowalski of the Sisters of Charity of Cincinnati, a school psychologist, counselor, diagnostician, and teacher of handicapped children, it differs from conventional therapies in that it is a behavioral approach as opposed to the psychodynamic Freudian approach. Sister Jackie and her colleagues use interactive therapy with parents, to enable them to decide the main issues and determine what changes they are willing to make, as well as contracting for a time in which they are willing to make those changes. Seton Center has had remarkable success in helping both handicapped children and their parents.

Sister Mary Sepeck, SC, designs and implements the Family-Based Treatment Program of care for emotionally disturbed children at St. Christopher Ottelie, a private, nonprofit agency for foster care in New York City. It was developed to serve children who repeatedly failed to make it in foster families – seriously disturbed children with severe behavioral problems. Families are recruited for a ten-week course in parenting skills and behavioral modification. Parents are taught praise without a price tag, positive time, catching a child at being good, helping a deeply troubled child to experience his or her gifts and capacities. A component of grief work was added to help both adult and child acknowledge and deal with losses. It matches children with families, giving children guided choices. Foster families and children are assured of all the services they need. Sister Mary Sepeck also developed the Home and Community-Based Waiver Program for children able to return to their own parents and home. In 1993 she designer the Crisis Respite Program targeting families in crisis, providing short-term foster care for special-needs children in all five boroughs of New York City. She served as President of the Foster Family-Based Treatment Association, representing New York nationwide as the model became the standard of care for seriously disturbed children.

The field of nuclear medicine has also been of interest to sisters studying medicine. Sister Bernard Ann Ruebusch, a Sister of Charity of Nazareth, Kentucky, was Founder and Director of the School of Nuclear Medicine Technology and the Department of Nuclear Medicine at

St. Vincent Infirmary Medical Center in Little Rock, Arkansas (1969-1993).

Her outstanding work in nuclear medicine at Radiation Center, Fort Worth, Texas, and Presbyterian University Hospital in Pittsburgh had brought her reputation to the fore. In the late 1980s the University of Arkansas School of Medical Sciences asked her to share with them in combining the two schools. When Sister Bernard retired in 1992, the University of Arkansas presented her with a plaque "In recognition of your outstanding contribution to Nuclear Medicine Technology Education in the State of Arkansas." Sister Bernard had excellent discussions with President Bill Clinton when he was Governor of Arkansas, and with his wife, Hillary Rodham Clinton, regarding the future of health care in the United States. Their genuine interest in trying to provide universal health care was a source of deep satisfaction to Sister Bernard, despite the failure of their efforts. Because they brought it to universal attention, she feels that it will eventually be achieved.

Sister Marie Therese Sedgewick, a Daughter of Charity in the St. Louis Province, was called a "catalogue person" because she entered the congregation after reading about them in a catalogue. As Executive Director of Health and Social Services to the Poor in San Antonio, Texas, she has had a stimulating career in health care. She has been a Physical Therapist in hospitals in Waco, Texas; a member of a government committee on nutrition for women; an occupational therapist; a worker for IDN (Integrated Delivery Network), which includes several hospitals, nursing homes, and psychiatric hospitals forming a network for strength. Her work with government officials has given her a firm belief that their efforts are genuine and will have lasting results.

Sister Agnes Connelly, R.N., is Director of Mission Effectiveness in the Alliance for Catholic Health and Human Services in the Archdiocese of New York. Former President of the Congregation (1979-1987), Sister Agnes has the organizational abilities for her present position, directing a network of forty-six health and human services organizations (hospitals, nursing homes, child-care and home-care agencies). To strengthen their sense of mission and hence their Catholic identity, she sets up a mission function in each, using strategies to insure that the mission is clearly expressed and accepted by all the workers and general public involved. Her message is to extend Jesus' healing mission by developing core values such as compassion and respect.

There are many Sisters and Daughters of Charity who are medical doctors, family physicians, and pediatricians. Among these is Sister Monteil Rosenthal, M.D., a Sister of Charity of Cincinnati and a family physician. She is involved as a doctor in ten county regions of Kentucky, from those who live in the "hollers," or narrow valleys, to those folks who live on the ridges in Elliott County, Sandy Hook. She offers a full range of services to these poor families, even minor surgery. Her home visits cover all ages, from those yet to be born to a 107-year-old woman who chews tobacco, spits, swears, and does not like being shifted around. She is being taken care of by her 85-year-old son. Sister Monteil describes the folks here as desperately poor, living hand to mouth, raising vegetables on scrappy plots, canning fruit and vegetables. They continue to live there because their folks lived there. The county school system, the largest employer in the county, reflects badly on the economic system. Doctor Rosenthal learns more in five seconds walking into a patient's home than in hours in an office. The terminally ill are in her hospice where they can die with dignity amid familiar settings and family. Sister Monteil supplies supportive care, pain control, and counseling. Just her presence is enough for them. Family ties are very strong there. Everybody is literally related to everybody else. They are very insular people, suspicious of outsiders, with more trust in the familiar than in anything new. If they go to a grocery store and do not know every person in there, they will leave and never return. They do everything by the signs of the moon, even to weaning the baby from its bottle. They have their own home remedies such as an excellent one for gallstones. TV keeps them in touch with the outside world. They have bizarre notions of Catholics but do not hold them against Sister Monteil. She teaches Family Medicine, Obstetrics, Midwifery, and Nursing. Sister Monteil Rosenthal, M.D., is beloved by the people in the hollers and the ridges, as well as by her colleagues in medicine.

Sister Cynthia Loeffler, M.D., is a Daughter of Charity and a medical doctor. Her vocation to the religious life is significant. Recipient of an American College of Surgeons Scholarship, she came from her hometown in Minnesota to the National Cancer Institute in Maryland to do research. A friend brought her to the Basilica of St. Elizabeth Ann Seton in Emmitsburg. There in the Basilica she experienced an incredible sense of peace difficult to contain. Seeing a Sister praying at Our Lady's Altar, Dr. Cynthia Loeffler decided then and there to enter the congregation. Returning to her apartment, she looked up a Catholic Church in the Yellow Pages of the telephone directory. She visited the church and again experienced the same incredible sense of peace. The Presence of God in the Eucharist seemed to her to be a palpable reality in which she had never previously believed. She entered the Company of the Daughters of Charity in 1992 and finished her Formation in 1995. Her medical research had been immunology. She dovetailed into cancer research, trying to stimulate T cells and recognize tumor cells in order to destroy them. Her experience in her formation years as a Daughter of Charity brought her to a realization that she had to begin living by faith – God's presence in nature and in other people. The religious life was far more sacrificial than she had expected. Her present expectations are much more realistic than when she entered. The life of a doctor who is also a religious is for her an enriching experience. The changes in religious life are very challenging – how religious women today are perceived by the male hierarchy of the Church. The Church is addressing it but slowly. New ministries for religious women are evolving quickly – working with AIDS, drugs, child abuse. Female religious are in the forefront. Dr. Loeffler feels that we must, as Sisters and Daughters of Charity, share the network with one another while keeping a clear vision of who and what we are.

Another ministry of the sisters in the area of health care is homes for incurable patients. Sister Prudentia Bornak is a Vincentian Sister of Charity of Pittsburgh, Pennsylvania, General Secretary of the congregation and now historian. The sisters have always been in charge of the Diocesan-owned Vincentian Home, a home for incurables, run on charity, opened before the Great Depression. In 1987 they bought the home from the diocese. At last it was theirs. They did not want to lose this ministry. When the schools closed, they still had four nursing homes, several day-care centers, and a Slovak tradition of hard work. It is their work in health care that has kept their tradition of service alive and significantly healthy.

Sister Agnes McPhee, a Daughter of Charity of the Province of the West, manages Seton Guest Center at St. Vincent Medical Center, Los Angeles, California. Many of the patients are high-risk surgery patients, and Seton

Guest Center, opened in 1994, accommodates the families of those patients from out-of-town as well as families of patients in the Intensive Care Unit. The Center has twenty-two rooms, each complete with small refrigerator, phone, private bath, queen-sized bed and sofa bed. Families can now be a vital part of the healing process. Then too families can reach out to other families with similar problems and needs. They develop their own support system. Sister visits the families each day in an effort to support and encourage them.

From the initial founding of religious congregations in North America, children have been the focus of their attention, particularly orphans. But in the latter half of the twentieth century mentally retarded and emotionally disturbed children have replaced the orphans as the focus of those most in need of help. Orphanages have by and large disappeared as infants and children are placed in foster homes or given for adoption. Care of the mentally retarded, multihandicapped, and nonambulatory infants and children has been, since 1976, the dedicated profession of Sister Marianne Van Vurst, an educator and administrator, and Sister Lynn Heper, a nurse. These two Sisters of Charity of Cincinnati established a Home for Severe and Profound Mentally Retarded Infants and Children who are multihandicapped and nonambulatory. Their needs were so great and the number that the sisters and their helpers could assist was so small that in 1989 they initiated a $6.6 million fund drive, thus increasing their capacity by 50%. There are now eighteen buildings interconnected, with six cottages and eight children to a cottage. There are 140 paid employees. They care for forty-seven children and adults, male and female. The youngest is two, the oldest, thirty-six. They are funded by Medicaid, by wills, bequests, and fund drives. The home provides twenty-four-hour nursing care. Only two of the forty-seven can feed themselves. They have continually to be moved and stimulated in a variety of ways to use their senses. They love music and will try to do anything to have music played to them. All are visually impaired and ten are blind. The sisters provide education in three different handicapped schools and a workshop. Eight school buses are provided for thirty-four children, all in wheelchairs. In the reciprocal love between caregivers and children, they are a joy to the caregivers who feel that to walk into this "Home" is to experience heaven.

Institutional health care, although given up by many congregations who have divested themselves of their hospitals in favor of individual ministry, or who have not sufficient numbers of sisters to staff their hospitals, is not the case with the Daughters of Charity of the East Central Province with its Provincial House in Evansville, Indiana. They continue to emphasize the needs of the poor from an institutional base. Sister Dorothea Huber is the Visitatrix. Through her leadership and the dedicated efforts of her nurses and other health-care workers, their commitment to institutional health care continues to be successful. Owning and operating eleven large hospitals, the Daughters of Charity are seen as strong and viable in this field. Four sponsored social agencies, three large day-care centers and one home for emotionally disturbed children bring their charity care to more than $92 million (Medicaid, actual giving of food, clothing, medicine, staff-education for those who cannot afford it). They have a "sister-province" in Venezuela and support it financially. Being very conscious of new needs, such as AIDS patients, single mothers, battered and abused children, they also focus on the elderly in their own homes in an outreach program for the poor who live alone. They point out that it is their hospitals that provide them with the financial means to carry out their many programs for the poor.

POLITICS AND EDUCATION

Sister Gemma Del Duca, a Sister of Charity of Seton Hill, Greensburg, Pennsylvania, because of her awareness of what she calls "the centrality of the relationship of the Jewish people with the Church in the work of renewal," received permission to study in Israel in 1975. While there, in 1977, she became associated with a Benedictine priest, Father Isaac Jacob, OSB, at Tel Gamaliel, Bet Shemesh, about twenty miles from Jerusalem. There the study, work, and community focused on the Church within the modern State of Israel. Father Isaac was a creative leader who took the teaching of the Church since Vatican II as the framework for a Torah-Gospel community while using the Rule of Benedict (translated into Hebrew through his efforts) to work out specifics for day-to-day living in Israel. He encouraged Sister Gemma to study the history of the Shoah (the Holocaust) with Professor Yehudah Bauer at the Hebrew University. In 1987, as a result of a proposal made by Sister Gemma to the President of Seton Hill College, Dr. JoAnne Boyle, the College initiated a program for Catholic Education at the World Center for teaching the Shoah, Yad Vashem, Jerusalem. Sister Gemma has been the representative of the College at Yad Vashem for this program. At Seton Hill College the sisters set up the National Catholic Center for Holocaust Education. Sister Gemma maintains that living in Israel, where she "experienced the blessing of living the Word, Torah, and Gospel with religious lay women and men," is central to her religious life. In 1995 when Father Isaac Jacob died, Sister Gemma and her group vowed to hold fast to his teachings and to the Israeli model of community in the kibbutz.

Sister Jeanne de Valois, a pioneer in the development of education for several generations of Acadian women and a member in Moncton, New Brunswick, Canada, of the Congregation of Les Religieuses de-Notre-Dame-du-Sacré-Coeur, of which she was one of the founding members, lived until her ninety-fifth year in 1995. "She was the midwife of a whole generation of young women who went on to become doctors or lawyers and teachers," said well-known novelist Antonine Maillet, who was one of her students.[6] Sister Jeanne was instrumental in founding College Notre Dame d'Acadie, which eventually merged with the University of Moncton. The Educational Building on the campus is named for her. Sister was also Superior General of her Order. Sister Marie-Dorotheé quoted her as saying, "Strike while the iron is hot!" She knew when the time was politically ripe to initiate a new project. Sister Jeanne, not afraid of dying, said during those last hours, "Death isn't hard; it's very normal." Maillet said of her that she was ". . . a thoroughly modern woman while being a religious of deep Christian convictions. She was avant-garde and a non-conformist who had a *joie de vivre*, a joyous response to life."

New advances in education have been made in many spheres by the sisters. Sister Kathleen Dalton, a Sister of Charity of Halifax and recently a teacher of children with Downs Syndrome in Ireland, discovered a method of teaching them to speak. Throughout her teaching career, Sister has been deeply immersed in the Kodaly Music Methodology, with a long history of involvement with it in international schools and colleges. She discovered that this method with its emphasis on motifs of rhythm patterns and simple children's chants, with the mother tongue closely wedded to the music of the culture, might help children with Downs Syndrome to speak. The Monastery of Killarney had a large school for the handicapped, and the priests offered her the facilities to teach there. Today children with Downs Syndrome are speaking as a result of Sister Kathleen's experiment with the Kodaly methodology.

In the Diocese of Salt Lake City, Utah, Sister Stella Marie Zahner, a Daughter of Charity of the Province of the West, works as coordinator of a new program to assist poor families who desire a Catholic education for their children. She informs pastors and principals that this assistance is available. She then interviews families referred to her by them. Applications are reviewed and financial aid is provided for the most deserving. Sister visits the homes of those being aided, monitors their progress in school, tutors them when necessary. She will assess their needs – clothes, transportation, material needs at home – and do whatever is possible for them. She keeps records in the files of family visits, report cards, progress reports. Currently there are sixty-five children from forty families, thirty of whom are minorities, single parents, or both, with incomes below the poverty level.

Sister Joan Holmberg, a Sister of Charity of Halifax, former Provincial of the New York Province, is a resident staff member of WHW, Women Helping Women, and a sociologist with a doctoral dissertation, "The Changing Occupational Status of Women, 1950-1970." Chair of the Sociology Department at Wagner College (Lutheran affiliated), she was asked to be a consultant with the Lutheran Church on the economy. This resulted in an eighteen-year association in which she coordinated Global Institutes for Lutheran college faculties. Global Studies became part of their curriculum. Asked to join a Task Force on Peace and Justice Education for the Evangelical Lutheran Church in America, she initiated an international conference on consciousness-raising issues in Namibia, which was attended by the President-in-exile and over 1,000 people. When South Africa achieved its independence, this proved a highly influential group. She was a member of an International Study Committee for ELCA to develop sites in third world countries for students and faculty, an immersion in third World Countries in order to incorporate this into their curricula. They established these sites in India, Africa, Botswana, Namibia, and Brazil. Her local work consisted of establishing an Urban Immersion Workshop in South Harlem, and in the Bushwick section of Brooklyn. She also set up one for the migrant workers of California. Sister Joan has visited the places in which these programs were established and is a professional speaker on the subject of the status of women in third world countries. She firmly believes we should use our corporate power as a Federation for systemic change.

Sister Mary Teresa Orbegozo, a Sister of Charity of Convent Station, New Jersey, is Principal of the Paterson Adult and Continuing Education Programs for the City of Paterson, N.J., funded by local, state, and federal governments. These Programs include English as a Second Language, Basic Skills/GED (General Education Development), GED Testing Center, N.J. Youth Corps, AmeriCorps Program, Adult High School Program, and Medical Secretary Training Program. The scope of Sister's responsibilities also extends to five public schools where evening classes are held for adults. The Program serves approximately 3,200 students per year and represents thirty-six different nationalities, the majority being Hispanic. Many others are Haitians and African-Americans while increasing numbers are from the Middle East, India, and Poland. Those involved in the program are opened to new initiatives and challenges. Sister Mary

Teresa negotiates grants and establishes relationships of collaboration with other institutions and grant foundations. The sisters firmly believe that through education they can and do effect changes in people's lives, especially the disadvantaged and new immigrants lacking literacy skills requisite to effective citizenship and productive employment.

The media image of sisters today has been a source of much concern. Directors of films, both movie and television, tend to depict sisters in the old-time image of the naive, oddly innocent nun in long religious habit and veil who must be protected from the world at all cost. To replace this image with the reality of today's postmodern sister, a group has been formed to educate the public and the media. MIRA, the Media Image of Religious, is an association in which the member sisters write and publish articles on contemporary nuns and their work. They meet with people in the media, people actively engaged in television, radio, and journalism, to discuss and try to change the old concept of the sister. Sister Irene Fugazy, a New York Sister of Charity is a very active member of this group. The recent film *Dead Man Walking,* with Susan Sarandon, who won an Oscar for Best Actress, is a realistic depiction of the postmodern nun – the image which MIRA advocates.

A consultant of the Head-Start and Follow-Through office in Washington, D.C., is a Kentucky Sister of Charity, Sister Catherine Doyle. She is a developer of the Catherine Spalding Center and a coordinator of day-care centers with more than thirty in Louisville and Jefferson County, Kentucky. Supervisor of Elementary Education and Professor of Education at Catherine Spalding University, Sister Catherine has been actively engaged in dialogue with government officials in education, with positive results in many cases.

POTPOURRI

There are an innumerable variety of works that one cannot put under a general heading, in which sisters today are engaged. These surprise and interest laypeople who are often astonished to find religious women in these fields. Sisters are archivists, printers, phone-line respondents, sculptors, artists, retreat directors, healers, physicists, and ecologists, to mention but a few.

All thirteen congregations in the Federation have their professional archivists. Sister Marion Murray of the Sisters of Charity of the Immaculate Conception in Saint John, New Brunswick, Canada, is their archivist. With a background of ten years as a canon lawyer in Edmonton, Alberta, and a number of years as a teacher and principal, sister returned home to her native New Brunswick to become the community's archivist. She found this the most enriching period of her life, as the research brought her deeply in touch with not only the history but also the spirituality of the congregation and its individual members. She learned about the first women who entered the congregation in the early years of the nineteenth century – their charism that revealed itself as "no fanfare." Sister Marion said: "They saw a job to be done and they just plain did it." As an archivist, she has been called upon to function in a very wide area. Sister Marion traveled to all the houses of the community from the East to the West Coasts and was impressed with the wide variety of new and unusual services that they are presently undertaking. With a genuine grasp of the congregation's history, from archival material, letters, and memorabilia preserved since 1854, she is a valuable consultant on the past but also on evolving new directions that religious women will take.

The busy, ongoing lives of sisters today with constant demands on their services require the assistance of practical nuns who will provide in large houses their expertise in the day-to-day chores. Sister Maurice Wayda of the Pittsburgh Vincentian Sisters of Charity is one of these invaluable members. Sister is a buyer and a printer. As buyer for the community, Sister Maurice, in the early hours of the morning, each Wednesday at 5:30 a.m., drives a large cargo van to the "strip district," the covered market, where she purchases wholesale cartons of fruit and vegetables for the sisters and those under their care. The farmers have grown to know and like Sister Maurice. Her wholesome and outgoing personality has made for her many friends among them. When the Vincentian Sisters have their annual raffle for the poor, the farmers buy many raffle tickets from Sister Maurice. As a printer, Sister does all the printing for the congregation as well as her hobby – printing greeting cards with handset type.

Sister Gabrielle Charest of the Notre-Dame-du-Sacré-Coeur congregation, a retired sister in her eighties, works on a Prayer-Line Project. Begun in 1985, it is a local and long-distance phone line for people in the Maritime Provinces who need to talk to someone. The phones are staffed by two sisters answering from 10 a.m. to 10 p.m. Altogether there are eight sisters, most of them retired, running this project. They average about fifty calls a day. People phone in who are depressed, ill, lonely, worried, and in need of prayers. Some callers require as much as forty-five minutes; others a shorter time. The retired sisters find this a very fulfilling project connecting them to the world in which they had worked and from which they now feel excluded.

Silver Burdett Ginn Religion Division of Simon & Schuster Publishing Company employs a Sister of Charity of Seton Hill, Greensburg, Pennsylvania, as Resource Specialist/Summer Seminar Coordinator. Sister Mary Denise Diethrich plans, coordinates, designs brochures, and teaches two sessions at approximately twenty "Silver Seminars" across the country every summer. These are professional catechetical workshops provided to dioceses throughout the United States and recently in Panama and Germany. Sister works with catechists in the Army and Air Force in Germany. She and a colleague also work closely with a professional video company to produce a series of videos to accompany their elementary textbook series, *This Is Our Faith*. Sister Denise also coauthored the *Parent/Parish Guidebook* to accompany their Family Life Series, *Fully Alive*.

Sister Marie-Helene Allain, of the Notre-Dame-du-Sacré-Coeur community is a full-time artist and sculptor, formerly an art teacher at the University of Moncton. She studied at L'Ecole de Beaux Arts de Montreal (1967-1971). Her work, especially as a full-time sculptor, has been deeply fulfilling. Cistercian nun Sister Jean Marie Howe, OCSO, has written in her Preface to Caroll Gagnon's book on this sculptress that Sister Marie-Helene is immersed in the substance of her artistic world. She finds depth and transformation in the very elemental nature of her material, especially stone. She sees a co-naturality, an affinity between the elemental and the spiritual.[7] Sister Marie-Helene is aware of the values of pure form, showing life organically in a balanced and harmonious way, suggesting movement, the phenomenon of growth. Her faith in nature is at the center of her creative work. She tries to release the primal life of the stone she is sculpting. She "calls herself a daughter of nature . . . but nature as an implacable and unavoidable force . . . that power to which we must submit or which will cause us to perish" (Carolle Gagnon, p. 19).

Some areas of education, formerly relegated only to priests, has gradually opened to sisters. Sister Zoe Glenski, a Daughter of Charity in St. Louis, has been Professor of Church History at Kenrick-Glennon Seminary for twenty-four years. She has also been active and dynamic, giving over 100 retreats in the British Isles, Canada and the U.S.; promoting institutes on religion and mission to hospital administrators; currently doing an in-service program at a hospital in St. Louis. Sister Zoe asks for a dynamic Federation that will in future create a new congregation. She says: "The Sisters and Daughters of Charity have, in the past, been dynamic workers but old congregations die out and new ones fill their place. We can rise from the ashes of the old. Let us light the spark!"

While serving as Councilor for Apostolic Service, Sister Patricia Hughes of the Seton Hill, Greensburg, Pennsylvania Sisters of Charity, became a very active member of the National Association of Church Personnel Administrators. NACPA is an organization for human resource managers and ministry directors, dedicated to the development of just practices rooted in gospel values. In 1993 she joined the National Staff as Director of Program Services, conducting workshops, serving as consultant, writing and editing publications, affording her many opportunities to work with Church leaders. She conducted workshops for Catholic Charities, for NATRI, NCEA, NCCL, and CMSM, as well as dioceses and religious communities. As consultant to religious congregations, she advised on how to restructure governance, develop personnel systems, utilize physical facilities, implement a mission effectiveness plan, and create a safe and healthy workplace. Fifty percent of her time is devoted to planning and managing national meetings. She chooses a theme and contacts speakers knowledgable of Church teachings on human resource management. Her goal is to establish a program that motivates, informs, inspires, and pleases those in attendance. Catholic organization leaders are led to reflect on how they comply with the principles articulated in *Just Treatment for Those Who Work for the Church*. This is NACPA's premier document. It is the only opportunity leaders of Catholic organizations have to share wisdom, find support, and network with one another. Sister Patricia Hughes exudes enthusiasm and an intelligent grasp of justice in personnel practices. She has recently been offered the Vice Presidency of NCEA (National Catholic Education Association) to which she can bring her wide experience and knowledge of just practices from personnel managers to educators.

Doctor Nuala Kenny, a Sister of Charity of Halifax, is a pediatrician, scholar, researcher, writer, and noted public speaker, with a twenty-five year background as Doctor and then Chief of Pediatrics in some of Canada's outstanding hospitals. She has been, as well, Professor and then Chairperson in Departments of Pediatrics of Canadian Medical Schools. There her experience and expertise has been much appreciated. From 1975 to 1996 Dr. Kenny has given over 250 presentations and workshops on such subjects as child abuse, the needs of the hospitalized child, pediatric care programs, health care for children and families, moral ethical and legal issues, economic limits, and bioethics. She has published over fifty papers on related subjects and has served on some eighty professional committees, boards, and societies. Her most innovative work today as Director of Bioethics Education and Research at Dalhousie University, Halifax, is the setting up of an office to focus on ethical dilemmas facing doctors today. With research grants amounting to almost $200,000, Dr. Kenny is presently working on "Curriculum Development for Postgraduate Ethics Education." As a founding member of the National Council of Bioethics in Human Research; International Scholar of Hastings Center for Ethics in New York (1991), with a Continuing

Medical Education Fellowship at the Royal College of Physicians and Surgeons of Canada, and at the Kennedy Fellow Institute of Ethics at Georgetown University, Washington, D.C. (1993-1994), Dr. Kenny is eminently fitted for her present position at Dalhousie University. She will focus on such ethical dilemmas as euthanasia and assisted suicide, the vulnerable such as children, the elderly, and those with Alzheimer's disease, decisions on high-risk medical surgical procedures, on in-vitro fertilization, on the use of aborted fetuses to help cure Parkinson's disease, on research involving human subjects, on living wills, the huge advances in medical technology that use extraordinary means to help keep patients alive. The focus is on specific issues in pediatrics, gerontology, internal medicine, and surgery. Not limited to the Medical School, Dr. Kenny's Office will also address other related faculties: education, law, nursing, theology, philosophy. Dr. Kenny will offer "Ethics on the Street" – informal brown-bag lunch discussions for students and faculty on international ethical dilemmas. Dr. Kenny says, "The public expects doctors to be able to deal with ethical as well as scientific issues, competently and compassionately." As a Sister of Charity, doctor and researcher, Dr. Nuala Kenny, SC, is richly endowed to head such a timely program.

Another new direction in education is the combination of ecology and spirituality. Sister Mary Bookser, a Sister of Charity of Cincinnati, devotes her time and energy to literature, women, and ecospirituality. She points out that literature tells the story of women. Alternative modes of healing come through women (midwives, healers). Women are deeply tied to justice and the earth. She contends that music, and talking to plants, rocks, crystals helps the earth. Her spirituality is eclectic. She lives with environmentalist Sister Paula Gonzalez in

Solar House (La Casa del Sol) on the Motherhouse grounds of the Sisters of Charity of Cincinnati. Sister Mary is involved in the learning center called "Earth Connection." She wants to connect women mystics, women alive in the Spirit, with Shaman visioning and healing techniques. Religious women with a disciplined prayer life can use this tool for the healing of people and the earth, maintains Sister Mary.

An exciting way of viewing life on this planet is proposed by Sister Constance Dahinden, an Evansville, Indiana, Daughter of Charity, and Physics teacher. She sees life and even the life of the Federation as a microcosm of the larger universe. She states that we are preparing for a world we don't even know about, which will have its own energies. Sister Constance recommends the book *Belonging to the Universe* by Fritjof Capra and David Steindl-Rast (San Francisco: Harper, 1992) exploring how theology and physics match. It suggests starting with the universe and finding its parts, discovering the many holes in the universe and the realization that these holes have to be working together too. Sister Constance says: "Since Physics is a study of matter and motion, it can be used to study the Federation, its evolution ever-moving, ever-changing." She tells us to "see what the Federation is by looking at all its parts. If we can get all the forces of thirteen congregations working together, we will have connection and development, and possibly the creation of a new community."

A very serious earth-watcher is Sister Maureen Wild, a Sister of Charity of Halifax, the daughter of a successful farmer. Sister Maureen was brought up on the family farm in Berwyn, Alberta. She is today a good Director of Genesis Farm in Blairstown, New Jersey. Maureen's concern for the earth attracted her to this ecology center. The continuation of life for human beings, for animals, plants, water, attracted her to Genesis Farm, a gift to ecological development, of the Dominican Sisters of Caldwell, New Jersey. Women from various continents (of whom 80% are sisters) have been drawn to this 140-acre farm, a community-supported garden of fruits and vegetables grown without the use of chemicals that is used as a learning center. One hundred eighty families are shareholders and receive their produce from it every week. Sister Maureen's role is liaison between the community-supported garden and the ecological learning center, directing all the community service programs. The challenge is for the human community to live in a mutually enhancing way with the entire earth community. "Religious women since Vatican II are delving into ecology and social analysis, reinterpreting our vowed commitment to the preservation of all forms of life on the earth," says Sister Maureen. The planet is dependent on professional ecologists and on women such as Sister Maureen, who are dedicating much of their life and time to the preservation of all life on our planet. They understand Sister Elizabeth Johnson's words: "We are connected in a most profound way to the universe, having emerged from it."[8] Her thesis is "that the exploitation of the earth, which has reached crisis proportions in our day, is intimately linked to the marginalization of women, and that both of these predicaments are intrinsically related to forgetting the Creator Spirit who pervades the world in the dance of life."[9]

A scholar and a scientist in earth ministry is Sister Paula Gonzalez, who has an international reputation in this field. A freelance futurist, educator, and environmentalist for the past twenty-five years, she is the founding Director of Earth Connection. She is a full Professor with a Ph.D. in Cellular Physiology. Her intense concentration is on Earth Ministry sponsored by her congregation, the

Sisters of Charity of Cincinnati. Sister Paula combines the intellectual with the practical. Her lectures on futuring, a sustainable future, emphasize changing the uses of the earth's resources, restructuring waste and consumerism, restoring and healing the damage to soil, oil, water, a more organic form of agriculture, use of daylighting instead of electricity, promoting renewable energies (solar, wind). The house she designed, Solar House, is passive solar super-insulated. Sister Paula helped design her new building, Earth Connection, where they use rain and sun for heat, cooling, light. They store summer heat in a huge insulated bank of earth – seasonal thermal storage. In winter they withdraw it into a heating system. They convert solar energy into direct current electricity. There are also solar hot water heaters, but all this must be made cost-effective. Based on ecospirituality, Sister Paula Gonzalez is devoted to the principles of ecology – the universe as the primary mystery of the revelation of the mystery of God.

Sister Barbara Aires, a member of the Sisters of Charity of St. Elizabeth, Convent Station, New Jersey, works full-time for the Sisters of Charity of the Incarnate Word, Houston, Texas, 275 sisters engaged in health-care, education, retreat ministry, and social services. Her position is Coordinator of Social Concerns. This involves a number of areas, but the Texas Congregation's primary interest and first priority is "to do something to impact ecology." She and the General Superior and Council developed an "Environmental Policy and Statement of Principles," hoping to enflesh their own aspirations and some of the challenges put forth in the Bishops' USCC Pastoral "Renewing the Earth." A sisters' Ecology Committee was formed, and the members began an internal education process in their religious community to internalize the values inherent in the statement. A conference on the environment took place in October 1996. The Congregation also conducted an independent environmental audit of its Motherhouse complex. Recommendations presented have lead to remediation, a facilities' assessment and a Five-Year Plan. They instituted a recycling program and a partial recycling purchasing program. They also established an Employee Environmental Committee. Their Environmental Policy and Statement of Principles was sent to the Sisters of Charity Health-Care System (SCH System). After Sister Barbara Aires and her co-workers conducted education sessions with CEOs, administrations, and senior management, the system is using it to require environmental action on a number of issues. The Committee on Ecology provides ongoing information to local communities. The sisters celebrate with the employees Arbor Day in January, Earth Day and Texas Recycles Day in November. Currently Sister Barbara Aires and the Sisters of Charity of the Incarnate Word are educating the employees with in-service programs, one of which is on energy-savings ideas. Sister Barbara admires the commitment of the Congregation to follow through on their enactments and to share their resources.

Notes

1. The individual ministries described in this chapter are based almost entirely on interviews with each of the sisters represented here. There are a few exceptions based on correspondence with sisters.
2. Sister Noreen Neary, SC, Interview with the author, Convent Station, New Jersey.
3. Sister Mary Rose McGeady, DC, Interview with the author, Covenant House, New York City.
4. Sister Noreen Neary, SC, *Dimensions*, Sisters of Charity, Convent Station, New Jersey.

5. Sister Deborah Humphreys, SC, *The Stink Tree,* Sisters of Charity, Convent Station, New Jersey.
6. Antonine Maillet, as quoted by Andre Veniot, "Nun Was Pioneer in Women's Education," *Evening Times Globe,* May 12, 1995, p. A13.
7. Sister Jean-Marie Howe, OCSO, Preface to Caroll Gagnon, *Marie-Helene Allain: Symbolism of Stone* (Moncton: Les Editions d'Acadie, 1994), pp. 7, 8.
8. Sister Elizabeth Johnson, *Women, Earth, and Creator Spirit* (New York: Paulist Press, 1993), p. 34.
9. *Ibid.,* p. 2.

Chapter Six

The Vocation of Associates

Just as the work of the Church in the past many centuries seemed to be the prerogative of priests, nuns, and brothers, defining and upholding the Church's standards in liturgy, education, health care, social work, parish ministry, so today in this post-Vatican II era, it is the prerogative of the laity. As religious congregations of lay women and men dwindle in numbers and fewer young men and women opt for the priesthood and the sisterhood, so proportionately do the numbers of laymen and women increase as they take active roles as pastors, deacons, parish ministers, missionaries, educators, health-care workers, social service administrators, and workers. According to Sister Marlene Lehmkuhl, a Sister of Charity of Nazareth, Kentucky, in her ongoing study, "Probing the Relationship between Associates and Their Congregations":

> It was Yves Congar, OP, in his massive two volumes, *Lay People in the Church: A Study for a Theology of Laity (1959)* and *Laity, Church and World* (1960), who delineated in our time the vocation of lay persons. . . . That theology teaches that the gift of Baptism directs all believers to one basic vocation: to follow Christ, Whose union with God and ministry with God's people were inseparable.
>
> Vincent de Paul and Louise de Marillac's Ladies of Charity and Company of Charity understood why they did not belong to a religious order. Their mission with the poor flowed out of their personal un-

ion with God and their praying with the community. Vincent and Louise's foresight predated by three centuries the recent development of the theology of the laity.[1]

After Vatican II increasing numbers of religious congregations of women turned to an Associate Program to augment the decreasing numbers of sisters as large groups of sisters left religious life and fewer entered the convent. Many of the thirteen congregations of Sisters of Charity in the Federation did likewise.

THE SISTERS OF CHARITY OF NAZARETH, KENTUCKY[2]

One of the first Associate groups was initiated by the Sisters of Charity of Nazareth, Kentucky. Laywomen and men who felt called to an associate membership and loose affiliation with the work and prayer of the Sisters of Charity, while living diverse lifestyles and striving to be faithful to the mission of the Church, were admitted to Associate membership. Sisters and Associates are thus united in a relationship of mutual support and enrichment. Officially initiated in 1971 and approved by the SCN Executive Committee in January 1972, the Associate Program became part of the Congregation of Sisters of Charity of Nazareth, Kentucky. Associates differ from sisters, who make public vows of poverty, chastity, and obedience. Associates, who have not relinquished the privileges of their lay state, do not have full and complete status in the congregation. Rather they are extensions of the congregation, who noncanonically affirm the mission and spirit of the congregation in their desire to share in the congregation's charism, goals, and ministries.

Energized by a common charism and bonded in a relationship of trust, commitment, and accountability, Sisters and Associates together seek to carry out the mission of the Church in a spirit of simplicity, humility, and love. Together they discover new ways of bringing Gospel values into the marketplace. A 1994 count the Associates in the Congregation of Sisters of Charity of Nazareth, Kentucky, showed that fifty fall into the age group of thirty to forty-nine years; 150 in the age group of fifty to sixty-nine years, and approximately forty in the age group of seventy to ninety years. Most of these men and women are single, divorced, widowed, or never married. There are, however, eighteen married couples in the Associate Program. The Associates come mainly from the following states: Kentucky, Arkansas, Maryland, Massachusetts, Ohio, Tennessee, and Belize, Central America. There are one or two SCNAs in Alabama, Arizona, California, Iowa, Indiana, Louisiana, Maine, Mississippi, Montana, New York, Texas, and Virginia. This does not count the numbers of Associates in the same states belonging to Associate Programs in other Congregations of Sisters of Charity.

Since the beginning of the Associate Program in Kentucky, the number of Associates has gradually grown larger until today they number 252. What draws them to the program is their desire for community and spirituality. They want to be part of a group who have similar ideals. When the Sisters of Charity of Nazareth first began the program, each Associate was given a Sister contact person, but as the program progressed the sisters found that a faith community can better replace the contact person. The Sisters are quick to note that from the very beginning of their congregation in 1812, laywomen and men have collaborated with them in mission, but no formal structure such as the Associate Program had ever been introduced.

Of the present 252 Associates a variety of jobs and professions are represented. These range from Directors of large hospitals to lab assistants, state officers in health care, computer programmers, addiction counselors, school principals, teachers, chaplains, politicians, college presidents, firefighters, city water workers, former missionary workers, and a number of retirees who have held administrative positions.

Two of their present Associates do most of their video work, making videos of their meetings and general assemblies. One woman Associate is a journalist who writes articles for them, publishing in such newspapers as the NCR (*National Catholic Reporter*) summarizing, for example, their June 1995 national Assembly. Another Associate has produced a video, *SCN Heritage of Health.* This same Associate has spent a month in India assisting the Sisters of Charity there in medical lab techniques. Two others have assisted the sisters in their missionary work in Belize. Another two have helped the sisters in their archives and media center, working on programs for them.

All the Associates are expected to participate monthly in a two-hour faith-sharing session. Imbued with the Vincentian charism, the Associates seek relationship with the Sisters of Charity in order to deepen their Baptismal call and to better effect their mission in Church and world. They look confidently to the sisters for formation, spirituality, mission, and community. The increasing number of Associates and their desire to work with the sisters is causing the sisters to examine their own place in Church and society. Vatican II and Rome's mandate, *Perfectae Caritatis*, accelerated the efforts of women religious to adapt to a changing world. In 1989 the CMSM/LCWR (Leadership Conference of Women Religious) identified the top two transformative elements for the future of religious life as a prophetic witness and a contemplative stance. One might see it for Sisters of Charity as a recovery of their initial history in the Vincentian tradition. Moving into the twenty-first century will require an engagement in an in-depth study and dialogue on the meaning and implications of those two transformative elements vis-à-vis the Associates. An Associate Membership Study in all religious congregations beginning with the Federation of Sisters of Charity is imperative, as is a study dialogue with the Associates. A first step might be the distribution of survey material to them regarding their understanding of their call and their hopes for the future of the Associate Program. Models for structuring the Associates' Program have existed from the twelfth-century Beguine Movement, the first women's movement in Western history, through the seventeenth-century Ladies of Charity into the present lay secular institutes. But the Associates are unique in their inclusion of both men and women. A new model must be created that will offer a structure actualizing the charism of charity in this post-modern age. The time is ripe for clarifying the relationship between vowed lifelong membership and dedicated temporary association. Lifestyles and intent of both Associates and Sisters must be examined; honest dialogue on the present structure with the possibility of creating a new structure must begin; the corporate ability for both social and ecclesial change must be recognized.

THE SISTERS OF CHARITY OF CINCINNATI, OHIO[3]

In 1973, one year after the Kentucky Sisters of Charity had inaugurated their Associate Program, the Sisters of Charity of Cincinnati initiated a similar program. It came about quite naturally when Blasa Rivera, a forty-seven year-old mother of four grown-up children and separated from her husband, asked to enter the Congregation of Sisters of Charity of Cincinnati. Because of her circumstances, they were not able to comply with her request for a vowed commitment, but offered to accept her as a comember. This was a new concept for the congregation. Two other women joined her and what was eventually to become the Associate Program was born. By 1978 the number had increased to forty-five from Cincinnati, Denver, Dayton, and the Great Lakes. The Cincinnati community introduced the term Auxiliary Membership, which refers to either (1) those living in community, "Associates," or (2) those living outside community, or "Auxilliary," later changed to "Comembers." The focus of program development included "Spiritual Companioning" booklets and video, along with workshops. In 1990 the name for all was changed to "Associates in Community" and "Associates in Mission." A Pictorial Directory was developed in 1991, and a new "Anima Christi" card was printed and sent to each Associate. In 1992 Sister Rita Hawk was appointed full-time Director of Associates and in 1993 an Associate in Mission Handbook was completed and distributed. In 1995 the first Associate Convocation was held in Cincinnati, attended by seventy-two Associates.

In 1994 two new forms of association had been formed by the Cincinnati Congregation: "Associates in Volunteer Ministry" and "High School Associates." As of March 1996 the Sisters of Charity of Cincinnati number 103 Associates in Mission and three Associates in Volunteer Ministry – all 106 Associates' ages ranging from mid-30s to mid-80s with the average age in the mid-50s. John O'Connor, a high school teacher and an Associate in Volunteer Ministry, served for six weeks as tutor and recreation organizer in Tipp City, Ohio, with the Sisters of Charity Migrant Ministry Program. The two other Associates in Volunteer Ministry served in Cincinnati. The Associates in Volunteer Ministry have a full-time service/Associate relationship with the Sisters of Charity for a specified period of time. After a year of volunteer service, this person may continue as an Associate in Mission. The sisters are surfacing potential service sites for the Associates in Volunteer Ministry.

The news bulletin, *Associates Connect,* offers an informative series of articles and pictures on the ministries of the Associates in the Cincinnati Sisters of Charity Associate Program. September 1993 marked the Twentieth Anniversary of the Cincinnati Associates Program and the Reception of Blasa Rivera and her two companions into the Associates. All three women are still faithful members. Eight states are represented by Associates: Ohio, Kentucky, Colorado, New Mexico, Texas, Michigan, Florida, and Tennessee. Although not a recruitment program, seven of the Associates have entered the Congregation of Sisters of Charity of Cincinnati.

Association in Mission is a commitment expressed by men and women in renewable agreements for specific periods of time to share in support of the mission and spirit of the Sisters of Charity and to enter into a mutually enriching relationship appropriate to their own state of life. They meet regularly with a contact Sister. This spiritual companioning component adds to the enrichment experienced by the Associate in Mission as he or she participates in local, regional, and congregational activities open to Associates in Mission. Associates in Volunteer Ministry embrace the values and vision of the Sisters of Charity as they strive to meet the needs of the poor and oppressed. The benefits to all Associates include an expansion of their life perspective, an experience of other cultures and geographic areas, personal fulfillment in service to others, spiritual and professional growth, a supportive community, and a small stipend for simple living. Types of service include education, social service, health care, pastoral ministry, and environmental ministry.

Another form of the Associate Program is developing with the Sisters of Charity of Cincinnati – "Associates in Community" – people who will live with the Sisters of Charity but will not be Sisters. For this form there will necessarily be a financial commitment.

THE SISTERS OF CHARITY OF NEW YORK[4]

Sister Ellen Rose O'Connell directs the Associate Program for the New York Sisters of Charity at Mount Saint Vincent-on-the-Hudson in Riverdale, New York. It is intended to foster a creative mutuality that can enrich, support, and challenge both Associates and Sisters in their response to the Gospel in our time. Their essential element of association is to widen and strengthen the bonds with others who affirm the Sisters of Charity's goals and mission, and who wish to live these from within their own lifestyles.

The Associate Program of New York began informally in the early 1970s when a former member of the congregation and her husband made inquiries about how they could continue ties with the Sisters of Charity. Both were involved in the ministry of education. The possibility was discussed by the Council and General Assembly. In 1975 the Assembly empowered the Council to implement an Associate Relationship Program according to the following guidelines: appointment of a Coordinator, a process of orientation and spiritual development for prospective Associates, processes for drawing up contracts and evaluation.

In 1976 the first Associates were received and the program continued to grow slowly and steadily. An Associates' Team, composed of Associates and Sisters, was appointed to provide education on Associates for the Congregation and the Church at large, to develop governing policies and procedures, to monitor evaluation and contract renewals, as well as to plan and implement the initial introduction of Associates to the Congregation. Associates gradually became involved in congregational committees and commissions, sharing their expertise with sisters. Over the years Associates have become part of the General Assembly by serving on committees and contributing their insights through a process of limited participation.

At the 175th Anniversary of the Congregation, they wore Associate pins for the first time, identifying themselves in a public way as Associates of Charity. At the present time Associates work side-by-side with vowed sisters as nurses, educators, family social workers, advocates for the poor, and volunteers in the New York Sisters of Charity's institutions. Through vision groups sisters and Associates share faith. They participate in congregational projects and live the charism of charity from within their individual lives.

In 1996 there are forty-six Associates of the New York Sisters of Charity, living mainly in New York but also coming from Nassau, the Bahamas (where the sisters have missions), and other parts of the United States. They are women and men, single, married, a Jesuit priest, working with the homeless, in hospices, in schools as educators. They identify with the values of Mother Seton and Vincent de Paul. There is a married couple, Roberta Lener and her husband, living in the North Bronx, both in their fifties with grown children, who are very dedicated Associates. They live very simple lives after the example of Vincent de Paul who said to his Daughters of Charity: "Your cloister shall be the streets of the city; the houses of the sick your convent." When Roberta and her husband moved here from the West, where they had already given up their car to missionaries, they became Associates. Roberta is a part-time hospice visiting nurse in the Bronx and a part-time parish minister in the RCIA Program, while her husband is a doctor's assistant.

Another couple, Miriam and Jack, started their married life together by working for the poor in Salvador. They learned Spanish and worked in a health station. Upon their return to New York, they became Associates. Jack works in a residence for homeless men, and Miriam works with AIDS patients in a clinic. She is the niece of Sister Ita Ford of Maryknoll, who was one of the four sisters martyred in El Salvador a few years ago.

Other Associates work in both traditional and nontraditional ministries and are supportive of one another in ties that bind them to the charism of Elizabeth Ann Seton and Vincent de Paul.

THE SISTERS OF CHARITY OF THE IMMACULATE CONCEPTION, SAINT JOHN, N.B.[5]

Sister Rose Mulholland is the Director of the Associates' Program for the Sisters of Charity of the Immaculate Conception in Saint John, New Brunswick, Canada. As far back as 1972 they discussed an Associates' Program and by 1981 the reality of comembership was accepted by the congregation. In 1981-82 research was begun and Father Cassian Yuhaus, CP, of CARA, Washington, D.C., addressed the sisters on comembership. A committee was established to develop guidelines, which were approved in 1984. Sister Rose felt they now had the book knowledge but not the flesh. She therefore gathered together some laymen and laywomen – five women and one man in their late twenties and thirties. She asked them to journey with the sisters and questioned them on how the sisters could be a support for them. They answered that in trying to live the Christian life they felt they were going upstream without a paddle. The sisters could offer mutual support in living the Gospel in everyday life. The first years of the Associates Program were years of searching. How best to function? What did they need to enrich their lives?

In 1985 a pilot program was inaugurated with the first groups of Associates meeting in Saint John, New Brunswick, and Edmonton, Alberta. Each year new members were invited to join, were introduced to the program, and were integrated into the larger groups. This was all in the preparation phase of the program. In 1987 they made a commitment for one year. By 1990 fourteen women and men in British Columbia were ready to make a commitment as Associates, eleven renewed their commitment in Edmonton, and seven in Saint John, bringing the total number of Associates in the Sisters of Charity of the Immaculate Conception of Saint John, New Brunswick, to thirty-two.

Over the years some Associates left the Program, but those who remained were challenged to transition, to refocus as new changes took place. Those who have journeyed together with the Sisters of Charity have experienced a deepening relationship with Jesus, a growing familiarity with Scripture, an expanding awareness of ministry within the Church, and a deeper appreciation of Vincent de Paul, Elizabeth Ann Seton, and Honoria Conway. Today they total twenty members: six in the Atlantic region, five in the prairie region plus three candidates, and six in the Pacific region. They continue to remain actively engaged in Gospel living through their lifestyle, ministry, and work.

The program aims to provide support, encouragement, and growth opportunities for women and men actively engaged in Gospel living. They meet regularly for sharing in prayer, discussions, workshops, and retreats, thus providing support as each member is committed "to build up and sustain by every means in their power, the Church of God on earth." Over the years they have had a variety of age groups, with the majority in their late 40s and 50s, some in their 60s, and one couple in their 70s. When they first began, each Associate had a companion Sister, but as the years passed that was seen as unnecessary. In their monthly meetings they focus on the Gospel, the teachings of the Church, Baptism, the charism of Charity, and ministry. Two or three times a year they have retreats. Today the focus seems to be on their jobs as ministry. The sisters in both East and West plan conferences with them.

In 1994 they were invited to attend the Sisters' General Chapter. Some of the Associates from Western Canada joined them. They journeyed with the sisters at Assemblies, at participation in the General Chapter proceedings. They were encouraged to speak at the microphone if they had any advice to give or anything they wished to share. At the end the Associates as a group thanked the sisters for allowing them to be with them at their most important discussions for the future of the Congregation. During the General Chapter they participated with the sisters in forming the native Indian "Talking Circle." The Associates joined in that tradition also. There were some 150 or more sisters and Associates present. The Sisters of Charity of the Immaculate Conception have truly drawn their Associates into their congregation in a way not yet experienced before.

THE SISTERS OF CHARITY OF SETON HILL, GREENSBURG, PENNSYLVANIA[6]

Sister Kathryn Palas is the Director of the Associates Program for the Sisters of Charity of Seton Hill, Greensburg, Pennsylvania. In 1983 the original group of women interested in spiritual development met with Sister for Bible Study and discussion. These women soon expressed a need for prayer. In response to their request and with the encouragement of the Church to involve laity in the Congregation, the Sisters of Charity formed a committee to research the feasibility of an Associate Membership Program. With the blessing of the Community Council and the support of the Congregation, guidelines, invitations, a membership agreement, and a formal ceremony were approved.

In July 1985 six women were accepted as Associates. A Sister of Charity as Director and a team of six sisters volunteered to pioneer the group. It was organized to enable laywomen and laymen to share in the spirit and the mission of the Sisters of Charity of Seton Hill. The Associates meet regularly to pray, to study the charism of Elizabeth Ann Seton and Vincent de Paul, and to endeavor to "carry Christ to the world."

While living full Christian lives as professional people, parents, busy women and men serving God in their homes and in the workplace, they are challenged to bring the Gospel to others. Today there are twenty-nine Associate members. They receive the *Newsletter of the Sisters of Charity* and are invited to participate in the Congregation's special events. They are also welcome to visit local houses where the sisters live, to pray with the community, and to share in their daily life. The Church as well as the Congregation of Sisters of Charity of Seton Hill, Greensburg, Pennsylvania, is blessed with the spiritual support of the Associates.

THE SISTERS OF CHARITY OF LEAVENWORTH, KANSAS.[7]

Sister Noreen Walter is the Associate Director for the Sisters of Charity of Leavenworth, Kansas. In the fall of

1987 the Associate Program began a pilot year as a result of the 1986 General Chapter deliberations and decisions. A task force was formed of four sisters to study the possibilities, and from this emerged the Sisters of Charity of Leavenworth Associate Program. The Associate is perceived as a person who wishes to further the mission of the Church by collaborating with the sisters in a formal and mutually enriching way. "Close collaboration with the laity is reflected in the life and ministry of the sisters so that, in mutuality, the mission of the Church may be furthered by the talents and gifts of all."[8]

The purpose of the SCL Associate Program is to acknowledge in a concrete way the common call to holiness of all baptized persons; to extend and enhance the Gospel message and the Kingdom of God through the mutual response of believers from varied walks of life; to enrich mutually the lives of the sisters themselves and of women and men who are drawn to the spirit of the Sisters of Charity of Leavenworth; to call forth the resources of the sisters and of their Associates in such a way as to benefit both; to unite sisters and other persons, lay or ordained, in their search for the fundamental values of Christian life, especially as that life reflects a counterculture in today's society.

From its beginning in 1987 the Associate Program has grown in numbers, presently numbering 116 members, of which ninety-three are women and twenty-three men. Membership continues to grow monthly in spite of the fact that no advertising or recruitment is done for the Program, which is under the direction of Sister Noreen Walter, who works half-time in this capacity. She is responsible for new members and works with the sponsors so that ongoing formation is taking place. This generally is handled through annual or semiannual gatherings of Associates in regional areas. Associates seem to fall into two categories (although the program is not technically defined in this way): (1) "Praying Associates" who support the others in prayer, and (2) "Active Associates" who minister with the sisters or in some way support them in their ministry. There is no doubt that this Program will continue to grow as more and more women and men have been asking to join.

THE SISTERS OF CHARITY OF SAINT ELIZABETH, CONVENT STATION, N.J.[9]

Sister Julie Scanlon is Director of the Associates of the Sisters of Charity of Saint Elizabeth, Convent Station, New Jersey. Through a Mandate of the 1987 General Assembly, "That the General Assembly endorse a congregational program of lay affiliation for those who wish to join in our mission and charism of charity,"[10] the Office of Lay Affiliation opened in 1989. The Seton Volunteer Program, which had begun in 1975, became a responsibility of this new office. But its main work was to design a new process by which men and women could be invited to become lay affiliates of the Sisters of Charity of St. Elizabeth. In 1990 Seton Affiliates officially opened, and its first member was Katherine Kiernan, sister of the late Sister Anne Kelly. A longtime friend of the sisters and a dedicated volunteer, giving years of service to the ministries of the sisters, Katherine was proud of her title as first Affiliate. Although she died shortly thereafter, others soon followed, two of whom had been the first long-term Seton Volunteers in 1975.

In July 1993 the name "Affiliate" was changed to "Associate" for this new bonding of laypersons and sisters. Today there are over 117 Seton Associates, men and women, married and single, teachers, nurses, home health aides, housewives, businesspeople, priests, social workers, counselors, volunteers, and retirees. They feel they have established a firm relationship sharing their spiritual life and contributing their services to the sisters and their ministries. Each Seton Associate writes a "Commitment Contract" explaining why he or she became an Associate and how the new relationship will be lived out, either through prayer or through active ministry. At an annual Commitment Service new Seton Associates are welcomed into a formal relationship with the Congregation of Sisters of Charity of Saint Elizabeth, and current Seton Associates renew their commitment. Seton Associates each have a Sister of Charity sponsor who welcomes them to local community events and accompanies them to gatherings planned specifically for Seton Associates. Arlene Kleissler, a member of the Seton Advisory Group for three years, reflected on her experience as an Associate. She said:

> The Sisters of Charity have long been, for me, a group of dedicated religious women whom I have admired and been connected with in various ways for most of my life. The connection I experience as a Seton Associate allows a formalization of that connection and calls me to a more conscious commitment to join the Sisters of Charity in this way, bringing the mission of charity to the world in which I function. . . . As an Associate I am joined in partnership with members of the Congregation, thus strengthening the impact of charity in today's world.[11]

Seton Associates are involved in many different ministries: twenty-two in education, and many others feeding the hungry in soup kitchens or serving the poor, the neglected, or the destitute. Some Associates serve on parish staffs, and many are Eucharistic ministers, lectors, RCIA leaders or CCD teachers. Three are doctors and several volunteer to work with elderly retired sisters. Two are priests in the Hartford Diocese and one is a

Deacon in the Paterson Diocese. Mary Marinucci, a social worker and psychotherapist, said as an Associate:

> I feel a part of a succession of sisters . . . who were a vital and dynamic force in the world. I carry their good into the future. Although alone at any given time doing my job in an unlikely place, I feel part of this united force of Sisters of Charity from all times, making that moment in time bigger than the obvious in its value.[12]

Seton Associates come from several states – California, Georgia, New Jersey, New York, Connecticut, Massachusetts, Mississippi, Florida – wherever the Sisters of Charity of Saint Elizabeth have missions. Patricia (Boyd) Clifton, Director of Adult Education and Christian Initiation at St. Angela Merici Church, Brea, California, said: "My life is about bringing folks into the Church, and where the seed was planted for that was in the Sisters of Charity."

THE VINCENTIAN SISTERS OF CHARITY, PITTSBURGH, PENNSYLVANIA[13]

Sister Elena, a Vincentian Sister of Charity of Pittsburgh, Pennsylvania, is Director of the Associate Program that began formally in 1990. In the late 1980s the Vincentian Network of Prayer was initiated to connect the sisters with those laypeople interested in praying for community intentions, who wished to be in a prayer relationship with the sisters. The main intention was to pray for religious vocations. The group was remembered weekly at liturgy and received a semiannual newsletter. Once a year the community hosted a gathering at the Pittsburgh Motherhouse for all members of the Network. The sisters give talks on the Network in parishes as an ideal way for homebound and elderly individuals to stay connected with the prayer life of the sisters. Presently there are over 500 members in Canada, the United States, and Peru. With that background, the Vincentian Sisters of Charity decided to offer an Associates' Program as well. In 1992 the first group, three men and five women, made a commitment during a Community Liturgy Celebration. Since then the group has grown to thirteen very active Associates, volunteering their services with the sisters' ministries, at the annual Community Festival, and in summer ministry programs. Monthly they gather for prayer and discussion. They are also invited for Community days of prayer, retreats, and lectures.

In 1995 a formal Associate Formation Program was instituted for those in discernment about becoming Associates. New members are welcome to join the group at monthly meetings. Presently the group is exploring further participation with the sisters in volunteering at the Motherhouse to care for the retired and ill sisters. A core group of two Associates and two sisters helps to make plans for the future and directs the group. Discussion about writing a handbook is currently on the table. For virtually everyone involved, the experience of the Associate Program has been a positive one. While the spiritual bond is what binds the group, individual members have grown in relationship with one another and with other sisters in the Community. Both sisters and Associates are constantly challenged by new ways to give life to the Vincentian charism.

THE DAUGHTERS OF CHARITY OF ST. VINCENT DE PAUL, UNITED STATES[14]

The Daughters of Charity in the United States have an original and unique Affiliates' Program with the Vincentian priests, the Vincentian Service Corps (VSC), of laymen and women. Traditionally, since their foundation, the Daughters of Charity have always been associated with the laity in ministry. In fact the Ladies of Charity, a lay organization initiated by St. Vincent de Paul in 1617, preceded the Daughters of Charity in their service to the poor. It was because of the multiple forms of poverty and sickness in France at that time that these ladies of social means began to find it impossible to meet all the human suffering that St. Vincent brought to their attention. As a result St. Vincent turned to the rural village girls for help. It was one of the Ladies of Charity, Louise de Marillac, whom Vincent chose to train these girls and to cofound the Daughters of Charity in 1633.

Although the two groups, the Ladies and the Daughters of Charity, have, through the centuries, worked closely in their endeavors to the service of the poor, each has remained a separate organization. In August 1981, an associate program was formally established in the United States by the Daughters of Charity in St. Louis, Missouri. It was called the Daughters of Charity – Associates in Mission (DC-AIM) Program. First sponsored by the sisters of the West Central Province, it was then cosponsored by the Daughters in the East Central Province.

In 1981 the Vincentian Priests of the Eastern Province also started the Vincentian Service Corps (VSC). Likewise in 1990 the Vincentian Priests and Brothers on the West Coast began a service group called Vincentian Lay Ministry (VLM). The Daughters in both areas cooperated with these programs by providing placement for service projects and helping to offer retreats and times of renewal.

At a meeting in February 1992 the five Provincials of the Congregation of the Mission (Vincentians) and the five Provincials of the Daughters of Charity, merged the three Associate Programs in a combined program called the Vincentian Service Corps (VSC). This new affiliation has three regional offices: VSC East, Jamaica, New York;

VSC Central, St. Louis, Missouri; VSC West, Los Angeles, California. The VSC is "for men and women who want to serve the poor, live in Community with other VSC members and experience a simple lifestyle. They are called to deepen their faith, grow in charity, work for justice, celebrate life, and develop close bonds. Service is geared to helping people help themselves."[15]

The service commitment is for one to two years and is renewable. Summer programs are also available. They may serve in urban or rural areas throughout the United States. The types of placement are in adult literacy, advocacy, casework for shelters and for the mentally ill, childcare, community organizing, computer programming, coordinating volunteers, crisis counseling, legal aid, maintenance, nursing homes, outreach to the homebound elderly, work with the physically handicapped, parish ministry, pastoral care, skilled labor, social work, teaching, and youth ministry.

VSC is open to men and women, single, married, and widows, aged twenty or older. A college degree or significant life/work experience is required. Experience for persons with disabilities is possible. The VSC member receives room and board, a monthly stipend, medical insurance, and VSC and work-related travel costs. VSC members participate in a one-week orientation program "to get to know one another, look at issues regarding service, justice, community, lifestyle, spirituality, racial sensitivity, cultural diversity, and to set goals for the year." There is on-site training at each placement center. VSC members gather several times throughout the year for weekend retreats or workshops. During the year, personal and community support is given. Year placements begin in August, and summer placements in June.

Balance is a necessary and regular part of the lives of the VSC Volunteers. Retreats and renewal days help to provide for rest, prayer, reflection, discussion, exercise, and play. Retreats have been held in Princeton Retreat Center, New Jersey; the Daughters of Charity Provincialate in Evansville, Indiana; St. Louis, Missouri; the annual California Yosemite Retreat "*Come apart with me and rest awhile.*" Most volunteers seem to recognize that the values discovered and nurtured in their service year are both transforming and life-directing. One retreatant said:

> Our experiences were awesome . . . The very beauty . . . of Yosemite spoke to our hearts of the wonders of our Creator and the love He has for us . . . There was a time to share on a deep level our Vincentian heritage . . . We walked, talked, climbed, laughed, cried, ate and played. Each evening we closed the day with a beautiful liturgy.[16]

Volunteers come from many different backgrounds. A newlywed couple from Paris, France, served in a facility for the mentally and physically impaired in Indianapolis. A married couple (grandparents) from Erie, Pennsylvania, worked with children in Learning Clubs in Hope, Arkansas. A registered nurse (widow and grandmother) from Cheboygan, Michigan, serves in an adult day-care facility. A young woman from Sligo, Ireland, working in Washington, D.C., found the Vincentian Service Corps as an answer to prayer and a challenge to her desire to serve. A young male volunteer, working at a transitional housing geared toward helping struggling families become self-sufficient, is inspired by those he helps and by other volunteers whom he calls "a small army of dreamers."[17] Volunteers live together to form communities in former convents or residences for religious. A former VSC Volunteer, presently Manager of a Communications Office in Washington, D.C., said that her life changed through her VSC experiences by "meeting and becoming friends with some of the most incredibly nice, decent, caring, friendly people . . . undoubtedly my best friend from VSC is my husband. When I saw him impersonate Monsieur Vincent, I knew he was the one for me!"[18]

Another volunteer said:

> A year of volunteer service challenged me and my housemates to be creative, to invent fiscally prudent means of entertainment, to carry out non-violent solutions to conflict within the community . . . illuminated by the fact that we chose to live simply, in community, in service to others.[19]

A young man from New York said: "After the VSC you return with . . . a rejuvenated set of priorities, and a self as different from your old one as are the friendships and people you encountered along the way."[20]

THE SISTERS OF CHARITY OF HALIFAX, NOVA SCOTIA[21]

The Sisters of Charity of Halifax conduct Associate Programs in two of their five provinces, New York and Vancouver, B.C. The New York program has been in existence since 1980, when a small group of sisters in Forest Hills was graced to recognize this call in the men and women with whom they came in contact. There was an energy in their coming together, of people who shared the same charism, the love and service of the poor reflected in the lives of St. Vincent de Paul and St. Elizabeth Ann Seton. The bond was the love of God. From a small beginning grew a community of sixteen men and women of various backgrounds, ethnic diversity, age, and careers. These men and women began to meet every other week to share their faith and common call. Besides the hosting sisters, other sisters would come, as well as Professors from Queens College and St. John's University, as well as people from other diverse, ministries, to share with the group their views of a wider world. They met for seven years but eventually dissolved in 1988. Some joined other communities; other stayed loosely connected to the Sisters of Charity. The movement seemed to die but suddenly it came alive again when Sister Maryann Seton and a few other sisters challenged the Congregation of Sisters of Charity by drawing up by-laws and a document clearly stating the role of the laity as collaborators, separate and distinct, yet joined by mission to the Sisters of Charity. Susan McMahon, a laywoman and long-time friend of the sisters, joined Sister Maryann in creating the "team approach" with the two as codirectors. The leadership team consisted of sisters and laypeople. Three young women joined the group, and Sister Maureen Skelly returned to it. Between 1993 and 1995 nine laywomen joined, and in 1996 an additional thirteen women became Associates. The total number of lay Associates is presently twenty-six people committed to service of the poor. They live in the New York area – Brooklyn, Nassau, Suffolk, Staten Island, and New Jersey.

A person interested in becoming an Associate applies for formal membership, is sponsored by a Sister of Charity, and is interviewed by a team member and by a member of the Leadership Team. At the Ceremony of Acceptance each person promises to keep in contact with a Sister of Charity or the community of Sisters of Charity and to bring to his or her place of work or home the charism of charity. "Associates are those women and men who are attracted to the charism of the Sisters of Charity of Halifax, and have a desire to commit themselves with the Congregation to community, prayer, and its mission of loving service."[22] The person is then affirmed by the community, other Associates, and the congregation present, and receives a medal of St. Elizabeth Seton. The

Associates are invited to take part in the life of the Congregation by participation in Assemblies, joining focus groups, and volunteering in established works of service to the poor. Ten more people are preparing or discerning formal acceptance into the program.

Some works of the Associates include service at Xavier Society for the Blind, compassionate visits with families of victims destroyed by disasters such as the TWA Flight 800 crash, work at St. Vincent's in Staten Island, work with HIV/AIDS victims at Mount Manresa in Staten Island, service at Alba House, volunteer work at the Staten Island prison, assisting the elderly with shopping, phone calls, and other tasks. Special ministries include those to immigrant Philippine and Hispanic families. Some Associates are Parish Ministers, cancer ward visitors, activists in political letter-writing campaigns for the rights of the poor, challenging the government, raising the consciousness of peoples to peace and justice issues. Sister Maureen Skelly is the present Coordinator of the Associate Program.

The Sisters of Charity of Halifax, in their Province of Western Canada, have in 1995-96 just begun to form an Associate Program. For the past year Sisters Cecilia Hudec and Gertrude McGovern have been journeying with fifteen persons exploring association with the Sisters of Charity of Halifax. They are discerning whether their personal charism resonates with that of St. Elizabeth Seton, using the book *Praying with Elizabeth Seton,* as a framework for their reflection. Four persons are now ready to make formal request to commit themselves as Associates for one, two, or three years. The others plan to continue their journey of reflection. The Associates will make their commitment to the Congregation as a whole, not to the Western Province, which is phasing out. Among the fifteen are two men, husbands of two women who are exploring the commitment. The members come from widely separated areas of western Canada – Vancouver, British Columbia; Edmonton, Alberta; and Kelowna, B.C. One gentleman indicated that with fewer sisters in Kelowna, he felt moved to carry on the work of the sisters. Obviously it is the work of the Spirit moving people to continue the ministry of charity.

LES RELIGIEUSES DE NOTRE-DAME-DU-SACRÉ-COEUR[23]

An outcome of the General Chapter of July 1984 was the proposal to examine the possibility of accepting Associate Members into the Congregation of Les Religieuses de Notre-Dame-du-Sacré-Coeur. In the autumn of that year, a study of the CRC-N document on this subject that related experiences of other Communities encouraged us to outline such a program. In the autumn of 1987, two community groups agreed to work with laity who were interested in our spirituality and charism. Later, three other groups were formed to give the present total of fifty-three women and twelve men.

An Associate in this program is defined as any person who, living and working in his or her daily environment without vows, endeavors to deepen his or her faith by practicing the spirituality and works of the Congregation of Les Religieuses de Notre-Dame-du-Sacré-Coeur. The Aim of the Associates is to answer the needs of persons who wish to deepen their faith, and in company with others, to study and practice the Evangelical counsels. The community must support the Associates by prayer and assist spiritual development by conferences, retreats, workshops, etc. The Community is free to cancel the engagement at any time.

The Associate promises to live as a witness to the Christian faith in his or her workplace; take time to grow spiritually; familiarize himself or herself with the spirit and mission of the Congregation; attend the meetings, and actively follow the formation program; be familiar with the rights, privileges, and duties of Associates and the Congregation. The Associate is free to cancel the engagement at any time.

There are two stages: preparatory and engagement. Each Associate is under the direction of a coordinator in a designated locale. During the preparatory period, which may last from three months to a year, the Associate is given appropriate assistance to deepen his prayer life and the sense of his engagement. He has the opportunity to learn the history, spirituality, charism, and mission of the Congregation. During this period, meetings are held once a month from September to June. Each meeting consists of prayer, teaching, and fraternity. The program will be based on the particular needs of the group. Following the preparatory period, an evaluation of the candidate is made. If accepted, an engagement that may be renewed annually is signed. Both parties agree there are no legal or financial obligations on either part. The Associate has no vote in Council elections. Les Religieuses de Notre-Dame-du-Sacré-Coeur and the Associates assist each other in fulfilling their Baptismal promises and their duties as members of the Church. The Associates, being yet young, rely on the assistance of other Congregations and the experiences of Congregational groups. Periodic evaluations and adjustments must be made. During the next four years the General Council proposes to study in depth the problem to fit particular needs.

THE SISTERS OF CHARITY OF OUR LADY OF MERCY, CHARLESTON, S.C.[24]

In 1976-77 the Lay Associates program was inaugurated by the Sisters of Charity of Our Lady of Mercy and continued until 1989, when only one associate remained in the program. That same year an exploratory meeting was held for the purpose of discussing ways in which the laity and Sisters might share prayer life and ministry. Any volunteers were formed primarily for the Outreach program. In May 1990, a revised Associate Program and Handbook were formulated and sent to and approved by the Council. Six candidates were received and accepted as Associates on September 22, 1991. Three more were accepted in 1993 and another candidate in 1994. Three women applied then and were received into the program in 1996. As of October 1996 there are fourteen Associates. Sister Marcella Zwingmann, OLM, is the Associate Director.

An Associate Member of the Sisters of Charity of Our Lady of Mercy is a person who desires to extend the mission of the Church by committing herself or himself to the mission and charism of the Sisters through prayer and service. The purpose of the Associate Membership Program is to extend and to strengthen the mission of the Church by offering persons who are not vowed members of the Congregation the opportunity to participate in the life of the Church and in the life and ministry of the Sisters of Charity of Our Lady of Mercy. Associate Membership is open to women and men, married or single, religious or clergy of any denomination who feel called to participate in the life of the Church by sharing in the mission of the Sisters through prayer and service. Part of their commitment is service, and this can take many forms. We encourage Associates to pray the Liturgy of the Hours, Prayer of John England, and the Vocation Prayer as the Sisters do each day. Associates are welcome to join the sisters for Morning and Evening Prayer and Eucharist at any time. On all special days they will be formally invited.

Associates' ministries are varied and take many forms. They are invited to serve in any way possible with the Sisters in their area. This may be in direct service to others or to the Sisters themselves. Also, spreading the message by their involvement in Parish and other Service Organizations is most important. They try to let others know that they are OLM Associates. Spiritual Programs organized for the Community are held at May Forest, and the Associates are invited to these. Bimonthly meetings provide another opportunity for growth and spiritual enrichment.

There has been much sharing with the gathering of Associate Directors from four congregations of the Federation from Kentucky, Cincinnati, New Jersey, and New York. The Directors from the Federation's Associates' programs meet together, spawning wonderful ideas for the Associates. Sister Ellen (New York) used Cincinnati's pamphlet on Companioning for their Associates' program. They in turn adopted Sister Ellen's Formation of Associates packet.

They also meet with the Company of Charity Formation personnel. Groups of Associates seek community to share common Christian values and to have a place in which to share them. All the Associate groups are in localities where there are Sisters of Charity. In some Associate groups each member has a Contact Sister, a link. Some groups meet with their Contact Sisters on a monthly basis. They pray and socialize together and have some kind of learning input, enrichment focused around some aspect of spirituality, community history, or charism. Developed by Associates and Sisters, the Associates are taking the leadership. In the tri-state area (Ohio, Indiana, and Kentucky), they have the Tri-State Conference of Directors and Associates where they share common concerns and ongoing education. The future of the Associates' program may be greater interaction between Associates and Sisters of Charity.

Notes

1. Sister Marlene Lehmkuhl, SNC, "Probing the Relationship between Associates and their Congregations," Sisters of Charity of Nazareth, Nazareth, Kentucky.
2. Sister Marlene Lehmkuhl, SCN, Nazareth, Kentucky.
3. Sister Rita Hawk, SC, Cincinnati, Ohio.
4. Sister Ellen Rose O'Connell, SC, New York City.
5. Sister Rose Mulholland, SCIC, Saint John, New Brunswick, Canada.
6. Sister Kathryn Palas, SC, Greensburg, Pennsylvania.
7. Sister Noreen Walter, SCL, Leavenworth, Kansas.
8. *Constitution of the Sisters of Charity of Leavenworth*, Norm 1.4.
9. Sister Julie Scanlon, SC, Convent Station, New Jersey.
10. Sisters of Charity of Saint Elizabeth, Convent Station, N.J., 1987 General Assembly mandate.
11. Arlene Kleissler, *Ubi Caritas*, p. 21.
12. Mary Marinucci, as quoted by Sister Julie Scanlon, SC, Convent Station, New Jersey.
13. Sister Elena Almendarez, VSC, Pittsburgh, Pennsylvania.
14. Sister Margaret Flynn, DC, archivist, Daughters of Charity, East Central Province, Evansville, Indiana.
15. The Congregation of the Mission and the Daughters of Charity, *Vincentian Service Corps*.
16. A Retreatant, Annual California Yosemite Retreat, Spring 1995, Newsletter *VSC-WEST*.
17. Male Volunteer, Philadelphia parish, transitional housing program, *VSC News: East*, Spring 1996.
18. Former VSC volunteer, Manager of a Communications Office, Washington, D.C.
19. Volunteer, *VSC News*, Winter 1995.
20. Volunteer, New York, *VSC News*, Winter 1995.

21. Sister Maureen Skelly, SC, New York; Sister Cecilia Hudec, SC, North Burnaby, British Columbia.
22. Associates Program, Sisters of Charity of St. Vincent de Paul, Halifax, Nova Scotia, Canada.
23. Sister Imelda Guignard, NDSC, and Sister Odette Leger, NDSC, Moncton, New Brunswick, Canada.
24. Sister M. Anne Francis Campbell, OLM, Charleston, S.C.

Chapter Seven

The Sisters of Charity and the Twenty-First Century

The Daughters and Sisters of Charity have made astonishing progress during almost two hundred years since Mother Seton gave birth to that first American congregation in 1809. The expansion of the Daughters of Charity and the Sisters of Charity throughout the United States and Canada has been phenomenal, enhanced as it has been by the many congregations evolving from Mother Seton's initial group and its branches, which became diocesan communities and pontifical institutes. The two Vincentian congregations have added to their number and to the diversity of their missions. At their peak period in the 1960s the thirteen congregations, now members of the Federation, numbered over 14,000 living and productive Sisters and Daughters with an average age in the early forties.

Today the number has diminished to 7,000 with an average age in the late sixties. yet this older group of women continue to be a vibrant, dedicated, hard-working and creative group, still imbued with the early spirit of Elizabeth, Vincent, and Louise. The future of these congregations and the Federation is a mystery, dependent in large part on the cultural and spiritual changes in the next century. What will not change is the spirit of charity, the charism that is the foundation of their lives and works. Interviews with the General Superiors of these congregations have elicited some stimulating conjectures in this regard.

Sister Carol Barnes, past President of the New York Sisters of Charity, notes:

> The Federation of Sisters of Charity is today grappling seriously with its identity and purpose as new programs are introduced and evidence of real creativity is manifest. Sisters today respond in new ways to the needs of the poor, to developing new partnerships, new ways of mission. Diversity is the key.

Sister Mary Kathleen Stefani, Community Director of the Sisters of Charity of Leavenworth, Kansas, sees the Federation as a loosely-knit but bonded group, sharing opportunities and using their united clout to effect systemic change, particularly by influencing legislation.

Sister Mary Canavan, past General Superior of the New Jersey Sisters of Charity, recognizes the maturing process of the Federation's growth and its essential goal of bonding more closely the family of Elizabeth Seton and the broader family of Vincent de Paul. It is an ongoing activity in which the group has deepened its understanding of the roots of the charism of Elizabeth, Vincent and Louise. A kindred spirit exists among the Sisters and Daughters of Charity different from all other gatherings. As they plumb the issues of religious life in today's Church, as well as their mission in the future, they bring together both the common charism of charity and the diverse traditions of each congregation, providing them with a richness unequaled in their past experience.

Sister Louise Gallahue, Visiatrix of the Northeast Province of Daughters of Charity in Albany, New York, notes that the spirit of charity is also one of survival. She points out that the congregations in the Federation survived the American frontier, responded to wars and epidemics, answered the needs of poor immigrants with free health care, education, and social services, opening hospitals, schools, orphanages, homes for young women and the elderly throughout North America. They ministered in third world countries and developed similar experiences on parallel courses. The thirteen congregations discovered that they have much in common; they recognize a common culture and a common goal.

Sister Bridget Sullivan, former General Superior of the Sisters of Charity of Our Lady of Mercy in Charleston, South Carolina, has the all-embracing vision of a good CEO, aware of the great potential of the sisters in the Federation for the future.

Sister Nanette Gentile, Visitatrix and Provincial for the West Central Province of the Daughters of Charity in St. Louis, Missouri, is committed to the Federation's collaborative activities. She sees the flexible bonding of the thirteen congregations providing opportunities to respond in future. Some congregations may merge; others may not. But all thirteen collaborate, thus providing a large contingent who together can combine their talents. For example, in health care alone they are trying to balance institutional health care with community-based health-care centers. They are all committed to involving the leadership of the laity.

Sister Charlene Reebel, General Superior of the Vincentian Sisters of Charity in Pittsburgh, Pennsylvania, sees the Federation as an adventure in grace, a journey in hope, an interaction with sisters on the level of leadership in guiding their congregations toward the future. It is a kaleidoscopic experience merging with so many different congregations, all impelled by the spirit of Vincent, Louise, and Elizabeth. Not competitive but supportive, networking in an enriching experience – the greater picture of a Federation sharing and meshing the beauty of the charism of charity as a force for renewal and revitalization.

Sister Margaret Mach, General Superior of the Vincentian Sisters of Charity of Bedford, Ohio, sees the members of the Federation called to transformation, conversion, creating something new – what is being signaled today in terms of present needs and changes.

Sister Virginia Ann Brooks, Provincial of the Daughters of Charity in the Southeast Province, Emmitsburg, Maryland, spoke of the purpose of the Federation today as one of support, reaching out to all the communities with the charism of Vincent, Louise, and Elizabeth. It brings all these congregations together to celebrate the charism and foundations, to plan how sisters can share even more. "We are products of our history but it's what we do with it now to change the future history that is important."

Sister Gertrude Foley, Major Superior of the Sisters of Charity of Seton Hill, Greensburg, Pennsylvania, emphasizes the importance of scholars in the future of these thirteen congregations. She calls for an intellectual response that is reflected on in writing. Sister Gertrude says:

> We have in the past failed to highlight our scholars. As Sisters and Daughters of Charity we do not have an intellectual tradition that is reflective in writing. Yet Mother Seton was a reflective person – a thinker and a writer. We never fostered the intellectual life. Our service has been pragmatic. We seemed suspicious of ideas in the past. Yet every congregation had and still has its scholars. Let us highlight them. Women's history in the Church in the past has been non-intellectual but we are today at the turning point. The future looks bright. The Federation itself is sponsoring intellectual papers, articles and books on our history, spirituality, and the richness of our tradition.

> By converging the many strains of the thirteen congregations we reclaim the whole tradition as it really was with all its varied interpretations. The more intense convergence and the addition of new members into the Federation is thrilling. We must help sustain the on-going conversions of the Federation. In a way, the Federation has something analogous to the Ecumenical movement – to come together but not to lose the richness of traditions. We have a family trait coming from Mother Seton, our sense of ourselves. Even in our most repressed times we say it's OK to be ourselves – the individuality, the lightness of heart, the humor, the warmth, the friendliness, the lack of affectation in the community, taking for granted what we have done. Our communities are not austere but very human.

Sister Dorothea Huber, DC, Visitatrix of the East Central Province in Evansville, Indiana, said, as she was leaving office on August 3, 1996:

> If the Vincentian spirit is to be kept alive I believe we must spread the good news of the gospel, not only by preaching and teaching the actual Scriptural Word of God, but even more by living the good news and by witnessing the love of God; love to serve the poorest and most marginalized persons – these should be our priority, as they were Vincent's and Louise's; inculturate the Vincentian charism through our spiritual efforts, deeply loving God and our neighbor, be they our Sisters, our collaborators, our poor or our global community; love to live community. Community life is part of our Vincentian charism; we need to commit ourselves to our core group; understand and accept ourselves as church and inculturate the Vincentian charism by being committed Daughters of the Church.

Sister Mary Ellen Murphy, SC, General Superior of the Sisters of Charity of Cincinnati replied that her vision of Sisters of Charity in the twenty-first century would be

Gospel women, each knowing, believing in, and loving herself as a gifted woman, in her commitment to: living out the gospel values of truth, justice, love; modeling interdependent, nurturing relationships; reverencing the earth and all creation; being a source of peace in her local, civic, religious community; reclaiming, expressing her feminine leadership as gift to the Church.

They would express this together in their commitment to challenging those things that block peace, truth and charity; modeling church community; living out of a passionate awareness of our connection to all creation; learning from the poor by being in relationship with them; responding to unmet needs of the poor and alienated.

Sister Margaret Toner, SCIC, General Superior of the Sisters of Charity of the Immaculate Conception in Saint John, New Brunswick, expressed her vision in these words:

> I see a future full of hope, notwithstanding the diminishment that is taking place. We will be found in the company of the dispossessed, castaways in a culture that places profit over people. We will continue to seek out, learn from and support the disenfranchised, the voiceless, the reviled. With no power but that of the Gospel, we will know the need and value of community. We will offer solidarity to others along the way. Material things will be held in common, sharing with the poor what is rightfully theirs. Reliving the experience of our founders – a total reliance on Providence – we will know God in new and wonderful ways. Whatever its function, the Company of Charity we know as the Federation will have served to give expression to the vision.

From varied other interviews of Sisters and Daughters of Charity have come repeatedly such telling statements as the idea that changes in religious life are possibly God's instrument for the laity to take its proper place in the Church. Religious sisters had to decrease in order that the laity might increase. Yet the Federation, the real solidarity that it inspires among Sisters and Daughters of Charity, will prosper because we are helping each other. There is mutual recognition, encouragement, inspiration from similar ideals, history, and founders.

Our college residences are becoming homes for the elderly; our college buildings are becoming retreat centers. We have good collaboration with our Associates and other secular people. It is our call to service in an active charism that is the witness that will attract people and the bonds that will hold us together. What will attract people is the life we live and the service we give.

As we attempt to solidify the Federation's focus in the future we must capitalize on the links that bind us. There is a uniqueness in the Federation that needs to be probed. The future for the Federation members is global. With new technologies such as E-mail, FAX, conference calls, and the Internet, sisters can communicate quickly and easily. They can work together on new projects in every Charity congregation and in other countries where these congregations have established missions. We can publish ministry employment opportunities and fill positions with Daughters and Sisters of Charity in all thirteen congregations, collaborating on projects for the poor. It is time now to gather our forces and regroup, go out again but this time as members, not of one's own individual community but of a united Federation.

Regarding our corporate responsibilities, we should combine our efforts as a Federation, filing shareholders' resolutions with corporations in which we hold stock and attending shareholders' meetings to present resolutions. We should act as a combined entity to speak and advocate for the poor, particularly today when the massive welfare reform program in the United States is fast being destroyed. The good, feminine corporate voice has to be heard more clearly – feminine power used corporately.

There are ever more meaningful ways for a Federation working together in ministries, celebrating our affiliation with an annual Elizabeth Seton Federation Day in the regions televised through satellites, get-togethers also for the missionary sisters in Korea, the Orient, and India, as well as another for those in Latin American countries.

A network to affect health-care systems of the Sisters and Daughters of Charity in the United States is essential today, with the focus on political advocacy for the poor.

Our Mission Statement as Federation should translate key values into concrete behavior for decision-making, development evaluation, budget, policies, final planning. It should incorporate them into job descriptions and job evaluations. It should expand our ecological and eco-spiritual horizons on the environment of the future, and our earth ministry on the use of the earth's resources. It should address global social justice in its condemnation of the overuse of energy.

Leadership is needed for all of this – leadership embodied in a Federation President, one whose zeal and vision is all-encompassing. Her term of office of four to six years, supported by a good team of advisers, can energize and transform the Federation in the future.

Sister Maryanna Coyle, SC, of the Cincinnati Sisters of Charity, in her paper, "How to Plan for Ministry in the Year 2000," writes: "Our possible future may be one of refounding . . . picking up what is essential to our identity and moving it into new areas, new structures and new signs if we are to be relevant in the year 2000."

Sister Audrey Gibson, Assistant of the Daughters of Charity Province in Los Altos, Calfornia, writes:

> Religious life was never meant to be "fixed" in any particular age. As with all life, ours is in process and will ebb and flow as time goes on. New challenges will emerge and we will meet them with an whomever God provides us.
>
> As for the future of the Federation – I believe that our strength is in our shared charism. If we remain true to the reason for our being, we will be open to greater collaboration for the purpose of working tirelessly to improve life for the impoverished. This in itself is reason enough to envision great promise for the future.

Sister Bernice Gaudet, NDSC, General Superior of Les Religieuses de Notre-Dame-du-Sacré-Coeur in Dieppe, New Brunswick, notes that:

> Religious communities are entering the twenty-first century faced with new challenges. In this era of rapidly growing technology, the world has become globally interconnected. World problems, social issues are part of everyday living; computer technology is posing serious problems to human development; people are less and less in touch with each other; values are endangered. In this period of upheaval, both in the Church and in the world, religious are called to witness Christ, to take on his attitudes and to bring love and hope to humankind. Our lifestyle must lead to a life that portrays certain values: respect for life, unconditional love, acceptance of others, attentiveness, justice, solidarity, concern for the downtrodden and marginalized. We are called to be witnesses who reveal by our presence, by our "being," even more than by our works, the living God of Jesus Christ. The mission to which the twenty-first century calls us is more than action, more than a task to be accomplished, it is our whole life, our whole being that must become mission.

The future of the Federation lies with the younger members and their potential as future religious. If they face the future creatively, planning ahead for concerted ministries, using professional expertise in its growth, these highly energized self-starter women are bound to explore new territories of ministry. As one young woman, Sister Michelle Grgurich, of Croatian descent, a member of the Pittsburgh Vincentian Sisters of Charity said:

> The Federation must have a major impact on the future – the pioneering spirit come alive again in the twenty-first century – mavericks on the cutting edge of change, huddling around the campfires of charity, envisioning a new breed of religious out there, right in the midst of the energy. The ideas and possibilities for the future are limitless.

Sister Mary Louise Brink, Congregational Leader of the Sisters of Charity, Halifax, Nova Scotia, responds to the future of the Federation in these words:

> Over the past eight years that I have been in congregational leadership, I have come to know and to appreciate all the benefits of belonging to the Federation of the Sisters of Charity in the Vincentian-Setonian tradition. I have found great joy and hope in meeting so many women who live out the same charism of charity that I do. During these eight years there have been many grassroots events in which members of all thirteen congregations have participated. Not just leadership but many sisters have experienced firsthand the energy and enthusiasm that emerges when Sisters of Charity get together to explore our common charism and mission. Although our federation has chosen to maintain only a loose affiliation among members now, as our numbers decrease, I can foresee that the shared experiences we have had are preparing the way for closer bonding, and, perhaps, for a union like that of the

> Sisters of Mercy of the Americas. Since our charism of charity is dynamic and timeless, I expect that it will continue to live on in many others who will also feel its attraction.

Sister Elizabeth Wendeln, SCN, President of the Sisters of Charity of Nazareth, Kentucky states:

> The future of Charity is unlimited and the future of religious life rooted in charity is also unlimited. Women religious networking with others will spiral many circles of charity. These many spirals are integral to the work of the gospel. The Charity Federation is one facet of our networking. Laity, religious and clergy will once more become one body, with few distinctions. The synergy created by our joint efforts will keep the fire of the life of Charity alive.

Bibliography

Boyle, Sister Mary Electa, SC. *Mother Seton's Sisters of Charity in Western Pennsylvania.* Seton Hill, Greensburg, Pennsylvania: Sisters of Charity, 1946.

Buckner, Sister Mary, SCL. *History of the Sisters of Charity of Leavenworth.* Kansas City: Hudson-Kimberly, 1898.

Campbell, Sister M. Anne Francis, OLM. *Bishop England's Sisterhood: 1829-1929.* Ph.D. dissertation, St. Louis University, 1968.

Conroy, Sister Mary Carol, SCL. *The Historical Development of the Health Care Ministry of the Sisters of Charity of Leavenworth, Kansas.* Manhattan, Kansas: Kansas State University Press, 1984.

Dirvin, Joseph I., CM. *Mrs. Seton: Foundress of the American Sisters of Charity.* New York: Farrar, Straus and Giroux, 1962, 1975.

Gilmore, Sister Julia, SCL. *Come North.* New York: McMullen Books Inc., 1951.

_________. *We Came North.* St. Meinrad, Indiana: Abbey Press, 1961. (Sisters of Charity of Leavenworth, Kansas)

Hannefin, Sister Daniel, DC. *Daughters of the Church: A Popular History of the Daughters of Charity in the United States, 1809-1987.* Brooklyn: New City Press, 1989.

Hennessey, Sister M. Genevieve, SCIC. *Honoria Conway: Woman of Promise. Foundress of the Sisters of Charity of the Immaculate Conception, Saint John, New Brunswick.* Saint John: Sisters of Charity, SCIC, 1985.

Kremenik, Sister Anne, VSC. *History of the Vincentian Sisters of Charity of the Diocese of Pittsburgh*. Pittsburgh: Vincentian Sisters of Charity, 1976.

Mahoney, Sister Benedicta, SC. *We Are Many: A History of the Sisters of Charity of Cincinnati, 1898-1971*. Cincinnati: Sisters of Charity, 1982.

Maillet, Soeur Marie-Dorothee, NDSC. *Une Pierre de la Mosaique Acadienne*. Ottawa: Les Editions Lemeac, 1984.

McEniry, Sister Blanche Marie, SC. *Woman of Decision: A Life of Mother Mary Xavier Mehegan*. New York: McMullin Books, Inc. 1952.

__________. *Three Score and Ten*. Convent Station, N.J.: Sisters of Charity of St. Elizabeth, 1969.

McGann, Sister Agnes Geraldine, SCN. *SCNs Serving Since 1812*. St. Meinrad, IN: Abbey Press, 1986.

Power, Sister Maura, SC. *The Sisters of Charity of Halifax*. Toronto: Ryerson Press, 1956.

Sharkey, Sister Mary Agnes, SC. *The New Jersey Sisters of Charity, 1859-1933*. (3 vols.) New York: Longmans, Green & Company, 1933.

Slavik, Mother Mary Joseph, VSC. *History of the Vincentian Sisters of Charity of Bedford, Ohio*. Bedford: Vincentian Sisters of Charity, 1975.

Spillane, Sister James Maria, SCN. *Kentucky Spring*. St. Meinrad, Indiana: Abbey Press, 1968. (Biography of Mother Catherine Spalding and early history of the Sisters of Charity of Nazareth, Kentucky, 1812-1858.)

__________. *Summer Winds*. St. Meinrad, Indiana: Abbey Press, 1991. (In conjunction with *Kentucky Spring*, it relates the history of the Sisters of Charity of Nazareth, 1859-1912.)

Walsh, Sister Marie de Lourdes, SC. *The Sisters of Charity of New York, 1809-1959*. (3 vols.) New York: Fordham University Press, 1960.

Index